Syllabi for Music Methods Courses

Barbara Lewis, Editor

Production Editor: Teresa K. Preston

© 2002
MENC–The National Association for Music Education
1806 Robert Fulton Drive
Reston, VA 20191
Printed in the United States of America.
ISBN 1-56545-151-1

SYLLABI
FOR MUSIC METHODS COURSES

SECOND EDITION

EDITED BY BARBARA LEWIS

MENC MENC
MENC
MENCM

The National Association for Music Education

CONTENTS

INTRODUCTION

This new collection of syllabi has been published in response to MENC's request to the Society for Music Teacher Education (SMTE) for an updated version of the original 1992 edition. After SMTE agreed to undertake the project, a Call for Syllabi was printed in various MENC publications in the spring and fall of the year 2000.

Music education professors from around the country submitted syllabi for various types of music education courses. These syllabi were sent to a panel of reviewers comprised primarily of the members of the board of the Society for Music Teacher Education and some members of the board of the *Journal of Music Teacher Education* who were selected because of their area of expertise.

The reviewers completed a rating sheet for each syllabus based on the criteria in the Call for Syllabi (see page ix). The syllabi receiving the highest ratings and most favorable comments were selected for inclusion in this publication.

Some features of note in this 2002 version that reflect the changing times are attention to the National Standards for Music Education and the inclusion of innovative activities involving technology.

SMTE hopes that this compilation of what is currently being taught in graduate and undergraduate music education courses will be an invaluable resource for instructors in the field. On behalf of SMTE, I would like to thank those who submitted course syllabi for making this publication possible.

Barbara Lewis
University of North Dakota

CALL FOR SUBMISSION
OF GRADUATE AND UNDERGRADUATE COURSE SYLLABI
FOR THE MENC/SMTE SYLLABUS PUBLICATION

Teachers of music education courses are invited to submit copies of their syllabi to be reviewed for inclusion in an upcoming syllabus publication. Syllabi that address implementation of the National Standards are especially sought.

Criteria for the Evaluation of Syllabi are as follows:

- Syllabus includes all course topics; could serve as a review of the course

- Clear delineation of course content including attention to the implementation of the National Standards

- Evidence of systematic organization of course content

- Includes statement of course objectives

- Includes list of required texts, materials, suggested texts, and reserve readings

- Provides clear expectations of student course performance:

  - Indication of all assignments with due dates

  - Indication of all dates of examinations and performance proficiencies

  - Indication of special projects/field experiences/activities related to technology

  - Percentages of credit given for categories of course work

    (Example: Projects = 30%)

  - Includes absentee policy

Please submit a clean copy of each syllabus, as well as an electronic copy in Microsoft 5.1 or Microsoft Word 98 on a Mac disk. If you do not have access to the Mac platform, send the electronic copy in the body of an e-mail to the following address: barbara_lewis@und.nodak.edu. as soon as possible. Send the hard copy and disk to: Barbara Lewis, Box 7125 University Station, Grand Forks, ND 58202. For further information, contact Barbara Lewis, book editor, at the University of North Dakota (701) 777-2820.

SYLLABI REVIEWERS

Sara Bidner
Southeastern Louisiana University

David Brinkman
University of Wyoming

J. Bryan Burton
West Chester University of Pennsylvania

Jeffrey Bush
Arizona State University

William Fredrickson
University of Missouri—Kansas City

George Heller
University of Kansas

Randi L'Hommedieu
Central Michigan University

Mary Leglar
University of Georgia

Paul Mortenson
University of North Dakota

David Teachout
University of Minnesota

Kimberly Walls
Auburn University

GENERAL MUSIC

MUSIC 262: MUSIC IN EARLY CHILDHOOD
DR. CAROLINE PERKINS
DEPAUW UNIVERSITY, SCHOOL OF MUSIC
SPRING 2000

Instructor: Dr. Caroline Perkins
Office: 658-4503, Room 225E
e-mail: ckperkins@depauw.edu
Class Hours: Mon., Wed., 1:30–2:20
Location: Room 17 PAC
Office Hours: Mon., Wed., 11–12; Mon., Wed., 2:30–4, and by appointment

COURSE DESCRIPTION
Detailed consideration of the music programs in nursery schools and kindergarten. Topics include the nature of early musical responses, objectives, experience levels of the program, methods of teaching, and materials. Observation of music teaching and participation in music teaching are included in course-work.

COURSE OBJECTIVES
Through a variety of in-class activities and outside assignments, the students will
- understand the value of music education in the lives of young children
- become familiar with music materials appropriate for young children
- gain knowledge of teaching aids and methods of teaching music to preschool children
- gain knowledge of appropriate strategies for integrating music with other subject areas
- become cognizant about child development, maturation patterns, and learning styles of normal and exceptional learners
- acquire knowledge of trends in the music education of young children and their philosophical and historical framework

COURSE TOPICS
- Child Development
- Musical Development
- Music Learning Environments
- Instructional Strategies
- Learning Centers
- Learning Theories
- Evaluation
- Music and Materials
- Music in an Integrated Curriculum
- Musical Experiences
- Music Concepts

MATERIALS
Required Materials
- Andress, B. (1998). *Music for young children.* New York: Harcourt Brace College Publishers.
- Palmer, M., & Sims, W. L. (1993). *Music in prekindergarten: Planning and teaching.* Reston, VA: MENC.

Relevant Periodicals in the Music Library
- *General Music Today*
- *Journal of Research in Music Education*
- *Music Educators Journal*
- *Teaching Music*
- *Update: Applications of Research in Music Education*

Relevant Periodicals in Roy O. West Library
- *Childhood Education*
- *Children Today*
- *Children's Literature Association Quarterly*
- *Educational Leadership*
- *Journal of Research in Childhood Education*
- *Phi Delta Kappan*
- *Teaching Pre-K–8*

Materials on Reserve in the Music Library
- *Dimensions of Musical Thinking* MT 1 .D55 1989
- *First Steps in Music for Infants and Toddlers* MT 1 .F441 1995
- *First Steps in Music for Nursery and Preschool* MT 1. F443 1995
- *Kindergarten Kupboard* MT 1 .K56 1979
- *Leading Young Children to Music* MT 1 .H13 1996
- *Music: A Way of Life for the Young Child* MT 1 .B35 1991
- *Music for Fun, Music for Learning* MT 3 .C35 B6 1982
- *Music for Very Little People* MT 1 .M875 1986
- *Music in Preschool* MT 1 .F6713 1995
- *Musical Games, Fingerplays, and Rhythmic Activities for Early Childhood* MT 1 .M87 1983
- *Readings in Early Childhood Music Education* MT 1 .R364 1992
- *Strategies for Teaching: Prekindergarten Music* MT 925 .S87 1995
- *What? Me Teach Music?* MT 920 .L38 1982

GRADING SCALE

A+ = 98–100	A = 94–97	A- = 90–93
B+ = 88–89	B = 84–87	B- = 80–83
C+ = 78–79	C = 74–77	C- = 70–73
D+ = 68–69	D = 64–67	D- = 60–63
F = 59 and below		

EVALUATION
Grading will be based upon data obtained from the following sources and will be weighted as indicated:

25% Exams. Midterm and Final

5% Quizzes. Unannounced quizzes over reading assignments

15% Observations. Observations of six different preschool settings are required:
- Kindermusik
- Head Start
- Special Needs Students
- Prekindergarten
- Kindergarten
- Younger Learners (ages 2–4)

25% Presentations. Three presentations to preschool students are required:
* Music Time   • Story   • Learning Center

Components of Grade for Observations and Presentations: Attendance, evaluation by cooperating teachers, write-ups of observations and self-reflections of teaching. Lesson plan observation write-up should consist of a summary of the observation, descriptions of behaviors and characteristics you observed, comparison of behaviors and characteristics observed with readings and class discussion, and any additional comments you may have.

15% Learning Center. Design a learning center appropriate for preschool children. Will be shared with class and presented to students.
Grading Criteria: Age-appropriateness, content, presentation, appeal to students

5% Story. Using a sequencing program such as *Cakewalk* or *Mastertracks Pro,* create a soundscape to accompany a story. Will be shared with class and presented to real students.

10% Integrated Unit. Select a theme and incorporate it into four curriculum areas (one must be music).
Ideas: Food, sounds, transportation, seasons, etc.

Other Requirements.
* Assigned readings and/or video viewings. Prior to coming to class, post a summary, observations/thoughts, questions, and/or comments pertinent to the assignment to our bulletin board.
* In-class activities
* In-class participation

Written work is to be word processed. Any work turned in otherwise will be returned to you ungraded. All assignments are due at the beginning of class on the assigned day. Grades for late work will be lowered one letter grade for each day late. This policy is designed to help keep you on track.

Due Dates

Several of the due dates are in the second half of the semester because they require an application of the information gained in the first half of the semester. I recommend that you begin your assignments early (at least generate some ideas) and allow ample time for completion. Keep in mind that it is perfectly acceptable to turn in assignments prior to their due dates.
* Story: March 6
* Midterm: March 13
* Learning Center: April 26
* Integrated Unit: May 3
* Observations and Presentations: May 8 (May is a busy month here on campus and at the preschool centers because things are winding down and wrapping up. Therefore, I recommend that you complete your observations and presentations prior to May 1.)
* Final: May 10

Attendance Policy

Attendance, preparation, and participation are expected and required. Each student is responsible for contacting the instructor if and when an absence is unavoidable. Each student is responsible for checking with the instructor or a classmate when an absence occurs in order to stay on schedule with class assignments, readings, etc.

This course is designed to be a seminar which requires active participation by everyone. Thus, the success of the course depends on the contributions made by each of you. It takes all of us working together to form an effective learning community.

Excused absences include family emergency, illness, and university-approved activities. Unexcused absences include other classes, vacation plans, computer problems, sleep deprivation, Greek activities, etc.

One point will be subtracted from your final grade for each unexcused absence and for each unreported absence. Absences prior to and following school recesses (i.e., leaving early for and/or returning late from break) will be counted as two absences.

Punctuality is a professional courtesy and allows for the smooth start of each class session; therefore, three tardies will equal one absence.

PROFESSIONAL RESPONSIBILITIES FOR SCHOOL OBSERVATIONS

Attendance. If you must be absent from any of your observations due to illness or emergency, you must inform the people affected by your absence (i.e., placement teacher and carpool members, if applicable). You are expected to reschedule missed observations with your placement teacher.

Privacy Issues. We need to be cognizant of the importance of respecting the privacy of the children observed. Do not discuss classroom scenarios that might be embarrassing to teachers, parents, or children or that might include sensitive information about a child or family. During class discussions, use pseudonyms. Use professional judgment when discussing students, situations, etc., at your observation site.

Deportment. You will be viewed and judged as an adult by students, parents, and teachers. Dress appropriately. Do not wear jeans or hats. Do not chew gum. Be polite and considerate to everyone you encounter including the director, secretaries, custodians, teacher assistants, parents, etc. Arrive a few minutes prior to your scheduled observation. Please continue the tradition of representing yourself and DePauw in a professional manner.

Please Note: If you have a disability and require auxiliary aids, services, or accommodations, please contact me in my office so that we may talk about your particular needs.

Please do not hesitate to ask questions or contact me if you are unclear about assignments, readings, etc. I am looking forward to a GREAT semester, I hope you are too!!

TENTATIVE SCHEDULE OF CLASS TOPICS

January 31   **Introduction**

February 2   **The Young Child**
Read Ch. 1, Andress

February 7   **The Preschool Center**
Guest Speaker: Vicki Small, The Learning Castle

February 9   **The Young Child and Music**
Musical Characteristics
Read Ch. 2, Andress; pp. 7–13, *Music in Prekindergarten*

February 14   **Developmentally Appropriate Practice in EC Programs**
Music in the Prekindergarten Classroom.
Read pp. 15–25, *Readings in Early Childhood Music Education;* pp. 3–5, *Music in Prekindergarten*

February 16   **Musical Play**
Read Ch. 3, Andress

February 21   **Developing Musical Concepts**
Musical Thinking
Read pp. 29–32, *Music in Prekindergarten;* Ch. 6, *Dimensions of Musical Thinking;* pp. 9–12, *The School Music Program.*

February 23   **Setting the Environment**
Read Ch. 4, Andress.

February 28	**Children's Literature**
March 1	**Kindermusik** Guest Speaker: Pam Smith. Presentation may need to be rescheduled to accommodate the guest speaker.
March 6	**Story Presentations**
March 8	**No Class (National MENC Conference)** Read pp. 47–65 and 71–72, *Music in Prekindergarten*. Watch video: *Music and Early Childhood* (ML 83 .M87 1991).
March 13	**Midterm Exam**
March 15	**Guidelines for Music Activities and Instruction** Read pp. 19–27, *Music in Prekindergarten*.
March 20	**Singing** Read Ch. 6, Andress; "Let's Sing It Again!" by Jan Wolf.
March 22	**Instruments** Read Ch. 7, Andress.
April 3	**Movement** Read Ch. 8, Andress.
April 5	**Music Play Centers** Read Ch. 9, Andress; "The Birth, Care and Feeding of an Early Childhood Music Learning Center" by Grace Morris.
April 10	**Teacher's Role** Read Ch. 5, Andress.
April 12	**Long-Range Program Goals** Read pp. 15–18, *Music in Prekindergarten*.
April 17	**Integrating Music Throughout the Curriculum** Read Ch. 12, Andress.
April 19	**Music for Young Children with Special Needs** Read Ch. 10, Andress; pp. 33–36, *Music in Prekindergarten*.
April 24	**Multicultural Music in Early Childhood** Read Ch. 11, Andress.
April 26	**Learning Center Presentations**
May 1	**Evaluation in Early Childhood Music** Read pp. 37–43, *Music in Prekindergarten*.
May 3	**Presentations of Integrated Units**
May 8	**Discussion of Observations and Presentations**
May 10	**Final Exam**

MuE 412/512: Teaching Methods
Elementary General and Choral
Dr. Kathleen Jacobi-Karna
University of Oregon, School of Music
Fall 2000

Instructor: Dr. Kathleen Jacobi-Karna
Office: Music 132
Phone: 346-3769
e-mail: kjacobik@darkwing.uoregon.edu
Office Hours: Mon., Wed., Thurs., Fri., 10–10:50; Tues., 2–2:50, or by appointment

Course Description
Concerns of music teachers in the elementary school. Observations, procedures, instructional materials; planning and teaching lessons for analysis and criticism. [UO Catalog]

Purpose of the Course
MuE 412/512 is designed for those who will be teaching general/choral music in an elementary school. This course will include a review of major concepts and philosophies of music education, exposure to a variety of teaching materials and song literature for the general music class and many singing, playing, movement, and exploratory activities.

Because of the nature of this course and the emphasis on in-class activities and demonstrations, students are required to attend all class sessions. Even though there are textbooks, the student's comprehension of the materials also depends upon class participation. As a corequisite for MuE 412/512, students must also enroll in MuE 409 Practicum: Elementary School Music.

The student will be responsible for all assignments, whether or not he or she is present when the assignment is made. There may be unannounced group assignments which cannot be made up if the student is not present. Late assignments, if accepted, will receive lowered grades. In preparation for each class session, read assignments for the texts, as well as supplementary materials as required. Class attendance is expected of those choosing the teaching profession. Poor attendance and/or tardiness will affect the final grade.

Required Textbooks/Materials
Campbell, P. S., & Scott-Kassner, C. (1995). *Music in childhood: From preschool through elementary grades.* New York: Schirmer. ISBN 0-02-870552-1.

Recommended (But Not Required) Textbooks
Consortium of National Arts Education Associations. (1994). *National standards for arts education.* Reston, VA: MENC. ISBN 1-56545-036-1.
Stauffer, S. L., & Davidson, J. (Ed.). (1996). Strategies for teaching K–4 general music. Reston, VA: MENC. ISBN 1-56545-081-7.

On Reserve–Knight Library: Reserve Reading Room
Edelstein, S., Choksy, L., Lehman, P., Sigurdsson, N., & Woods, D. (1980). *Creating curriculum in music.* Menlo Park, CA: Addison-Wesley.

Good teaching, like good learning, is not something achieved, but something ever in process.
Judith Wells Lindfors

REQUIRED JOURNAL READINGS

Music Teacher

Brand, M. (1990). Master music teachers: What makes them great? *Music Educators Journal, 77*(2), 22–25.

Classroom Management

Bartholomew, D. (1993). Effective strategies for praising students. *Music Educators Journal, 80*(3), 40–43.

Buck, G. H. (1992). Classroom management and the disruptive child. *Music Educators Journal, 79*(3), 36–42.

Merrion, M. (1991). Classroom management for beginning music educators. *Music Educators Journal, 78*(2), 53–56.

Nutter, K. (2000). The keys to classroom management. *Teaching Music, 7*(6), 24–30.

Evaluation

Draper, A. (comp). (1998). Making the grade: Authentic assessment in music, K–8. *Teaching Music, 6*(2), 34–35, 48.

Lange, D. M. (1999). Practical ways to assess elementary music students. *General Music Today, 13*(1), 15–18.

Wells, R. (1998). The student's role in the assessment process. *Teaching Music, 6*(2), 32–33.

Whitcomb, R. (1999). Writing rubrics for the music classroom. *Music Educators Journal, 85*(6), 26–32.

MuE 412/512 Course Objectives

The MuE 412/512 student will

- research issues regarding the elementary general music classroom through professional journals and texts
- demonstrate a knowledge of the elementary general music curriculum regarding content and construction
- plan and implement elementary general music mini-lessons
- discuss the musical behavior, development, and ability of children in an educational setting
- develop instructional materials appropriate for the elementary general music classroom
- demonstrate a knowledge of classroom management techniques
- articulate a rationale for music education in the K–5 environment
- discuss major topics and issues presented throughout the quarter

MuE 412/512 Projects and Assignments

(1) **Professional Article Reviews.** Read one article each week for six weeks from the *Music Educators Journal* (current or past issues are fine, but not an article from the required journal readings list). Choose articles that focus on an aspect of the elementary general music classroom. Write a one-page summary of the article stating major points, teaching ideas, etc. (10 points each)
Due Date: Six consecutive Mondays beginning October 2, 2000

(2) **Curriculum Construction.** Construct a year's curriculum for one grade level (elementary general music class). Use *Creating Curriculum in Music* to determine concepts and instructional objectives. Document the relating National Standard(s) and Oregon Standard(s) for each instructional objective. (50 points)
Due Date: Friday, October 27, 2000

(3) **Lesson Planning and Implementation.** Upon completion of your curriculum, plan one 15-minute lesson. Begin by choosing one or two concepts, corresponding instructional objectives, and state and national standards. This lesson should be conceptual in approach (teaching to the concepts) through several activities/experiences. (75 points)
Due Date: The lessons will be taught in class the week of November 27, 2000. Your lesson plan will be due on the day you teach.

(4) **Instructional Materials—Lesson Strategies.** Create ten lesson strategies for use in the elementary general music classroom. Include the following information:

> Grade Level
> Concept(s)
> Instructional Objective(s)
> National Standard(s)
> Oregon Standard(s)
> Materials
> Procedure
> Evaluation

Remember to include notation and directions for any games/activities. (30 points)
Due Date: Friday, November 17, 2000

(5) **Classroom Management Profile.** Describe your future elementary general music classroom. Include your room setup (physical environment), the expectations you have of your students regarding overall general behavior, classroom management issues you will be facing (rules, consequences, procedures, etc.), and how you will deal with possible disruptions during a lesson/class. (20 points)
Due Date: Monday, November 27, 2000

(6) **Philosophy of Music Education.** Throughout the quarter, compile your observations, ideas, and expectations concerning music education. These will become a basis for an essay regarding your philosophy of music education. This paper should be a synthesis of the topics we discussed in class—current methods and techniques, the child's voice, curriculum design, etc.—as well as a discussion on the value of music education and justification of music in the schools. Your paper should be approximately 8–10 pages in length and should include citation references according to the APA handbook. (75 points)
Due Date: Rough Draft, Wednesday, November 15, 2000; Final Draft, Friday, December 1, 2000

(7) **MuE 412/512 Notebook.** Organize the materials from this course (notes, handouts, assignments, etc.) into a three-ring binder (or similar method of collection). Consider categorizing the materials in a way that suits your learning/teaching style. Bring to the final exam. (15 points)
Due Date: Friday, December 8, 2000; 10:15 am

(8) **Final Exam.** The final exam for this course is a comprehensive essay exam. Organize your notes through the quarter to assist in preparing for this exam. (75 points)
Due Date: Friday, December 8, 2000; 10:15 am

MuE 412/512 Calendar
Week **Topics/Assignments**

Sept. 25   Course outline and requirements; Profile of a music educator; National Standards for
            Arts Education; Oregon State Standards; Curriculum construction
            Textbook Reading: *Music in Childhood,* Ch 1 & 11
            Journal Reading: Brand

Oct. 2   Learning development; Rote poem/song process; The child's singing voice
            Textbook Reading: *Music in Childhood,* Ch. 2, 5, & 6
            Due: Professional Article Review #1 (Monday)

Oct. 9   Singing experiences in the music class; Rote process presentations: song
            Textbook Reading: *Music in Childhood,* Ch. 5 & 6
            Due: Professional Article Review #2 (Monday)

Oct. 16	The elementary school chorus; Movement experiences in the music class
	Textbook Reading: *Music in Childhood,* Ch. 8
	Due: Professional Article Review #3 (Monday)
	Instructional Materials—Rhythm Instruments (Friday)

Oct. 23   Listening experiences in the music class; Methods and techniques: Introduction
            Textbook Reading: *Music in Childhood,* Ch. 7 & 3
            Due: Professional Article Review #4 (Monday)
                    Curriculum (Friday)

Oct. 30   Methods and techniques, cont.
            Textbook Reading: *Music in Childhood,* Ch. 9
            Due: Professional Article Review #5 (Monday)

Nov. 6   Methods and techniques, concl.; Planning a lesson
            Due: Professional Article Review #6 (Monday)

Nov. 13   The exceptional child in the music class; Assessment
            Textbook Reading: *Music in Childhood,* Ch. 14
            Journal Reading: Draper, Lange, Wells, Whitcomb
            Due: Philosophy of Music Education—Rough Draft (Wednesday)
                    Instructional Materials—Lesson Strategies (Friday)

Nov. 20   Classroom management; Review for final exam
            Friday: No class (Thanksgiving Holiday)
            Journal Reading: Bartholomew, Buck, Merrion, Nutter

Nov. 27   Teaching Presentations
            Due: Classroom Management Profile (Monday)
                    Philosophy of Music Education (Friday)

Dec. 4   **Final Exam:** Friday, December 8, 2000; 10:15 am; Room 105
            Due: MuE 412/512 Notebook

MuE 412/512 Grading Policy
Letter Grade/Points

A	400–369	B-	328–317	D+	276–265
A-	368–357	C+	316–305	D	264–249
B+	356–345	C	304–289	D-	248–237
B	344–329	C-	288–277	F	236–0

Students who have special needs or disabilities that may affect their ability to access information and/or materials presented in this course are encouraged to contact me and request that the Counselor for Students with Disabilities send a letter verifying the disability.

MUS 351: Elementary General Music Methods, Materials, and Curricula
Dr. Caroline Perkins
DePauw University, School of Music
Fall 1999

Instructor: Dr. Caroline Perkins
Office: 658-4503, Room 225E
e-mail: ckperkins@depauw.edu
Class Hours: 2:00–3:50 Tues., Thurs.
Location: Room 17 PAC
Office Hours: 10:00 M W F, 2:00 M W, and by appointment

Course Description
Methods and materials suitable for teaching vocal music in the elementary school. General survey of elementary music curricula. Includes analysis of texts and literature relevant to the elementary music program. Incorporates theories of learning; curriculum development, organization and evaluation; and teaching strategies and techniques. Observation of music teaching and participation in music teaching are included in coursework.

Course Goals
The music education student should develop skills and understandings necessary to plan, implement, and evaluate a comprehensive general music program at the elementary level. This course is designed to enable the future music educator to (1) acquire pedagogical skills for use with children, (2) develop a working knowledge of practices in current use in elementary music education, (3) develop a working knowledge of materials employed in the teaching of elementary general music, and (4) become acquainted with some of the theoretical constructs on which elementary music education is based.

Course Objectives
Through a variety of in-class activities and outside assignments, the student will
- gain fluency in curricular issues and in lesson planning
- explore and evaluate repertoire, basal series, software, and materials appropriate for use in an elementary general music classroom
- gain an understanding of various methods of teaching music to elementary school students
- apply principles of teaching, learning, and classroom management to the elementary music environment
- become cognizant about the musical development, maturation patterns, and learning styles of elementary students
- become familiar with various theories of learning
- identify and sequence appropriate teaching materials and strategies for various types of learners
- become familiar with techniques for evaluation of musical growth
- prepare, teach, and evaluate music lessons that incorporate a variety of musical activities directed toward the development of a musical concept
- develop a personal philosophy of music education

Course Topics
- National Standards for Arts Education
- Lesson Planning and Sequencing
- Musical Development of Children

- Repertoire and Materials Selection
- Technology for Music Instruction
- Process for Securing a Teaching Position
- Music Teaching Evaluation
- Exceptional Students
- Experiences with Music
- Approaches to Music Teaching
- Music in an Integrated Curriculum
- Curriculum Models
- Curriculum Development, Organization, and Evaluation
- Theories of Learning
- Teaching Strategies

COURSE MATERIALS
Required Materials
- Consortium of National Arts Education Associations (1994). *National standards for arts education.* Reston, VA: MENC.
- Campbell, P. S., & Scott-Kassner, C. (1995). *Music in childhood: From preschool through the elementary grades.* New York: Schirmer Books.
- VHS tape
- MENC membership
- Binder for class materials

Relevant Periodicals in the Music Library
General Music Today
Journal of Research in Music Education
Music Educators Journal
Teaching Music
Update: Applications of Research in Music Education

Texts on Reserve in Music Library
Music in the Elementary School by Nye, et al.
The Eclectic Curriculum in American Music Education by Carder
The Experience of Teaching General Music by Atterbury and Richardson
Teaching Music: Managing the Successful Music Program by Darwin Walker
Music Education: Historical Contexts and Perspectives by Labuta and Smith

Miscellaneous Materials on Reserve in the Music Library
- *Music for a Sound Education: A Tool Kit for Implementing the Standards* by National Coalition for Music Education
- *The Generative Approach to Music Learning* by Boardman and Pautz (manual for use with video)
- Curriculum Guides (Des Moines Independent Community School District, Greencastle Community Schools, Minneapolis Public Schools, Omaha Public Schools, State of Tennessee, Vigo County School Corporation, and Wichita Public Schools)
- Indiana Fine Arts Proficiency Guide

GRADING SCALE

A+ = 98–100	A = 94–97	A- = 90–93
B+ = 88–89	B = 84–87	B- = 80–83
C+ = 78–79	C = 74–77	C- = 70–73
D+ = 68–69	D = 64–67	D- = 60–63
F = 59 and below		

EVALUATION
Grading will be based upon data obtained from the following sources and will be weighted as indicated.

25% Teaching Episodes
Components of Grade: Lesson presentations, lesson plans, and reflective self-evaluations
Songs must be memorized. Do not teach with your lesson plan in hand. On the day of your peer-teaching, arrive early to locate and organize all of the materials required for your lesson so that we may begin class promptly.

- *Teaching Episode 1.* Teach an unfamiliar, unaccompanied song. Properly give pitch and tempo. Model appropriate vocal quality for children. Rote or note approach. Includes informal lesson plan. Contents of informal plan should include intended grade level, lesson materials, assumptions about student knowledge and skills, and procedures detailing the introduction, body, and closure of the lesson. (15%)
- *Teaching Episode 2.* Teach an unfamiliar song and provide an accompaniment with one of the following instruments: Autoharp, guitar, bass xylophone or metallophone, or piano. Includes informal lesson plan. (20%)
- *Teaching Episode 3.* Teach a lesson focused on the concept of your choice. Include at least two musical activities (singing, moving, playing instruments, creating, listening). Includes formal lesson plan. (40%)
- *Teaching Episode 4.* Tag-team teaching. Includes Plan of Possibilities. (25%)

20% Exams
Midterm and Final: 10% each

5% Quizzes
Unannounced quizzes on assigned readings

40% Assignments
(1) What is elementary general music?—written and pictorial (5%)
(2) Written assignment that addresses the following areas:
   (a) Why you want to teach
   (b) Your strengths and weaknesses as you see them
   (c) Description of the type of teacher you hope to become
   (d) What you want to accomplish with your future students (5%)
(3) Personal philosophy of music education (10%)
(4) Evaluation of music series (20%)
   Review and evaluate the following music series:

Share the Music by McGraw-Hill	*The Music Connection* by Silver Burdett Ginn

(5) Review of music software (15%)
   Review and evaluate *eight* of the following software packages:

A Little Kidmusic	*Alice's Adventures in Musicland*
Allie's Playhouse	*Beethoven Lives Upstairs*
Children's Song Book	*Early Music Skills*
Instruments of the Symphony	*Juilliard Music Adventure*
Making Music	*Menlo the Frog*
Music Ace	*Music Ace II*
Music Lessons	*Music Time*
Musical World of Professor Piccolo	*Rock, Rap, and Roll*

(6) Curriculum (20%)
   Listing/description of concepts and behaviors to be learned at each grade level from K–5.

(7) Resume and Letter of Application (5%)
(8) Reflective paper on your individual development and what you have learned about teaching (5%)
(9) Self-assessment of your vocal, instrumental, and communication skills (5%)
(10) What is elementary general music?—written and pictorial (5%)
(11) Are you ready—why or why not? (5%)

10% Field Experience
This field experience will take place in the local public schools. A write-up for each observation and a reflective self-evaluation for each teaching episode is required. There will be a total of six school visitations.
Components of Grade: Attendance, evaluation by cooperating teacher(s), write-ups, and self-reflections.

OTHER EXPECTATIONS

- Assigned readings
- In-class activities
- Informal assignments
- Active participation in student chapter of MENC
- Organized binder containing class notes, notes on readings, handouts, peer evaluations, and assignments. Consider putting class notes and notes from your readings on computer.

Written work is to be word processed. Any work turned in otherwise will be returned to you ungraded. All assignments are due at the beginning of class on the assigned day. Grades for late work will be lowered one letter grade for each day late. This policy is designed to help keep you on schedule.

DUE DATES

Assignments
(1) What is elementary general music?—written and pictorial: August 31
(2) Four-part written assignment: September 2
(3) Personal philosophy of music education: September 7
(4) Evaluation of music series: October 26
  Please Note: This assignment will take some time to complete.
(5) Review of music software: December 2
  Please Note: This assignment will take some time to complete.
(6) Curriculum: First Draft—November 4
        Second Draft—November 11
        Final Draft—November 18
  Please Note: This assignment will take some time to complete.
(7) Resume and letter of application: December 2
(8) Reflective paper: December 9
(9) Skill assessment: December 9
(10) What is elementary general music?—written and pictorial: December 9
(11) Are you ready—why or why not?: December 9

Peer-Teaching and Lesson Plans
September 14, September 28, November 11, November 30

Self-Evaluation of Peer-Teaching
Class period after your peer-teaching episode
September 16, September 30, November 16, December 2

Observation Write-ups and Self-evaluations of Micro-teaching
Class period after your observation/micro-teaching

ATTENDANCE POLICY

Attendance, preparation, and participation are expected and required. Each student is responsible for contacting the instructor if and when an absence is unavoidable. Each student is responsible for checking with the instructor or a classmate when an absence occurs in order to stay on schedule with class assignments, readings, etc.

Excused absences include family emergency, illness, and university-approved activities. Unexcused absences include other classes, vacation plans, computer problems, sleep deprivation, Greek activities, etc.

One point will be subtracted from your final grade for each unexcused absence and for each unreported absence. Absences prior to and following school recesses (i.e., leaving early for and/or returning late from break) will be counted as two absences.

Punctuality is a professional courtesy and allows for the smooth start of each class session. Three tardies will equal one absence.

This course is designed to be a seminar which requires active participation by everyone. Thus, the success of the course depends on the contributions made by each of you. It takes all of us working together to form an effective learning community.

PROFESSIONAL RESPONSIBILITIES OF FIELD EXPERIENCE

Attendance. If you must be absent from any of your school visitations due to illness or emergency, you must inform the people affected by your absence (i.e., placement teacher and carpool members if applicable). You are expected to reschedule missed visitations with your placement teacher.

Privacy Issues. We need to be cognizant of the importance of respecting the privacy of the children observed. Do not discuss classroom scenarios that might be embarrassing to teachers, parents, or children, or that might include sensitive information about a child or family. During class discussions, use pseudonyms. Use professional judgement when discussing students, situations, etc. at your field experience site.

Deportment. You will be viewed and judged as an adult by students, parents, and teachers. Dress appropriately. Do not wear jeans or hats. Do not chew gum. Be polite and considerate to everyone you encounter including the principal, secretaries, custodians, teacher assistants, parents, etc. Arrive a few minutes prior to your scheduled visitation. Please continue the tradition of representing yourself and DePauw in a professional manner.

Please Note: If you have a disability and require auxiliary aids, services, or accommodations, please contact me in my office so that we may discuss your particular needs.

Please do not hesitate to ask questions or contact me if you are unclear about assignments, readings, etc. I am looking forward to a GREAT semester, I hope you are too!!

TENTATIVE SCHEDULE OF COURSE TOPICS

Aug. 26   **Introduction**
                2:30 Visit the Technology Lab (Julianne Miranda)
                What is "General Music"?

Aug. 31   **The Multiple Meanings of Music for Children**
                Read Ch. 1
                Learning Theories
                Read Ch. 2
                Assignment 1 due

Sept. 2   **Toward a Philosophy of Music Education**
                Read Ch. 12 in *Teaching Music: Managing The Successful Music Program*
                Case Study: A Sound Decision
                Assignment 2 due

Sept. 7	**Selecting Music and Materials**
	Rhythm and the Child
	Read Ch. 4
	Assignment 3 due

Sept. 9	**Pitch and the Child**
	Read Ch. 5
	Read pp. 21–33, 234–40 in *Music in the Elementary School*
	The Singing Child
	Read Ch. 6

Sept. 14	**Peer-Teaching of Song**
	Informal Lesson Plan due
	Discussion of Peer-Teaching

Sept. 16	**The Listening Child**
	Read Ch. 7
	The Moving Child
	Read Ch. 8
	Self-Evaluation of Peer-Teaching due

Sept. 21	**The Playing Child**
	Read Ch. 9
	Classroom Instruments (Recorder, Autoharp, and Guitar)

Sept. 23	**Classroom Instruments (Pitched and Unpitched)**
	The Creating Child
	Read Ch. 10

Sept. 28	**Peer-Teaching of Accompanied Song**
	Informal Lesson Plan due
	Discussion of Peer-Teaching

Sept. 30	**National Standards for Arts Education**
	Read pp. 5–19, 26–29, 42–45 of *National Standards for Arts Education*
	Look at *Music for a Sound Education: A Tool Kit for Implementing the Standards*
	Self-Evaluation of Peer-Teaching due

Oct. 5	**Planning—The Parts of a Lesson Plan**
	Evaluation of Musical Learning
	Read "Assessment as a Class Activity," March '94 *MEJ*
	Read "Videotape as an Assessment Tool," Feb. '96 *TM*
	Read "Reporting Progress with Developmental Profiles," July '97 *MEJ*
	Read "Assessment—Applying the Yardstick to Musical Growth," Sept. '97 *Indiana Musicator*
	Read "Criteria for Evaluating Performance Assessment," Nov. '97 *Indiana Musicator*
	Read "Tools for Assessing Musical Skills," March '98 *Indiana Musicator*
	Read "Can Portfolios Be Practical for Performance Assessment," May '98 *Indiana Musicator*

| Oct. 12 | **Planning and Sequencing Music Lessons** |
| | In-class planning activity |

Oct. 14	**Critiquing of Student Plans**
	Individual lesson plans due. Provide a copy for the instructor and each class member
	Classroom Management

Oct. 14 (cont.)	Read "Judicious Discipline in the Music Classroom," Jan. '97 *MEJ* Read "Classroom Management for Beginning Music Educators," Oct. '91 *MEJ* Read "Classroom Management and the Disruptive Child," Nov. '92 *MEJ*
Oct. 19	**Midterm Exam** **Using Children's Literature in the General Music Classroom** Read "Music and Children's Literature: Natural Partners," Spring '94 *General Music Today*
Oct. 21	**Curriculum Design and Evaluation** Read Ch.11 Read Ch.3 in *Music Education: Historical Contexts and Perspectives* Read "Designing Curricula Based on the Standards," July '97 *MEJ*

Oct. 26	**Curriculum Models**
	Be familiar with the following curriculum materials:
	      National Standards for Arts Education
	      Indiana Fine Arts Proficiency Guide
	      Des Moines Independent Community School District
	      Greencastle Community Schools
	      Minneapolis Public Schools
	      Omaha Public Schools
	      State of Tennessee
	      Vigo County School Corporation
	      Wichita Public School
	Consider similarities and differences, usefulness, comprehensiveness, format, assessment of student growth, skills, concepts, etc.
	McGraw-Hill and Silver Burdett Ginn Series
	Read preface/introduction of a teacher's edition (any grade level between K–5) of the two basal series texts
	Assignment 4 due

Oct. 28	**What Should Students Know by the end of Elementary School?** **Music in an Integrated Curriculum** Read Ch. 15
Nov. 2	**Approaches to Music Teaching: Kodály** Read pp. 51–53 Read "The Kodály Approach," pp. 55–74 in *The Eclectic Curriculum* Watch video: *What is Kodály Music Education?* **Approaches to Music Teaching: Generative** Read introduction to *Holt Music* series and look through series Watch video: *The Generative Approach to Music Learning* Peruse manual: *The Generative Approach to Music Learning* Guest Speaker: Eve Harwood, University of Illinois
Nov. 4	**Approaches to Music Teaching: Dalcroze** Read pp. 48–51, 199–202 Read "The Dalcroze Approach," pp. 7–28 in *The Eclectic Curriculum* Watch video: *Dalcroze Eurhythmics with Robert Abramson* Guest Speaker: Tim Caldwell, Central Michigan University Thompson Recital Hall First Draft of Assignment 6 due

Nov. 9	**Approaches to Music Teaching: Orff**
	Read pp. 53–57
	Read "The Orff Approach," pp. 109–36 in *The Eclectic Curriculum*
	Watch video: *Orff-Schulwerk: A Simple Gift to Music Education*
	Music, Multiculturalism, and Children
	Read Ch. 13
Nov. 11	**Peer-Teaching of Activity of Choice**
	Formal Lesson Plan due
	Discussion of Peer-Teaching
	Second Draft of Assignment due
Nov. 16	**Music for Exceptional Children**
	Read Ch. 14
	Watch video: *Mainstreaming in Music Education*
	Self-Evaluation of Peer-Teaching due
Nov. 18	**Copyright Laws**
	Guest Speaker: Holling Borne, DPU Music Librarian
	Final Draft of Assignment 6 due
Nov. 30	**Tag Team Teaching**
	"Plan of Possibilities" due
Dec. 2	**Technology for Music Instruction**
	Read Ch. 12
	Assignment 5 due
	Securing a Teaching Position
	Assignment 7 due
	Read "Building a Professional Portfolio," July '98 *MEJ*
	Read "The Professional Portfolio...," March '98 *Musicator*
	Self-Evaluation of Peer-Teaching due
Dec. 7	**Real Teachers in Real Worlds**
	Read Ch. 11 in *The Experience of Teaching General Music*
Dec. 9	**Case Study: Up the Creek without a Paddle**
	Discussion of Field Experience
	Wrap-up
	Assignments 8, 9, 10, and 11 due
Dec. 16	**Final Exam**, 2:00–3:50

MUSIC ED. 52-367: MUSIC IN THE ELEMENTARY SCHOOL
DR. VERNA BRUMMETT
ITHACA COLLEGE
SPRING 2000

Credit: 2 hrs. (Tues. and Thurs., 8:00–8:50 a.m. and 11:00–11:50 a.m.)
Instructor: Dr. Verna Brummett, Studio #2205
Phone: 274-3386 (office)
E-mail: brummett@ithaca.edu
Office Hours: by appointment

COURSE DESCRIPTION AND CONTENT

This course emphasizes planning, implementing, and evaluating an eclectic curriculum based on conceptual pedagogy in the elementary general music classroom. Emphasis is placed upon practical application and the development of skills and knowledge needed by the general music specialist. The basic content of the course includes child development, planning and sequencing, and materials.

COURSE OBJECTIVES

- to develop an understanding of how children learn
- to develop an understanding of what elementary music is and should be and its importance in the total music education program
- to become familiar with age-appropriate sources, materials, and quality literature
- to become familiar with the National Standards for Music Education and their implications for teaching
- to develop an understanding of current assessment procedures by using a more authentic assessment approach to student learning
- to refine written communication skills

TEXTBOOKS

There are three textbooks required for this course and available at IC bookstore:
- Campbell & Scott-Kassner, *Music in Childhood*
- Schaberg, *TIPS: Teaching Music to Special Learners*
- MENC, *The School Music Program: A New Vision*

LIBRARY

There are three music textbook series available in their entirety. The *Holt Music* (1988 edition), *Silver Burdett Ginn Music Connection* (1995), and *Macmillan Share the Music* (1995) K–8 teacher manuals and student texts are on main floor reserve for your use. There are some supplemental materials as well. The entire sets of CDs are available on the fifth floor. See me to check them out overnight.

On the fifth floor are several older music textbook series and their accompanying recordings. Supplemental readings are on reserve in the library. See the calendar for due dates. Don't wait until the last minute to do assignments since there are usually only one or two copies available.

ABSENTEE POLICY

Your final grade will be dropped a step (e.g., from B to B-) for every class missed after the one excused absence. Contact me in case of emergency.

LAB SCHOOL

Immaculate Conception School (PreK–8), located on Buffalo and Plain Streets (in same block as GIAC and Beverly J. Martin Elementary School), serves as the IC Junior Vocal student-teaching early field experience site. Music classes are in session from 12:30 to 1:50 M, T, TH, F. *There are no music classes on Wednesday.*

Assignment #10 Lab School Observation
Dates below are the available dates to visit the lab school. You must arrange your own transportation. See me immediately if there is a problem. Details of this assignment will follow later on an assignment sheet. These are the *only dates available!*
- March 2, 3, 13, 14, 16, 21, 23, 24, 27, 28, 30, 31
- April 10, 11, 13, 14

Two classroom observations are required and can be done on one day. However, you are welcome to visit there anytime and as often as you like!

COURSE EVALUATION

As part of the educational reform movement and in conjunction with our National Standards in Music Education, alternative ways of assessing student learning are being developed and implemented. During this course we will use more "authentic" forms of assessment to assess your understanding. You may then in turn use these nontraditional assessment approaches with your students.

Evaluation will be ongoing, and you will play an active role in the process. There will be opportunities for revision of written assignments, as well as various small-group experiences and a considerable amount of reflection and self-evaluation. Hopefully, this approach can serve as a basis for evaluating your students' musical growth at some future date.

TECHNOLOGY ASSIGNMENTS

- Following your attendance at the lab school concert, respond on-line to the event.
- Visit the MENC Web site for information on MIOSM (Music in Our Schools Month). Jot down what you learned in your processfolio.
- Go to the computer lab and examine at least two software programs appropriate for prekindergarten through grade 6. Use the printed guidelines to help you assess the programs.

ASSIGNMENTS

Processfolio = 10%
Compilation of the coursework in *all its stages* including: class notes, notes from reading assignments, written assignments/revisions, articles/handouts.
Processfolio should be an organized, three-ring notebook.

Performance = 40%
Class application of assignments including daily assignments, guided journal entries, peer-teaching, and class contribution. Obviously, you are expected to be in class daily. More than one absence will be reflected in your semester grade.

Projects = 50%
- Mini lesson plan (Assignment #6)
- Special learner video and summary (Assignment #7)
- Full lesson plan and peer teaching from the plan (Assignment #8)
- Lab School observation and written summary (Assignment #10)
- Closure (Assignment #11)
- Technology Assignments

APPOINTMENTS

Please schedule an appointment to discuss any confusion, problem, or question with classes or assignments. Most problems can be solved if confronted early in the semester.

Welcome to one of the first phases on your journey as a music educator! I hope you find this a valuable experience no matter what your chosen professional path.

As teachers we stand for three things—three principles:

      (1) dignity of the individual

      (2) excellence

      (3) service

Many things will change, but these principles will not change.

Treat a man as he is and he will remain as he is. Treat a man as he can and should be, and he will become as he can and should be.

—Goethe

Calendar—Spring, 2000

T 1/18   **Introduction—Perform, Create, Describe**

TH 1/20   **Multiple Meanings of Music for Children**
Assignment: Read pp. xii–xiv and Ch. 1, textbook (Campbell & Scott-Kassner).

T 1/25   **Musical Concepts and Generative Teaching**
Assignment #1: Write your personal philosophy of music education. 1–2 pages typewritten.
      Read "Issues in Music Education" handout. (This may help you formulate
      your written philosophy, too!)

TH 1/27   **Modes of Understanding**
Assignment: Read text, pp. 15–33.
      Read "Generative Approach to Teaching" handout.

T 2/1   **Relating Theory to Practice**
Assignment: Read text, pp. 33–46. Be prepared to discuss questions on pp. 44–45.

TH 2/3   **Child Development**
Assignment: Read text Ch. 5, "Pitch and the Child," and handout on child development.
Assignment #2: Child development and music textbook series.

T 2/8   **Child Development (The Child Voice)**
Assignment: Read text Ch. 6, "The Singing Child."
Assignment #3: Select a song from text, Newman list, or any other source. Choose grade
      level for song and defend your choice!

TH 2/9   **Teaching a Rote Song**
Assignment #3 cont.: Select an action song to teach the class.

T 2/15   **Teaching a Rote Song**
Assignment #4: Select another song to teach the class. Focus on a musical concept.
      Study handout on musical concepts.

TH 2/17   **Teaching a Rote Song**
Assignment #4 cont.: Peer-teaching
Assignment: Read text Ch. 11, "Curriculum Design & Evaluation."

T 2/22   **Instructional Objectives and Planning**
Assignment #5: Summarize Leonhard & House reading. Write an instructional objective.
      The National Standards—What? Why?

TH 2/24   **Assessment Strategies**
Assignment: Read and be prepared to discuss handouts on authentic assessment.

T 2/29	**Guided Listening as Part of the Lesson**
	Assignment: Read text Ch. 7, "The Listening Child."

TH 3/2	**Guided Listening as Part of the Lesson**
	Assignment #6: Mini Lesson Plan and turn in processfolios.

T 3/7 & TH 3/9	**No Class—Spring Break**

T 3/14	**Music for Exceptional Children**
	Assignment: Read text, Ch. 14.

TH 3/16	**Music for Exceptional Children**
	Assignment: Be prepared to discuss questions on pp. 353–54.

T 3/21	**Music for Exceptional Children**
	Assignment #7: Schaberg *TIPS* summary and video summary.

TH 3/23	**Peer-Teaching**
	Assignment #8: Full written lesson plan. Teach portion to class.

T 3/28	**Peer-Teaching**
	Assignment #8: cont..

TH 3/30	**Peer-Teaching**
	Assignment #8: cont..

T 4/4	**Methodologies**
	Assignment: Read textbook, Ch. 3.
	Lab School Spring Concert in Ford Aud. at 7:00 p.m. Extra Credit!!

TH 4/6	**Methodologies**
	Assignment #9: Formulate three "common threads" among the various approaches. Discern distinguishing features of each methodology. Be prepared to apply each approach in a teaching example.

T 4/11	**Multiculturalism, Technology, and Integrated Curriculum**
	*Assignment:*Read text, Ch. 12, 13, & 15 for general ideas. Try to synthesize ideas from the semester within these contexts. What are the implications for your teaching?

TH 4/13	**Continuation of Tuesday's assignment**

T 4/18	**Selecting Quality Literature**
	Assignment #10: Lab School observations

TH 4/20	**Selecting Quality Literature and Music Textbook Series**

T 4/25	**Classroom Management**
	Assignment: Read selected passages from Rossman, *TIPS: Discipline in the Music Classroom*

TH 4/27	**Closure**
	Assignment #11: Closure: Synthesis! (by Monday, 5/1 by *10:00 a.m.*)
	Self-evaluations due *today* in class!

Tuesday, April 4, 2000, 7:00 p.m.
Lab School Spring Concert, Ford Auditorium Ithaca College
(Extra Credit: Turn in program with short paragraph giving your reactions to the experience.)

MUE 314: ELEMENTARY MUSIC METHODS
DR. VICTOR VALLO
ANDERSON COLLEGE
SPRING 2000

COURSE INFORMATION
Course Designation: MUE 314: Elementary Music Methods
Class Time & Place: Tues., Thurs., 12:30–13:45; Rainey Center 125)
Course Description: This course offers an application of teaching methods and materials relating to elementary school childrens' ability to learn musical concepts. Music educators must be aware of the role of music in early childhood development and must master the skills necessary to teach music at this critical age level. This course will allow you, the student, to master these vital competency-based skills.

INSTRUCTOR INFORMATION
Dr. Victor Vallo Jr., Associate Professor of Music
Rainey Fine Arts Center (Room 117)
(864) 231-2076
vvallo@anderson-college.edu
Office hours are immediately before and after class as well as by appointment. Check with instructor for daily office hours which may vary based on student-teacher visits in area schools.

COURSE GOALS AND OBJECTIVES
The goals of this course are that you will be able to
- Teach a singing, playing, listening, and movement activity
- Know, understand, and apply the nine National Standards for Music Education in your four required teaching activities
- Complete a computer research project based on topics found on the World Wide Web (Internet) (e.g., MENC Homepage)
- Compile a notebook of elementary music materials
- Complete a bulletin board that has an elementary music theme with musical concepts
- Complete musical analysis cards for both elementary music methods/materials and elementary musical instruments
- Learn to play and teach the recorder and Autoharp
- Make a musical instrument for use in an elementary class
- Observe and work with elementary music teachers in the area elementary schools

METHODS OF ASSESSING ACHIEVEMENT OF LEARNING OBJECTIVES
Students will be expected to fulfill all requirements of this course which are listed below. Written and oral feedback will be given to the student during the course of the semester.

(1) Teach the following activities at different K–6 levels:
    (a) Singing Activity
    (b) Playing Activity
    (c) Listening Activity
    (d) Movement Activity
Students should make these teaching activities as creative and as interesting as possible since they will be taught to the other members of the class. Use visual aids if possible and make copies of your typed lesson plan for each member of the class and for the instructor.

(2) Write a lesson plan for each of the above four activities where you list and/or explain the following components:

  (a) Title of activity (i.e., Singing Activity, etc.)
  (b) Level (K, 1st, 2nd, 3rd, 4th, 5th, 6th grades)
  (c) Materials used (include your sources)
  (d) Objectives (The student will be able to . . .)
  (e) Teaching procedure (include motivation, etc.)
  (f) Related activities (activities that augment learning)

(3) Make a musical instrument. Draw a master copy with a typed explanation of how you made it. Distribute copies of your handout to each member of the class and to the instructor.

(4) Design a musical bulletin board. Draw a master copy and make copies for the class. A bulletin board will be provided.

(5) Compile a notebook of the materials distributed in class by the instructor and your classmates. This notebook can and will be a ready sourcebook for your first elementary music job.

(6) Conduct a computer research project on an elementary music topic using the computer (World Wide Web and Internet). Write a two-page summary of your research.

(7) Fill out five elementary music materials and five elementary musical instrument analysis cards. Blank cards, music materials, and musical instruments will be provided.

(8) Observe elementary music teachers as part of your field experience prior to your internship. Select teachers who have agreed to having you visit and teach their students.

(9) **Extra Credit:** Write a one-page summary of any of the books in the Supplementary Readings section of this syllabus. These books are on Reserve at the Anderson College library.

STUDENT FEEDBACK AND GRADING POLICIES AND PROCEDURES

  A = 90–100
  B = 80–89
  C = 70–79
  D = 60–69
  F = Below 60

Late Assignments: A 10% late penalty will be deducted from the total amount of points for that assignment.

GRADE DISTRIBUTION

Course Content		Possible Points	Total Points
Singing Activity		50	_____
Preparation	_____		
Accuracy	_____		
Delivery	_____		
Musical Value	_____		
Lesson Plan	_____		
Playing Activity		50	_____
Preparation	_____		
Accuracy	_____		
Delivery	_____		
Musical Value	_____		
Lesson Plan	_____		

Course Content	Possible Points	Total Points
Listening Activity	50	_____
Preparation _____		
Accuracy _____		
Delivery _____		
Musical Value _____		
Lesson Plan _____		
Movement Activity	50	_____
Preparation _____		
Accuracy _____		
Delivery _____		
Musical Value _____		
Lesson Plan _____		
Handmade Musical Instrument	20	_____
Bulletin Board	10	_____
Notebook of Materials	20	_____
Computer Research Project	20	_____
Elementary School Visits	10	_____
Elementary Music Materials Cards	10	_____
Elementary Music Instrument Cards	10	_____
Mid-term Examination	100	_____
Final Examination	100	_____
Extra Credit Summaries	5 each	_____
Total Possible Points	500	
Final Numerical Grade	500/5	

Percentage of Credit for Categories of Course Work

Mid-term Exam	20%
Final Exam	20%
Teaching Competency	40%
Projects and Assignments	20%

METHODS OF INSTRUCTION

This course will be taught via lecture, demonstration, discovery, cooperative learning, and both individual and group participation. Outside observations and individual activities (i.e., supplementary reading) are strongly encouraged so that both group and individual learning may be optimized.

ASSIGNMENTS AND COURSE CALENDAR

Jan. 13	Course introduction; syllabus review	Syllabus
Jan. 18	Historical Foundations of Music Education	Lecture
Jan. 20	Ch. 1: How Children Learn	5–18
Jan. 25	Ch. 2: Guidelines for Teaching Music	19–37
Jan. 27	Ch. 3: Fundamentals of Music	37–83
Feb. 1	Ch. 4: Teaching Music through Singing	85–142
Feb. 3	Ch. 5: Integrating Songs with Other Subjects	143–220
Feb. 8	Piano: Applications: Practice teaching activity	Demos
Feb. 10	Elementary School Visits (no class)	
Feb. 15	**Singing Activity: Student Presentations**	

Feb. 17	Ch. 6: Teaching Music through Instruments	221–70
Feb. 22	Autoharp Practicum and Applications (guest Autoharpist)	
Feb. 24	Recorder Practicum and Applications	
Feb. 29	Orff Instruments Practicum and Applications	
Mar. 2	Playing Activity: Student Presentations	
Mar. 7	Elementary Music Video: "Kids Make Music"	
Mar. 9	**Mid-Term Examination**	1–270
Mar. 14	Ch. 14: Teaching Music through Listening	271–329
Mar. 16	Elementary School Visits (no class)	
Mar. 20	Spring Break (through March 26)	
Mar. 28	**Listening Activity: Student Presentations**	
Mar. 30	Ch. 8: Teaching Music through Movement	331–76
Apr. 4	**Elementary Music Teaching at Concord Elementary**	
Apr. 6	**Movement Activity: Student Presentations**	
Apr. 11	Ch. 9: Creative Experiences with Music	377–404
Apr. 13	Ch. 10: Integrating Music with the Study of Peoples, Places, and Cultures	405–55
Apr. 18	Ch. 11: Experience with Music and Other Arts Epilogue: The Continuing Place of Music	457–502 503–5
Apr. 20	Elementary Music Video: "Sing, Move, Listen"	
Apr. 25	Elementary School Visits (no class)	
Apr. 27	Measurement and Evaluation in Music	Lecture
May 2	Notebooks due with all contents (except class notes) Elementary Music Materials Analysis Cards due Elementary Music Instrument Analysis Cards due Handmade Musical Instruments due with demos Computer Research Projects due Review for Final Exam	
May 8	**Final Examination**	271–505

TEXTBOOKS, MATERIALS, AND SUPPLEMENTARY READINGS

Required Texts

Anderson, W. M.,& Lawrence, J. (1998) *Integrating music into the classroom* (4th ed.). Belmont, CA: Wadsworth Publishing Co.

Froseth, J. (1998). *Do it! Play recorder* (Book 1). Chicago: IL: GIA Publications, 1998.

Supplementary Texts (on Reserve in A.C. Library)

Campbell, P. S. (1998). *Songs in their heads: Music and its meaning in children's lives.* New York: Oxford University Press.

Hoffer, M. L., & Hoffer, C. R. (1987). *Music in the elementary classroom: Musicianship and teaching.* New York: Harcourt Brace Jovanovich.

McDonald, D. T., & Simmons, G. M. (1989). *Musical growth and development: Birth through six.* New York: Schirmer Books.

Newman, G. (1995). *Teaching children music* (4th ed.). Madison, WI: Brown & Benchmark.

Materials

> Soprano Recorder
> Three-Ring Binder (3"–4")
> Materials to make a musical instrument
> Materials to design and create a bulletin board
> Elementary Musical Instrument and Materials Analysis Cards
> Autoharp (provided by A.C.)
> Orff Instruments (provided by A.C.)

COMPUTER AND INFORMATION TECHNOLOGY AND USAGE

Students in this course are required to complete an elementary music research project using the World Wide Web and the Internet. Recommended Web sites are: www.menc.org; www.kindermusik.com; www.ars-nova.com.

COURSE POLICIES

(a) This is a course where group participation and interaction are essential. Your attendance is therefore important to the success of this course, as well as to your personal learning. Absences due to illness, emergency, and college-authorized activities will be excused. Unexcused absences may result in a lower overall grade. The following is a summary:

> 1 absence = A
> 2 absences = A
> 3 absences = B
> 4 absences = C
> 5 absences = D
> 6+ absences = F

(b) The reading assignments should be prepared before the class is given on that subject so that discussion will be enhanced by your knowledge and participation. The lecture will highlight the important points that are of particular relevance to you as you prepare to become music educators.

(c) The bulletin board must be an original creation. You are to use a wide variety of materials (e.g., crepe paper, etc.) and you will be graded on your creativity, originality, potential interest to elementary-level children, and attractiveness. Xerox copies of your bulletin board design are to be handed out to your classmates and instructor on the class day your bulletin board is due.

(d) The A.C. Education Division requires that MUE 314 (Elementary Music Methods) students have a practicum experience concurrent with this course. You are therefore required to have a minimum of 10 hours in the field visiting elementary music programs in the area elementary schools.

LEARNING FACILITIES AND RESOURCES FOR STUDENTS FOR COURSE

You are encouraged to use the computer labs on campus to do your research project on an elementary music topic. The music education closet (in Gambrill Choral Room) is also available for your use in completing your elementary music projects.

MUSIC 320: TEACHING MUSIC IN THE ELEMENTARY SCHOOL
DR. SHARON DAVIS GRATTO
GETTYSBURG COLLEGE
FALL 1999

Class Meetings: Tues., Thurs., 10:00–11:15, First Floor Music Education Curriculum Library
Instructor: Dr. Sharon Davis Gratto, Schmucker, Room 220, Extension 6135
E-mail address: sgratto@gettysburg.edu
E-mail alias: mus-320-a@gettysburg.edu
Office hours: by appointment

REQUIRED MATERIALS

Burakoff, G., & Hettrick, W. E. (1980). *The sweet pipes recorder book* (Book I, soprano). Levittown, NY: Sweet Pipes, Inc.

Campbell, P. S., & Scott-Kassner, C. (1995). *Music in childhood: From preschool through elementary grades.* New York: Schirmer Books, Inc. and accompanying CD recording of children's songs.

Consortium of National Arts Education Associations. (1994) *National standards for arts education.* Reston, VA: MENC.

Strategies for teaching series. Reston, Virginia: MENC.

(1) *Prekindergarten Music:* Compiled and edited by Wendy L. Sims, 1995.

(2) *K–4 General Music:* Compiled and edited by Sandra L. Stauffer and Jennifer Davidson, 1996.

Soprano Recorder (in C): Baroque Fingering System (available for purchase in the music office)

MENC/PMEA publications: the *Music Educators Journal, Teaching Music,* and the *PMEA Journal.*

Tuning fork (A=440) (also available for purchase in the music office)

Blank VHS videotape to record peer and practicum teaching. One blank tape should be sufficient for two semesters of the elementary and secondary methods classes. *Five points will be subtracted from the letter grade for each lesson a student teaches without his or her own videotape (including if another student's tape is used).*

Additional Course Materials

Basal music series, all books for elementary grades in the curriculum library. Focus should be on the most recent basal series of Silver Burdett Ginn and McGraw-Hill.

Recordings from the curriculum library, music department library, and college library.

Available music technology software and equipment in the music department technology lab and on the Internet.

Current music education journals, other print materials, videotapes, CDs, and audiotapes that are related to the course and that are available in the Music Department's curriculum library, in the college library, or are distributed in class.

RESOURCE BIBLIOGRAPHY

Resources for supplementary reading and future reference are available either in the music education curriculum library or on reserve in the main library.

Anderson, W. (1991). *Teaching music with a multicultural approach.* Reston, VA: MENC. (4 VHS tapes and a book).

Anderson, W. M., & Campbell, P. S., (Eds.) (1996). *Multicultural perspectives in music education* (2nd ed.). Reston, VA: MENC.

Andress, B., (Ed.). (1989). *Promising practices: Prekindergarten music education.* Reston, VA: MENC.

Campbell, P. S. (1996). *Music in cultural context: Eight views on world music education.* Reston, VA: MENC.

Choksy, L., Abramson, R. M., Gillespie, A. E., & Woods, D. (1986). *Teaching music in the twentieth century.* Englewood Cliffs, New Jersey: Prentice Hall, Inc.

Frazee, J., & Kreuter, K. (1987). *Discovering Orff: A curriculum for music teachers.* New York: Schott Music Corp.

Gardner, H. (1983). *Frames of mind: The theory of multiple intelligence.* New York: Basic Books, Inc.

Johnson, M. D. (April, 1993). Dalcroze skills for all teachers. *Music Educators Journal 79*(8). 42–45.

Kaplan, P. R., & Stauffer, S. L (1994). *Cooperative learning in music.* Reston, VA: MENC.

Mark, M. L. (1996). *Contemporary music education* (3rd ed.). New York: Schirmer Books.

MENC Committee on Standards. (1986). *The school music program: Description and standards.* Reston, VA: MENC.

MENC. (1990). *Choral music for children: An annotated list.* Reston, VA: MENC.

MENC Task Force on General Music Course of Study. (1991). *Teaching general music: A course of study.* Reston, VA: MENC.

Palmer, M., & Sims, W. L., (Eds.). (1993). *Music in prekindergarten: Planning and teaching.* Reston, VA: MENC.

Stauffer, S. L., (Ed.). (1995). *Toward tomorrow: New visions for general music.* Reston, VA: MENC.

Steen, A. (1992). *Exploring Orff.* New York: Schott Music Corp.

Warner, B. (1991). *Orff-Schulwerk: Applications for the classroom.* Englewood Cliffs, NJ: Prentice Hall.

Weikart, P. S. (1982). *Teaching movement and dance: A sequential approach to rhythmic movement.* Ypsilanti, MI: The High/Scope Press.

OBJECTIVES AND SCOPE

Students will study, evaluate, and utilize methods, materials, and techniques related to teaching vocal/general music in the elementary school. They will micro-teach lessons to their peers in class and children in the campus day care/preschool, as well as and the visiting Head Start children. In the process of doing this teaching, students will continue to develop a personal philosophy of music education, will become familiar with current trends in elementary music teaching today, and will develop skills and understandings necessary to plan, implement, and evaluate a comprehensive music program on the elementary level. The class will be taught using a combination of seminar-style lectures with discussion, peer-teaching, on-site observations, on- and off-campus practicum teaching experiences, electronic dialogues, Internet searches, reading, writing, and materials and equipment for exploration and investigation.

By the time the course is completed, students should

- be able to teach songs by rote and by note with and without accompaniment, including using a tuning fork
- be able to accompany songs with simple piano and Autoharp parts
- be able to play soprano recorder well enough to teach an elementary beginning recorder class and be familiar with the other instruments of the recorder family and related recorder methods and materials
- be able to research, write, and prepare comprehensive elementary general music lesson plans and units, using a standardized format
- be familiar with and able to select and utilize age-appropriate materials and activities for general music, Pre-K through grade 6, and upper elementary grade level choral music
- be able to use Kodály hand signs with corresponding vocal and rhythm syllables to teach song material and music reading
- be familiar with the instruments of the Orff-Schulwerk instrumentarium and other elementary classroom instruments
- be able to direct and sustain student attention to a piece of recorded music

- be able to plan and implement activities intended to encourage student creativity in the music class
- be familiar with the range of possibilities for using movement and dance in the elementary general music class
- be familiar with a varied selection of elementary song, listening, and reading material, including selections from varied cultures within and outside the United States
- begin to understand ways to integrate music with other disciplines in the elementary curriculum
- begin to be familiar with ways to handle the inclusion of children with special needs into the elementary general music class
- know the National Standards for Arts Education and how to apply the National Standards for Music Education to the elementary curriculum
- begin to be familiar with ways to assess student progress in the elementary general music classroom

GENERAL REQUIREMENTS

(1) Punctual attendance at and participation in *each* class session. Attendance in this course should be treated as if you were working in a school music teaching position. One absence *for any reason* will be allowed. The final course grade will be lowered five points for each unexcused absence after the first. Students are responsible for all class work missed due to excused or unexcused absences. Since no senior recitals are scheduled for class meeting days, they will not be considered for excused absences. Students whose peer-teaching lessons are not ready on the assigned day may not be given another class day to teach that lesson.

(2) Observation of and participation in practicum preschool and elementary classes off-campus.

(3) On-time completion of reading assignments and written work. Written assignments should reflect careful attention to spelling, grammar, and syntax, and must be prepared on a word processor. Late written assignments will receive a grade one level below the actual earned grade (i.e., A to A-, B- to C+, etc.). Peer-teaching assignments must be ready for presentation on the day scheduled, even if time does not allow the teaching to take place until the next class meeting. No written assignments will be accepted after the last day of classes.

(4) Because this is an upper-level class for majors, students who take it are responsible for information included in all assigned readings, whether or not the readings are discussed in class. Discussion of some readings will take place via e-mail dialogue.

(5) Timely and thoughtful responses to e-mail dialogues.

(6) Attendance at monthly meetings (scheduled for Sundays at 6:15 p.m. with light supper) of the Gettysburg CMENC chapter.

SELECTED ASSIGNMENT DETAILS

Details of additional assignments TBA.

Observations. During the semester, each student will be responsible for observing and preparing written reports on three music classes: one in general music, grades K–3; one in general music, grades 4–6; and one in elementary chorus or band, grades 4–6. In addition, written journals must be kept of all other observations, whether they are made independently or together as a class. The additional observations should include a preschool or Head Start class (which may or may not have much music teaching) and, if possible, an elementary assembly or concert presentation. Class observation trips must be written up at least in the journal and may also be used for the longer and more formal written reports. Assembly and concert presentations are available to view on videotape (see Dr. Gratto for this) if a live presentation is not available or convenient to attend. Be certain to record your observations for this course on the appropriate file cards in the music office.

Holiday Program Plan Information. Prepare a written outline of an all-school public holiday program for an elementary school, grades K–5. The program should be based on a theme or central idea and include ideas for connecting the material. Performances by school instrumental and choral groups should be part of the program. Each child in the school must have something to do in the program. Your theme idea should be discussed with Dr. Gratto before you begin work on this assignment.

Unit Outline. Prepare an outline of an integrated unit plan around an assigned theme, grades 4–6. Classes on each grade level in the group meet once a week for 45 minutes. The unit should last four weeks and should incorporate a wide variety of music class activities. Suggestions for integrating the unit into the regular elementary classroom curriculum should be included. Include multicultural material if possible and appropriate. This unit may form the basis for one that you teach during the student-teaching semester.

Collections of Materials and Resources. Each student will be expected to compile and submit the following by the last day of classes:
  (1) A large three-ring binder notebook sectioned off as follows to include:
      (a) Elementary Methods class notes
      (b) Articles handed out in class or collected independently
      (c) Three written observation reports
      (d) Peer-teaching lesson plans, both yours and those of other students in the class
      (e) Elementary basal series text evaluations in the form of general notes about series trends and changes over time, as well as specific details about the four most recent series books from Silver Burdett Ginn and Macmillan (considering layout, presentation/appeal, ease of use, index, content variety and quality, glossary, quantity of materials included, recordings, and other available supplementary materials)
      (f) A beginning list of your favorite general music song material, K–6, and the collection or basal series in which the songs are located (in order for you to locate them easily in the future)
      (g) A beginning list of children's literature materials, including folk tales, poems, chants, children's books about music, etc.
      (h) A beginning list of recorder materials appropriate for elementary school students
      (i) Copies of all written assignments and other work from this class
      (j) A beginning list of computer music software (CAI, writing, music games, etc.) and Internet Web sites that could be used with elementary music students
      (k) A beginning list (or actual octavo samples) of elementary choral music that you like and might consider using in your program
  (2) An inexpensive portable file box or milk crate containing:
      (a) Elementary music programs, both those personally attended and those collected
      (b) Music catalogs for vendors of elementary general music and choral materials and equipment

Teaching Practicum at Gettysburg Head Start. This pre-student-teaching experience will begin with observations of several Head Start classes that are within walking distance of campus. Following these class visits and a meeting with the Head Start director, Dr. Gratto will teach demonstration lessons in the classes where Methods students will work. For approximately ten weeks during the remainder of the semester, each student in the class will prepare and teach one 30-minute music lesson to the same Head Start group each week. Lesson plans will be discussed in class before and after they are taught. Each student is required to record the lesson for evaluation purposes and to maintain a regular tape "swap" with the Head Start classroom teacher to provide her with a body of song material that can be used after the semester ends. Head Start lessons should focus on developing singing and listening skills and include movement, classroom instrument playing, and creative activities.

Examinations

Midterm Competency Evaluation on recorder, piano, and Autoharp. Individual appointments will be scheduled for October 13, 14, 15.

In place of a written midterm examination, there will be five shorter announced tests during the semester. In the event of an absence on a test day, the test will not be made up, but the lowest test grade for the semester will be dropped and not included in the semester average.

Final Competency Exams. Scheduled by individual appointment during the examination period.

Written Final Examination. December 17, 8:30–11:30 a.m.

Extra Credit Assignments

(1) Attend a "Meet the Teacher" night at an area school (select from the Hanover, Gettysburg, Upper Adams, New Oxford, or Littlestown school districts) and report your experience back to the class via e-mail using the class alias. While this assignment is for extra credit, it is something that will be very helpful for you to observe. Focus on what is happening schoolwide and what the music teacher's role in the event is. You should be present when the evening's events begin and should attend any large-group general meeting that takes place. You may also contact Mrs. Gail Jones or Ms. Jill Marzolf for information about Beginner Band/Orchestra parent orientation in the Gettysburg School District, an event that may also be used to satisfy the requirements for this assignment. An area PTA meeting or a Board meeting that includes a musical presentation may be used for this assignment as well.

(2) Attend the concert by the flutist from South India in the recital hall on Friday, September 10, at 8 p.m. Write your observations about the concert in your observation journal and include a copy of the program in your files.

(3) Attend the Introduction to Orff-Schulwerk workshop with Orff clinician Sue Davis at Rice Elementary School in Mt. Holly Springs on Saturday, October 9, from 9–12 am. No registration fee or write-up required; this is Saturday of reading days weekend, but some of you may still want and be able to attend before setting off on a trip. (Heavy points are available here!)

GRADING

(1) Attendance/Participation, including school observations and MENC chapter meeting	5%
(2) Practicum teaching in a school setting	10%
(3) Peer micro-teaching (lessons taught in class)	15%
(4) Written assignments, including lesson plans, journal writing, e-mail responses, and other miscellaneous written assignments	15%
(5) Materials files and course notebook (graded on content and presentation)	5%
(6) Written observation reports (3)	15%
(7) Quiz average and midterm playing competency grade	15%
(8) Final exam and final playing competency grade	20%

CALENDAR

This calendar is subject to change as observation and practicum teaching opportunities become available and can be scheduled.

Please bring all books and recorders to every class. Read over the questions and activities at the end of each chapter in the Campbell text.

Observation Notes. Group observations and practicum experiences on Tuesdays and Thursdays will be scheduled beginning in the early morning before class, may include class time, and will not extend beyond 11:15 a.m., with the exception of one visit to the music technology and magnet program at Baileys Elementary School in Fairfax County, Virginia. Students not involved in Tuesday rehearsals of the Women's Chorus may use that time for off-campus independent observations. The Thursday time block from 11:15 a.m. to 1 p.m. is also available to be scheduled independently for observations and practicum experiences, except on Common Hour days. Check the Common Hour schedule carefully to avoid conflicts. Students must keep the time before class clear on days when school visits are scheduled.

Recorder Ensemble Playing Sessions. Six sessions will be held on Friday afternoons from 2–3 p.m. on 9/3, 9/10, 11/12, and 11/19 and from 3–4 p.m. on 9/10. Each student is required to attend at least two of these sessions or to make alternative arrangements in the event of a schedule conflict. Extra credit will be provided for students who attend more than two sessions. Meet in room 220 to receive your playing assignment for the day. Assignment selections will be made based on recorder playing experience.

Aug. 31 (T)   Course introduction, lesson plans, observations, National Arts Standards, basal series, Orff instrumentarium, other classroom instruments and materials, rote song teaching, student-teaching information.

Sept. 2 (R)   Setting up and organizing the elementary music classroom (slide presentation); classroom management and discipline; establishing guidelines and rules for the music classroom.
Have Sept. '99 *Music Educators Journal's* five articles on Assessment in Music Education read by today (pp. 19–44).

Sept. 7 (T)   **Have Campbell, Preface and Ch. 1, read by today** (meanings).
Go over the National Standards book, grades K–4.
Test #1 (including memorization of the nine music content standards in order).

Sept. 9 (R)   **Have Campbell, Ch. 2 and 3, read by today** (theory and methods).

Note: Attend all or part of the concert of South Indian music on Friday, Sept. 10, in the recital hall beginning at 8 p.m. Record your comments in journal for extra course credit. (See note above.)

Sept. 14 (T)   **Have Campbell, Ch. 5 and 6, read by today** (pitch and singing).
Be prepared to teach assigned song by rote using tuning fork and no accompaniment (3–4 minutes each; no written plan due).

Sept. 16 (R)   **Have Campbell, Ch. 7, read by today** (listening).
Test #2; Listening to music in the Western tradition and developing new ears for world music.

Note: CMENC meeting, Sunday, September 20, 6:15 p.m.

Sept. 21 (T)   Turn in ten classroom rules, five general and five musical ones

Sept. 23 (R)   TBA

Sept. 28 (T)   **Have Campbell, Ch. 9 and 10, read by today** (playing and creating).
Squonk Opera presentation, Kline Theatre (rear)

Sept. 30 (R)   Teach Prekindergarten Strategies Lessons (5–6 minutes each; no written plan).

Oct. 5 (T)   **Have Campbell, Ch. 7 and 13, read by today** (multiculturalism).
Pre-K Lessons, Part 2.

Oct. 7 (R)   Special guest in class: Professor Carol Richards from Australia.
Pre-K lessons conclusion, beginning at 9:00 am.

Reading Days
Note: Midterm playing competencies, October 13–15 by individual appointment.

Oct. 14 (R)   **Have Campbell, Ch. 11 and 15, read by today** (curriculum and integration).

Note: CMENC meeting, Sunday, October 18, 6:15 pm.

Oct. 19 (T)   Teach K–4 Strategies Lessons (8–10 minutes apiece; no written plan).
Test #3 (includes *Teaching Music* article on early childhood ed.).

Oct. 21 (R) K–4 Strategies Lessons, part 2.
Pre-K visit (Gettysburg's Growing Place) and demonstration teaching (meet at the West Building at 9:15 a.m.).

Oct. 26 (T) K–4 Strategies Lessons, continued.

Oct. 28 (R) No class.

Nov. 2 (T) K–4 Strategies Lessons, conclusion.

Nov. 4 (R) **Have Campbell, Ch. 4 and 8, read by today** (rhythm and moving).
10:30 a.m.–Aspers Head Start visit and teaching.

Note: CMENC meeting, Sunday, November 6, 6:15 p.m.—Folk dancing with Gail Jones.

Nov. 9 (T) **Test #4** on Text Ch. 4, 8, 11, and 15; recorder lesson.

Nov. 11 (R) **No class: Fall Convocation preparation.**

Nov. 16 (T) **Holiday program plan due.**

Nov. 18 (R) **Computer software and equipment sharing session—meet in computer music lab.**

Nov. 23 (T) **Test #5.**

Thanksgiving!

Nov. 30 (T) **Integrated Unit Plan due, including one complete lesson plan for a single class.**

Dec. 2 (R) **Internet Web site sharing session—meet in computer music lab.**

Dec. 7 (T) **Have Campbell, Ch. 14, read by today** (inclusion).

Dec. 9 (R) Final class; catch up, recap., and exam preparation.

Final Note. Open dates TBA as soon as they are finalized in terms of additional reading assignments, peer-teaching assignments, outside observations, and practicum teaching; school visits and practicum experiences in the campus preschool/day care center.

INSTRUMENT COMPETENCIES
Midterm Playing Exam
Piano. "America" in the key of F (from the basal series arrangement of your choice), and "Happy Birthday" with simple block chord accompaniment by ear in the key of C.

Recorder. "Hot Cross Buns," "Mary Had A Little Lamb," "Go Tell Aunt Rhody" (all songs by ear or from memory in the key of G; you may locate any of them that you do not know in a basal series text or in a beginning band method book).

Autoharp. "Happy Birthday" in the key of F.

Final Playing Exam (Note: selections will be chosen from the lists below)
Recorder. Seniors: anything in the Sweet Pipes soprano recorder method, Book I; Juniors: anything in the first half of the same book.

Use the piano accompanying books in the basal series texts as a resource for locating and learning arrangements of the following songs for piano and Autoharp.
Piano. "Bingo," "If You're Happy and You Know it Clap Your Hands," "Six Little Ducks That I Once Knew," and "The Star-Spangled Banner," plus two song accompaniments of your choice, one from *Share the Music* and one from *The Music Connection,* grades K–4

Autoharp. "Don Gato," "O, Susanna," "Skip to My Lou," "All Night, All Day," "Billy Boy," "Skin and Bones," and "Hush, Little Baby, Don't Say A Word."

MUSC 4363: MUSICAL DEVELOPMENT OF CHILDREN AND ADOLESCENTS
DR. DIANE PERSELLIN
TRINITY UNIVERSITY
FALL 2000

Catalog Statement: Programming, instruction, and organization of music in general music classes, prekindergarten through eighth grade

Prerequisite: MUSC 1161: Introduction to Music in American Schools or consent of the instructor

Credit: 3 hours of undergraduate credit

Meetings: 3 hours each week, Mondays and Wednesdays from 10:30 a.m.–12:00 noon.
Ruth Taylor Music Center Room 113

Instructor: Dr. Diane Persellin
Office: Ruth Taylor Music 104
Phone: 999-7265 (office)
E-mail: mailto:dpersell@trinity.edu   persell@trinity.edu
Office Hours: Monday and Wednesday 1:30–2:30.
      Tuesday and Thursday 11:10–12 noon and 1:00–2:00.
      Fridays by appointment.

REQUIRED TEXTS

Campbell, P. S. (1995). *Music in childhood: From preschool through the elementary grades.* New York: C. Schirmer Books.

Hall, L., Boone, N., Grashel, J., & Watkins, R. (Eds.). (1998). *Strategies for teaching: Guide for music methods classes.* Reston, VA: MENC.

REQUIRED JOURNALS

Music Educators Journal, Teaching Music, Southwestern Musician

SUPPLEMENTARY INSTRUMENTS

A classical guitar and an Aulos recorder

COURSE OBJECTIVES

This course serves as an introduction and overview of children's music in American elementary schools today. This course also provides the foundation for the music pedagogics courses and internships during the professional fifth year, which leads to the degree of Master of Arts in Teaching with teacher certification. Upon completion of this class, you will be able to demonstrate proficiency in the areas of knowledge, skills, and values. These will be based on class discussions, presentations, activities, teaching children, and on the readings. These areas of knowledge, skills, and values will continue to be developed during the professional fifth year.

Specific Course Objectives

Knowledge. As the student, you will demonstrate knowledge of
- singing, moving, listening, creating, describing, playing instruments, and analyzing in the elementary classroom
- the child's voice and how to select appropriate music for children
- the needs of exceptional students in music activities
- planning music activities for all children including children with special needs
- child development, learning theory, learning modalities, and metacognition when planning music activities

- materials that may be used in planning music activities such as music textbooks, children's literature, singing games, folk songs, recordings, and technology
- methodologies used in schools such as Kodály, Orff, Dalcroze, Gordon, Suzuki, and Comprehensive Musicianship
- music and its relation to the other arts and disciplines outside the arts
- music and its relation to history and culture
- the National Standards for Music Education

Skills. As the student, you will demonstrate skills in
- leading classroom singing with or without accompaniment
- playing the guitar, recorder, and Orff instruments
- devising and leading children in guided listening lessons
- leading children in movement activities such as expressive movement, patterned movement, action songs, and singing games
- writing an Orff-style setting of a folk song
- encouraging children's creativity
- teaching music reading based on child-developmental theories
- writing, teaching from, and evaluating lesson plans based on the lesson cycle presented in class and based on the National Standards for Music Education and the Texas Essential Knowledge and Skills

Values. As the student, you will gain an awareness of
- the importance of music for all children
- your own musical growth

Outside of class observations. I will be pleased to make arrangements for you to observe these fine teachers on days and times that fit your schedules and allow you to carpool with other students.
- Mrs. Janie Corley (Music educator who has developed a strong choral program. Her early morning—7:15 A.M!—4th and 5th grade choir has performed at Carnegie Hall. Encino Park Elementary School) Take Hildebrand west to I10. Go north (right) past Loop 410 and Loop 1604. Take a right turn on Encino Drive and follow the signs to the school. Allow 20 minutes.

- Mrs. Renee Meriwether (Music specialist who has developed an innovative K–5 program using folk dances from around the world. Redland Oaks Elementary) Take Hildebrand east to 281. Go left (north) past Loop 410 and Bitters. Turn right (east) on Anderson Loop 1604. Continue 3 miles and take the Redland exit. Go right (south) and follow the signs to the school.

- Mrs. Marguerite McCormick (Director of Children's Chorus of San Antonio). Go north on Stadium Drive to the Quarry. Take a right at Basse and go about one mile. Alamo Heights Methodist Church is on the left. Park in the back parking lot and enter through the door near the playground. Follow the signs to the choir room.

- Mrs. Valerie Thompson (Director of children's choirs at St. Mark's Episcopal Church). Go south on 281 and exit on Houston Street. Turn right on Houston and follow the street around until you see St. Mark's on the left. Park in the parking lot and follow the signs to the choir room.

- Mrs. Cora Hornish (Teacher of beginning strings at Cambridge Elementary School). Take Stadium Drive south to Olmos Drive. Turn left and go over the dam. Veer slightly right (don't take a sharp right turn onto Patterson) and continue to Cambridge. Park behind the school. The orchestra room is next to the cafeteria just off the playground.

ASSIGNED READINGS

On reserve at circulation desk of Elizabeth Coates Library.

Abrahams, F., & Head, P. (1998). *Up a creek without a paddle. Case studies in music education.* Chicago: GIA Pub. 30–36.

Chiodo, P., Frakes, L., MacLeod, S., Pagel, R., Schuler, S., Thompson, J., & Watts, D. (1998, October). Making the grade: Authentic assessment in music, K–8. *Teaching Music.* 34–35.

Choksy, L. (1986). *The Kodály method* (2nd ed.). Englewood Cliffs, NJ: Prentice Hall.

Hall, L. (Ed.) (1998). *Strategies for teaching: Guide for music methods classes.* Reston, VA: MENC.

McCoy, C. (1994, Spring). Music and children's literature: Natural partners. *General Music Today,* 15–19.

Phillips, K. (1992). *Teaching kids to sing.* New York: Schirmer Books.

Saliba, K. (1991). *Accent on Orff: An introductory approach.* Englewood Cliffs, NJ: Prentice Hall.

Shehan, P., Sinor, J., Jordan-DeCarbo, J., & Shamrock, M. (1986, February). Major approaches to music education: An accounting of method (Kodály, Gordon, Dalcroze, Orff, & Suzuki). *Music Educators Journal,* 26–55.

Spanko, J. (1985). *Taming the anthill: Zany alternatives for general music.* Memphis, TN: Memphis Musicraft Publications.

Stauffer, S. (1999, September). Beginning assessment in elementary general music. *Music Educators Journal,* 25–30.

Wong, H., & Wong R. (1998). *The first days of school.* Mountain View, CA: Wong Publications, Inc.

SUGGESTED READINGS

These readings have also been placed on reserve at the circulation desk of the library.

Bartholomew, D. (1993, November). Effective strategies for praising students. *Music Educators Journal,* 40–43.

Bissell, K. E. (1995, August). I'll write the words: You find the rhythm. *Teaching Music,* 40–42.

Bridges, M. (1993, Winter). The benefits of vocal exploration. *General Music Today,* 30–34.

Feierabend, J. (1995, Summer). Music and intelligence in the early years. *Early Childhood Connections,* 5–13.

Goodkin, D. (1994, July). Diverse approaches to multicultural music. *Music Educators Journal,* 39–43.

Gromko, J. E. (1995, Spring). A sound project in composition for young children. *General Music Today,* 27–30.

Hedden, S., & Ferguson, N. (1989, Fall). The ears of a seventh grader. *General Music Today,* 11–13.

Lewis, B. (1989). The research literature in movement-based instruction with children: Implications for music teaching and learning. *Update, 7*(2), 13–17.

Masterson, M. (1994, May). Moving beyond 'It's got a good beat.' *Music Educators Journal,* 24–28.

Moore, J. (1992, Spring). A multicultural curriculum for the middle school. *General Music Today,* 21–23.

Persellin, D., Pautz, M., Feierabend, J., Kenney, S., & Andress, B. (1994, August). Finding quality literature for young children. *Teaching Music,* 19+.

Single, N. A. (1991). Summary of research-based principles of effective teaching. *Update, 9*(2), 3–10.

Snyder, S. (1994, Spring). Language, movement, and music: Process connections. *General Music Today,* 4–9.

Stuessy, J. (1994, January). When the music teacher meets Metallica. *Music Educators Journal,* 28–32.

Upitis, R. (1995, Spring). Fostering children's compositions: Activities for the classroom. *General Music Today,* 16–19.

Walker, D. (1989, Fall). Using instruments in today's general music classroom. *General Music Today,* 14–17.

Webster, P., & Hickey, M. (1995). Challenging children to think creatively. *General Music Today,* 4–10.

Wheatley, S., & Mambo, M. (1994, Spring). Whole language and arts education. *General Music Today,* 10–14.

Wiggins, J. (1995, Spring). Learning through creative interaction with music. *General Music Today,* 11–15.

ASSESSMENT

Teaching children at Hawthorne Elementary School.	20–25%

Includes all written teaching strategies, videotaped teaching of the children, and the reflective assessment of the teaching and learning.

Music advocacy essay on "Why Teach Music"	10–15%

To be submitted to the TMEA undergraduate essay contest for possible publication in the *Southwestern Musician*. (Due Nov. 1.)

Written assignments not addressed by other projects	10%
Five observation reports (Due December 4)	10–15%
Term paper 8–10 pages (November 10)	10–15%

Need to use a minimum of eight books and periodicals and two Web sites.

In-class participation	10–15%

Includes in-class presentations and discussions. Energetic attendance is required. After two absences your grade will be lowered from an A to an A-, A- to a B+, etc. Unusual and extenuating circumstances will be dealt with on an individual basis.

Service Learning Project	10–15%

Develop a collection of songs and activities that you can share with children at the Battered Women's Shelter or the San Antonio Children's Shelter. Share your plans and experiences in class and write your personal reflections in your journal. (I am pleased to set this up for you according to your schedule.)

Guitar proficiency (November 18)	5%
Optional final exam (Final exam period)	0–10%
Journal entries (e-mail or paper; 6–8, one per week)	0–5%
Elementary portfolio notebook or files; due last day of class	0–5%

Rubrics will be used to assess each assignment. These will be distributed and discussed early during the semester so that you will understand the requirements to earn an A or a B, etc. for each project. Because we do not all learn the same way and vary in how we prefer to be assessed, you will have some leeway in how you wish some of the projects to be weighted in this class. At mid-semester you will be asked to evaluate your progress and give a tentative weighting to completed or uncompleted projects. These percentages can be modified during the final self-assessment due on the last day of class.

CALENDAR

Date	Topic	Reading	Due
8/28	Course Introduction. National Standards in Music. Playing the guitar (#2&3)*.		
8/30	The Multiple Meanings of Music for Children. Why Teach Music: Serving as an Advocate for Quality Music Instruction.	Ch. 1 (C & S), 2–14. MENC & TMEA advocacy literature: www.menc.org, www.tmea.org Abrahams & Head (*Case Studies in Mus. Ed.*), 30–36	Journal entry on your personal memories of music in your childhood. Include songs, teachers, individual lessons, and informal music-making experiences

9/6	From Theory to Practice in Teaching Music to Children. Learning Styles in Music Ed.	Ch. 2, 15–45	
9/11	Methods of Teaching Music to Children. The Kodály Method (#1 & 5).	Ch. 3, 47–70	Be prepared to play a cooperative learning strategy based on Table 2.1 on pp. 17–18 in C & S.
9/13	Observation/Guest lecture: Mrs. Kathy Palmer (MA in Kodály) Judson Montessori School.	Choksy *(The Kodály Method)*, Ch. 1 & 2.	
9/18	The Orff Approach (#1, 2, 3, & 5).	*Accent on Orff,* 1–29. Shehan et al., *Major Approaches to Music Ed.,* 26–55.	E-mail an essay on the Kodály method highlighting beginning melodic and rhythmic steps. Include suggestions of appropriate literature for each stage.
9/20	Observation/Guest lecture: Mrs. Carla Haynes (Orff-certified) Long Creek Elementary School.	*Accent on Orff,* 30–100 (includes many notated examples).	
9/25	Other Methods of Teaching Music to Children. (#1, 3 & 5).	*MEJ.*	First draft of three-part Orff arrangement due. Follow guidelines presented in class.
9/27	Rhythm and the Child (#5 & 6). Playing the guitar.	Ch. 4, 73–105.	Be prepared to play three-chord songs in D Major using a simple strum.
10/2	Pitch and the Child (#5 &6). Playing the guitar (#2 & 3).	Ch. 5, 106–24.	First draft of essay due: "Why Teach Music"(for TMEA undergraduate essay contest). Be prepared to play three-chord songs using several strums.
10/4	The Singing Child (#1).	Ch. 6, 126–57.	Title(s) of (possible) term paper topics due.
10/9	How to Teach Singing in Parts (#1). Inaccurate Singing.	*Teaching Kids to Sing,* 23–37.	One-page synopsis of video, *Growing and Singing.* Based on the model presented in class, prepare to teach a short kindergarten song in class.
10/11	The Listening Child (#6).	Ch. 7, 158–83. Hall, *Strategies for Teaching.*	Final draft of "Why Teach Music" essay due. Study the strategies to teach children to listen. Bring your book to class.

10/16	Planning to teach music to kindergartners.		Using the Listening Sequence on p. 175 of C & S and the model presented in class, write a listening lesson for young children. Be prepared to present your lesson in class with visual aids and/or movement activities.
10/18	Be at Hawthorne Elementary School by 10:30. I will teach a 25-minute lesson to a kindergarten class. Following this class we will stay at the school to discuss the class and to plan for next week.		Based on the model presented in class, write first draft of kindergarten teaching strategy. Bring copies for each member of the class to discuss.
10/23	The Moving Child (#6).		Ch. 8, 185–215.
10/25	Co-teach a 25-minute kindergarten class.		Write a teaching strategy for the Hawthorne kindergarten class that you co-teach. Rehearse your questions, songs, and activities so that you are very comfortable with them. Be prepared to be videotaped.
10/30	The Playing Child (#2 & 9). Teaching children how to play the recorder. Mr. Gerald Self, professional harpsichord builder and recorder artist/teacher.	Ch. 9, 216–44.	E-mail an analysis of your videotaped teaching of the kindergarten class using the rubric presented in class.
11/1	Co-teach a 25-minute kindergarten class.	Hall, *Strategies for Teaching.*	Study the strategies to teach children to play instruments.
11/6	The Creating Child (#2, 3, & 4).	Ch. 10, 246–65. Hall, *Strategies for Teaching.*	E-mail an analysis of your videotaped teaching of the kindergarten class. Study the strategies to teach children to create music. Bring your book to class.
11/8	I will teach a 25-minute fifth-grade class.		E-mail an analysis of two lessons in the state-adopted textbooks that deal with creativity in the fourth or fifth grades. Bring the *Strategies* book to class.
11/13	Curriculum Design and Evaluation (#7). The Texas Essential Knowledge and Skills (TEKS).	Ch. 11, 267–87. Chiodo et al. *(Authentic Assessment)*, Stauffer *(Beginning Assessment).*	Write a teaching strategy for the Hawthorne Elementary School fourth or fifth grade class that you will co-teach.

11/13 (cont.)	How the TEKS are directly related to the National Standards in Music Education.	The TEKS can be found and downloaded from the Texas Education Agency Web site: www.TEA.org.	Rehearse your questions, songs, and activities so that you are comfortable with them. Be prepared to be videotaped.
11/15	Co-teach a 25-minute fourth or fifth grade class.	Wong & Wong (*Lesson Mastery*), 197–267.	
11/20	Technology for Music Instruction. Guest lecturer: Mrs. Mary Terrell, Technology Specialist at Boerne Elementary School and former music educator at Jackson-Keller Elementary School.	Ch. 12, 289–306.	E-mail an analysis of your videotaped teaching of fourth or fifth grade class.
11/22	Co-teach a 25-minute fourth or fifth grade class.		
11/27	Music Multiculturalism and Children (#8 & 9).	Ch. 13, 310–29. Hall, *Strategies for Teaching*.	E-mail an analysis of your videotaped teaching of fourth or fifth grade class. Study the strategies on implementing multicultural music into the curriculum. Bring your book to class.
11/29	Co-teach a 25-minute fourth or fifth grade class.	Ch. 14, 331–54.	
12/4	Music for Exceptional Children.	Ch. 15, 356–82.	All outside observation reports should be completed by today. E-mail an analysis of your videotaped teaching of the fourth or fifth grade class. Term paper is due. Ten-minute poster presentation on paper is due.
12/6	Music in an Integrated Curriculum (#8 & 9). Closure.	McCoy (*Music & Children's Literature*). Hall, *Strategies for Teaching*.	Final self-assessment of progress during the semester due. Study the strategies to teach history and culture through music.
TBA	Optional Final Exam		

* The National Standards for Music Education will be addressed throughout this course. Although we rarely teach one concept, skill, or standard in isolation, the standard that is the focus of the learning has been noted above in the topics portion of this syllabus.

MUSE 201: Teaching K-8 Music
Dr. Marcelyn Smale and Dr. Margaret Schmidt
St. Cloud State University
Fall 2000

Instructors:	Dr. Marcelyn Smale	Dr. Margaret Schmidt
Office:	PA 147	PA 144
Phone:	(320)255-2285 (answering machine)	(320)255-2295 (answering machine)
E-mail:	smale@stcloudstate.edu	mschmidt@stcloudstate.edu
Office Hours:	as posted and by appointment	as posted and by appointment

REQUIRED TEXTS

Cornett, C. E. (1999). *The arts as meaning makers: Integrating literature and the arts throughout the curriculum.* Upper Saddle River, NJ: Prentice Hall, Inc.

Beall, P. C., & Nipp, S. H. (1981). *Wee sing and play* (audiotape and book). New York: Prince Stern Sloan, Inc.

Readings as listed in the assignments

The syllabus and all forms or additional information necessary for completing assignments can be found on the course Web page. Students are responsible for obtaining these materials.

The "Extra Resources Notebook," on reserve in the Learning Resource Center (reserve number SMF 053), contains a copy of all handouts and assignments, as well as resources to supplement the texts. It also contains a list of call numbers for all other course materials on reserve.

A list of additional resources is posted in three places: in the front of the Extra Resources Notebook (SMF 053) on the cabinet in PAC 140, and on the bulletin board outside PAC 144.

COURSE OUTCOMES

The prospective teacher will

- develop a repertoire of songs, games, and movement activities appropriate for teaching school-aged children in grades K–8
- demonstrate increasing competence in reading and writing melodic, rhythmic, and harmonic musical notation
- establish a foundation for continued development of performance skills: singing, listening, moving, and creating
- demonstrate principles of healthful vocal production by presenting speaking and singing activities appropriate for K–8 classrooms
- develop activities to integrate music with other disciplines within the K–8 school curriculum
- describe the purposes and content of a school music curriculum, grades K–8
- demonstrate understanding of a developmental sequence of musical concepts and skills by planning and teaching music lessons appropriate to children in grades K–8

MUSE 201 Web page: www.stcloudstate.edu/~.html
SCSU Conceptual Framework: www.stcloudstate.edu/~coe/about/cfgraphic.html
Minnesota Standards of Effective Practice: cfl.state.mn.us/teachbrd/8710_2000.html
INTASC Standards: www.ccsso.org/intasct.html

ASSIGNMENTS

(1) Consider your own experiences with music, your musical culture.

Assignment 1a. Write about three musical experiences you remember from your elementary years. These may be single events or long-term activities in school, family, or community. Describe the effect of these experiences on your attitudes about yourself and about music. (10)

Assignment 1b. Create a diagram to represent your own musical heritage and interests. (10)

(2) Read the two articles listed below, on reserve in the LRC. Write a brief synopsis (approximately one page for each article), including complete bibliographic citations as shown below. Add one or two paragraphs of your own response to the articles, emphasizing what you learned about your own singing or teaching. The paper may be typed or handwritten, but must look professional. (20)

> Bridges, Madeline S. (1993). The benefits of vocal exploration. *General Music Today 6*(2), 30–34.
>
> Bennett, Peggy. (1998). A responsibility to young voices. *Music Educators Journal 73*(1), 33–38.

(3) Select a poem to teach. Teach your poem to the class, videotaping your presentation. Turn in two copies of a written plan, including the poem and listing each step in the teaching process, and adaptations for a visually impaired student. Complete a self-evaluation based on the videotape.

(4) Read the text, pp. 334–46, and then watch this video or complete a few lessons of this computer program. Write a short paper (approximately one page) describing which of the musical elements listed on page 339–40 are emphasized in the video or the CD-ROM. Explain how the elements are illustrated. Add one or two paragraphs of your own response, emphasizing what you learned about music, or how you might use this media or ideas from it in your teaching. (10)

> *Behind the Scenes with JoAnn Falletta.* (1992). New York: Ambrose Video Publishing, Inc. (30 minutes; on reserve in the LRC).
>
> *Music Ace 2* (on reserve in the Teacher Development Curriculum Lab).

(5) Individually, sing a song suitable for use in an elementary classroom, using appropriate singing range for children. A cassette of additional songs (MU 668T) is on reserve in the LRC. (30)

(6) Read the article below, on reserve in the LRC. Write a brief summary (approximately one page), describing the benefits of using movement in the classroom, according to the author. List and briefly define each of the 15 movement concepts shown in the chart on page xii (1-2 sentences each). (10)

> Landalf, Helen. (1997). *Moving the Earth* (pp. vi–xx). Lyme, NH: Smith and Kraus.

(7) Individually, or in a two-member team, plan a short lesson for grades K, 1, 2, or 3. Teach your lesson to the class and videotape your presentation. Turn in two copies of a written plan, including adaptations for a hearing impaired student. Complete a self-evaluation based on the videotape. (50)

(8) Watch the video below, on reserve in the LRC. Write a short summary of the video, listing each culture presented and telling what music means in that culture, according to the featured presenter. Add one or two paragraphs of your own response, emphasizing what you learned about music, or how you might use this video or ideas from it in your teaching. (10)

> *Worlds of Difference: People in Harmony.* (1991). St. Paul, MN: KSTP-TV News. (50 minutes).

(9) Using information from the text, pp. 2–12 and 399–404, write a letter to the parent of one of your students who has politely told you that his or her child feels that doing music in school is a waste of time. In your letter, describe one or more music activities you use in your classroom, and explain why such activities are important for that student. (10)

(10) Choose two poems, each 16 beats long, one in duple subdivision (simple meter) and one in triple subdivision (compound meter). Determine their rhythm and notate them using rhythm notation. For one of the poems, print the musical notation, using the computer program *Music Mastery* (available in the Teacher Development Curriculum Lab.) (20)

Extra credit: Compose a melody for the poem, using *Music Mastery.* (5)

(11) Accompany the class and yourself with the Autoharp, while leading a two-chord or three-chord song. *Wee Sing and Play* is a good music source; there is also a list of songs with chord symbols and suggested transpositions in the Resource Notebook. (30)

(12) Compose contrasting spoken ostinati to accompany two poems. For each 16-beat poem, one ostinato should be four beats long, and one ostinato should be eight beats long. Write the composition in the assigned format. (30)

(13) Individually, or in a two-member team, plan a short lesson for grades 4, 5, 6, 7, or 8. Teach your lesson to the class and videotape your presentation. Turn in two copies of a written plan, including adaptations for a hearing-impaired student. Complete a self-evaluation based on the videotape. (50)

(14) In a group of one to four, develop an instructional tool or activity that integrates music and another elementary curricular area. Some examples are teaching a folk dance including its cultural background, compiling music to enhance a curricular area such as math, designing a whole-language activity based on a song, or designing a music/science station. Turn in one copy of a written plan, including adaptations for an academically accelerated student. (30)

(15) Attend a music program at an elementary school, or watch one of the concert videos on reserve. In a legible, two-page paper, answer these questions, as appropriate to the program you see:
   • Where was the program? Who participated in it?
   • Was there a musical or topical theme for the program? Were instruments, dance, solos, poetry, or acting used? Attach the printed program (if available) or a list of some of the music performed.
   • What academic and/or social learning objectives were reinforced?
   • Did you see or hear any evidence of awareness of cultural diversity as part of the program? Were you aware of the inclusion of special-needs students or any adaptations made for them?
   • In what ways do you think classroom teachers supported or assisted with the production of the program? What would you have felt comfortable doing to support this program if you were a teacher at this school?
   • How much time do you think it took to prepare the program? Do you consider that time spent to be beneficial to the students' education? Why or why not?
   • What impressed you about the program? How would you feel if you were a parent of a child in this program? (20)

(16) Develop a notebook of resource ideas for including music in your teaching. The notebook should contain your completed assignments, class notes, and handouts, organized so they will be useful when you begin teaching. You may choose to include other information you find or copies of your colleagues' lessons or projects, available in the Extra Resources notebook on reserve. (20)

(17) Participate fully in all class discussions and activities. You will lose five points for each absence, excused or unexcused; however, points lost for excused absences may be made up. For an excused absence, please talk with the instructor or leave a message at the instructor's office. (50)

EVALUATION

All work is to be completed in a professional manner. Habits of good grammar, spelling, and punctuation are important for a teacher; their absence will be reflected in reduced credit. Grades will be determined by number of points earned:

   90 % = A   80% = B   70% = C   60% = D

Assignments are due at the beginning of the class period on the day assigned. Late assignments will receive reduced credit ranging from 90% for assignments one day late to 0 for assignments five weeks late or after the class final. At the discretion of the instructor, students receiving less than 80% on an assignment may redo that assignment, resubmitting it within two class days.

ACADEMIC DISHONESTY

Academic dishonesty includes, but is not limited to, cheating, plagiarism, misrepresentation of student status, and resume falsification. Plagiarism includes, but is not limited to, the use by paraphrase or direct quotation, of the published or unpublished work of another person without full and clear acknowledgment, and unacknowledged use of materials prepared by another person or agency engaged in selling or otherwise providing term papers or other academic materials.

SPECIAL ACCOMMODATIONS

It is St. Cloud State University policy to provide, on a flexible and individualized basis, reasonable accommodations to students who have disabilities that may affect their ability to participate in course activities or to meet course requirements.

SCHEDULE OF ASSIGNMENTS

Wed. 9/6	Thurs. 9/7	Introduction
Mon. 9/11	Tues. 9/12	Assignment 1a (memories). Diagnostic
Wed. 9/13	Thurs. 9/14	Assignment 2 (article summaries)
Mon. 9/18	Tues. 9/19	Assignment 3 (teach a poem), bring videotape
Wed. 9/20	Thurs. 9/21	Assignment 3 (teach a poem), bring videotape
Mon. 9/25	Tues. 9/26	Self-evaluation for Assignment 3; Notes quiz
Wed. 9/27	Thurs. 9/28	Read text, 325–34. Assignment 1b (diagrams)
Mon. 10/2	Tues. 10/3	Assignment 4 (text, 334–46, and Falletta video or *MusicAce 2* program)
Wed. 10/4	Thurs. 10/5	Read text, 346–65. List/describe five activities you might use in your teaching (include page number with each)
Mon. 10/9	Tues. 10/10	Read text, 34–42, and complete WAIT worksheet
Wed. 10/11	Thurs. 10/12	Assignment 5 (singing a song)
Mon. 10/16	Tues. 10/17	Assignment 6 (article summary)
Wed. 10/18	Thurs. 10/19	Read text, 67–73
Mon. 10/23	Tues. 10/24	Assignment 7 (lower grade lesson), bring videotape
Wed. 10/25	Thurs. 10/26	Assignment 7 (lower grade lesson), bring videotape, counting worksheet
Mon. 10/30	Tues. 10/31	Self-evaluation of Assignment 7
Wed. 11/1	Thurs. 11/2	Assignment 8 (video)
Mon. 11/6	Tues. 11/7	Poetry Worksheet
Wed. 11/8	Thurs. 11/9	Read text, 2–12, 399–404
Mon. 11/13	Tues. 11/14	Assignment 9 (letter to parents)
Wed. 11/15	Thurs. 11/16	Assignment 10 (notated poems)
Mon. 11/20		
Wed. 11/22	Tues. 11/21	Assignment 11 (Autoharp)
Mon. 11/27	Tues. 11/28	Rhythm quiz
Wed. 11/29	Thurs. 11/30	Assignment 12 (ostinati)
Mon. 12/4	Tues. 12/5	Assignment 13 (upper grade lesson), bring videotape
Wed. 12/6	Thurs. 12/7	Assignment 13 (upper grade lesson), bring videotape
Mon. 12/11	Tues. 12/12	Self-evaluation for Assignment 13
Wed. 12/13	Thurs. 12/14	Assignment 15 (concert review), Assignment 16 (resource notebook)

The Final Examination (Assignment 14) is scheduled for: _____.

MUED 341 (84487): General Junior-High Methods
Dr. Ed Duling and Dr. C. Victor Fung
Bowling Green State University
Fall 2000

Instructors: Dr. Ed Duling, Room 2161 MMMAC
e-mail: eduling@bgnet.bgsu.edu   phone: 372-0281
Dr. C. Victor Fung, Room 1005, MMAC
e-mail: cvfung@bgnet.bgsu.edu   phone: 372-8104
Dr. Duling's portion of the course is 0.6 of your grade, and Dr. Fung's is 0.4.

Class Location: MMAC 1002
Times: 11:30–12:45 on Tuesdays & Thursdays
Office Hours: As posted on doors and announced in class
Course Logon Page: webcourse.bgsu.edu:8900/public/funmued341/index.html

**Kindly inform the instructors if you have any special educational needs of any type
(e.g., documented disabilities or special testing requirements).**

PREREQUISITES
MUED 240 or permission, GPA, and other criteria set forth in undergraduate catalog.

COURSE DESCRIPTION
Concentrated study of organization, administration, and teaching of general music in secondary grades (middle, junior high, high schools: grade 6–12); emphasizes correlation of methods seminars with clinical and field activities. The general purpose of the course is to furnish preservice music educators with materials and methods in content (music) and pedagogy (teaching). The development of specific segments of this pedagogical-content knowledge is achieved via the objectives and related activities listed below.

OBJECTIVES
Given the specific assignments outlined below, each music education major in MUED 341 will, to the satisfaction of the instructor:

(1) Identify physical, psychological, emotional, social, and general characteristics of the adolescent/young adult learner

(2) Read about/react to/demonstrate various plans of classroom management for students of various abilities

(3) Identify various curricular and scheduling configurations for teaching secondary general music

(4) Present a review of three articles on multicultural music education

(5) Plan and present, in pairs, a brief multicultural music lesson

(6) Write multicultural and technology lesson plans

(7) Create on disc a *Finale* file, a *Band-in-a-Box* file, and a *Vision* file

(8) Detail approaches that general music teachers may take in working with exceptional students from the general student population of a school

(9) Be prepared (in peer-teaching) to explain and demonstrate one or more of the following approaches to general music teaching: listening ("apprec." and DBME); singing (recreational and concept-related); playing (recreational and concept-related); integrating (various models/terms); composing (traditionally and creative technological applications); others as assigned

(10) Likewise, be prepared to explain and/or demonstrate one or more of these logistical pre-, inter-, and post-active teaching behaviors: organizing the classroom, organizing student groups, planning teacher movement in the classroom, making transitions among activities, distributing materials, ending a class or activity, and managing conflict. There will be a special emphasis on teacher collaboration (See assignment D7 below)

(11) Outline a unit of study on an American music topic for a secondary general music class connected to both the National Standards and State Arts model, and following instructor's outline in the packet
- Prepare media resources (see packet, pg. 1) for this unit, and utilize same in peer-teaching of one lesson
- List/collect resources and resource lists for the unit
- As part of the unit, create at least one full written lesson plan following a *pro forma* outline as part of the unit and present it on assigned day

TEXTS REQUIRED
- Duling/Fung, Handout packet for 341.
- Gilstrap. R. L., Bierman, C., & McKnight, T. R. (1992). *Improving instruction in middle schools.* Bloomington, IN: Phi Delta Kappa Educational Foundation.
- Hinckley, J. (1994). *Music at the middle level: Building strong programs.* Reston, VA: MENC. (H)

OTHER READINGS AND MATERIALS
As needed, these will be placed on reserve in the Music Education Curriculum Lab in MMAC 2115. Additional helpful materials/resources may be found at the Curriculum Lab, and in the Jerome Library's Curriculum Resource Center, second floor.

FUNG'S ASSIGNMENTS (F PREFIX)
F1. The World of Musics Review (due Sept. 12). [80 points] (Obj. 4) Students are required to submit a three-page combined review (not summary) of three articles (Fung, 1995; Fung, 1998; Goetze, 2000). The review should address issues related to general music teaching at the secondary level. The assignment must be typed with double-line spacing. Grading criteria include depth of insights, clarity of presentation/organization, and strength of support for any argument.

F2. Lessons Using World Musics (due Oct. 3–12). [60 points] (Obj. 5) Students work in pairs to prepare a 15-minute in-class teaching session incorporating world musics. A 5-minute in-class discussion will evolve after each 15-minute session. Students within the pair should work collaboratively and contribute equally. Students should make use of resources available in the Curriculum Lab, library, and any personal (students and instructor) collection of materials. These resources include videos, recordings, musical instruments, music, and books. Grading criteria include respectfulness and truthfulness of the musical activities, effective and creative instructions, and cooperative efforts.

F3. Multicultural Lesson Plan (due Oct. 19). [80 points] (Obj. 6) Students are required to submit a multicultural lesson plan using the references provided in this course outline. The lesson plan should be designed for a 50-minute lesson for a general music class at the secondary level (may be based on assignment F2, or on an observation of others' presentation of F2). The lesson plan should include (1) grade level and setting, (2) duration, (3) prerequisites (i.e., What do you expect students to know before the lesson?), (4) lesson objectives, (5) materials/equipment, (6) procedures, (7) additional/follow-up activities, (8) focuses of, as well as sources and ideas behind, the lesson plan (i.e., Why is the lesson plan designed the way it is? Is the lesson plan supported by any musical or educational models? Any references?). Figures may be included if they help clarify the lesson plan. Grading criteria include clarity of organization and presentation, appropriateness of materials selected, logic of procedures, depth of thoughts, and originality of the plan.

F4. *Finale* (due Sept. 21). [30 points] (Obj. 7) Students are required to submit a *Finale* file on disk of a "fake" piece of music. The disk should be labeled with the student's name and the file should be labeled "MuEd341Finale." This file should include: (1) title of the piece, (2) student name as composer, (3) at least two vocal/instrumental parts, (4) one repeat sign, (5) three dynamic markings, (6) three tempo-related markings (e.g., accelerando), (7) three phrase marks/slurs, (8) three articulation marking (e.g., staccato), (9) one change of meter, and (10) one change of key. This list of requirements plus musical common sense (e.g., correct number of beats in a given measure) form the basis of grading criteria. As in all important documents on disk, students should keep a copy of the assignment on another disk as backup.

F5. *Band-in-a-Box* **(due Sept. 21).** [30 points] (Obj. 7) Students are required to submit a *Band-in-a-Box* file on disk of an original piece that starts with the chord progression: C-Am-F-G. The disk should be labeled with the student's name and the file should be labeled "MuEd341Box." In addition, students should include a Microsoft *Word* file with a few lines of text describing the classroom activity that the *Band-in-a-Box* file would be accompanying. This Microsoft *Word* file should on the same disk and be labeled "MuEd341Word." Grading criteria include integrity of both "MuEd341Box" file and "MuEd341Word" file, musical senses of "MuEd341Box" file, and educational senses of contents in "MuEd341Word" file.

F6. *Vision* **(due Nov. 16).** [40 points] (Obj. 7) Students are required to submit a *Vision* file on disk of an original piece. The file should contain an arrangement of "Twinkle, Twinkle, Little Star" or variations of it with at least three tracks of different sounds. Students should use real-time recording and quintile function. Students should check the notation and see if the notes are "lined up." The disk should be labeled with the student's name and the file should be labeled "MuEd341Vision." Grading criteria include fulfillment of stated requirements, reflection of musicianship, and creativity.

F7. Technology lesson plan (due Nov. 28). [80 points] (Obj. 6) Students are required to submit a lesson plan involving the use of technology. Students should utilize some/all technology from *Finale, Band-in-a-Box,* and *Vision.* Students can also incorporate other types of technology if they wish. The lesson plan should be designed for a 50-minute lesson for a general music class at the secondary level. The lesson plan should follow the same outline as in F3 above. Grading criteria include clarity of organization and presentation, appropriateness of materials selected, logic of procedures, depth of thoughts, and originality of the plan.

DULING & FUNG (D&F) ASSIGNMENT

[60 points] Students are expected to attend and to actively participate in all class meetings. Students are allowed one missed class without penalty. Please stay in contact regarding personal illness, death in family, University-related off-campus trips, emergency, or other unavoidable circumstances. Beyond the one absence, the student is subject to loss of participation points. Three lates count as an absence. We reserve the right to ask for medical excuses.

DULING'S ASSIGNMENTS (D PREFIX)

D1. Exams (due as noted in outline below). Student shall complete midterm and final exams—in-class and take-home as appropriate—covering announced aspects of the course.

D2. Peer-Teaching (due Dec. 5 & 7). [75 points] (Obj. 9 & 10) "Full" lesson requiring a written lesson plan which covers at least one approach, uses some item/approach covered in the media session; due when you peer-teach.

D3. Unit Plan (due Dec. 12). [115 points] (Obj. 9, 10, & 11) A unit plan using some aspect of American music, within which there are one full lesson plan and nine summaries as part of ten lessons.

D4. Notebook (due Dec. 16). [55 points] A notebook of materials compiled during the course of the class.

D5. Checklist (due with unit plan). [25 points] (Obj. 11) Completed media skills checklist (from packet) with the American music unit.

D6. Papers (due as noted in outline below). [120 pts.; 24 each] (Obj. 1, 2, 3, & 8) Complete three in-class and two out-of-class reaction papers.

D7. Focus Group (due Nov. 30). [25 points] (Obj. 10) Complete a collaboration focus group with several "El. Ed." students from MUED 245.

ASSIGNMENT POLICY

Late work will not be accepted without prior arrangement with professor. Five points will be deducted from each assignment each day after the due date. No assignments will be accepted over seven days past the due date.

GRADING

D1. Exams	150		F1. Review	80
D2. Lesson plan/Pres.	75		F2. Lesson	60
D3. American Music Unit	100		F3. MC lesson Plan	80
D4. Notebook	40		F4. *Finale*	30
D5. Media Checklist	30		F5 *Band-in-a-Box*	30
D6. Papers	120		F6. *Vision*	40
D7. 245 Collaboration	25		F7. Tech. lesson plan	80
Duling Subtotal	**540**		**Fung Sub-total**	**400**
D&F Participation	60			
Grand total	**1,000**			

Final Grades out of 1,000 points for this course

900–1000	A (Outstanding)
800–899	B (Good)
700–799	C (Pass)
600–699	D (Barely pass)
599 & below	F (Fail)

TENTATIVE OUTLINE OF COURSE CONTENT BY DAY

Readings are due on the day for which they are listed. More specific readings for in- and out-of-class assignments will be given as the semester progresses, drawing on the list which follows, the texts, and other sources.

Date	Topics	Assignments
Aug. 29	Introductions, modus operandi, syllabus review; Methods Project packet; Policies; Why are we here?	
Aug. 31	Concepts of multiculturalism in music education.	
Sept. 5	Characteristics of the adolescent: Gerberian and other views; Assign OOC paper #1 (D6).	Skim Gilstrap et al., Hinkley 5–12 Read pkt. 3–8 (Coulter, 1984), 70–76 (Gerber, 1992), and H 13–17.
Sept. 7	Meet in Media Lab. room 206, in Education Bldg. Basic media work and checklist (D5).	
Sept. 12	Adolescence, conclusion; Technology hands-on (*Finale* and *Band-in-a-Box*).	F1 due.
Sept. 14	National Standards in the Arts (emphasis on music); Using the State Arts Model.	Read pkt. 17–28 (Atterbury, 1989). In-class reaction paper #1 (D6) with readings and responses.
Sept. 19	Exceptionality/special learners, pkt. 17–28; Sample of world musics and teaching approaches.	OOC Reaction paper #1 (D6) (Adolescence).
Sept. 21	Samples of world musics and teaching approaches; Exceptionality, cont.; Teaching phases and tasks (D2, 3).	F4 and F5 due.
Sept. 26	Lesson plans and planning; Listening lessons (DBME) and Copland mapped lesson demo; Bruner and Ausubel chart; Discussion of peer multicultural lessons and plan adaptation as needed (F2).	In-class reaction paper #2 (D6) (exceptionality).

Sept. 28	Discussion of unit (D3) and lesson (D2) planning from packet—American music in the GM classroom; Skim and read pkt. 76–99, 108–20; Further explanation of peer lesson and objective writing; Example lesson (Rick S.); Discussion of peer multicultural lessons and plans (F2).	Read pkt. 76–92, 108–120 (Ullom, 1990; Shirey, 1991; Dulling (sic), 1992).
Oct. 3	Listening lessons; Lessons using world musics I (F2).	F2
Oct. 5	Lessons using world musics II (F2).	F2
Oct. 10	Lessons using world musics III (F2).	F2
Oct 12	Lessons using world musics IV (F2).	F2
Oct. 17	No Class: Fall Break	
Oct. 19	Discipline/Management in the Classroom; Readings and responses, pkt. p. 100–7;138–42; Assign OOC paper #2 (D6); List topics for American music unit plans (D3); Diversity issues in music education.	F3 due Read pkt. 100–7 (John, 1996), 138–42 (Goodson & Duling, 1996).
Oct. 24	Midterm Exam material given (D1); Management, cont.; The National Standards; Comprehensive general music teaching—or not; DBME (Quartet); Diversity and learning styles in general music.	
Oct. 26	The Ohio Arts Model as needed; "Comprehensiveness debate in *MEJ*; Collaboration project MUED 245 explained (D7).	In pkt. skim 29–69 (Fallis, 1994; Barry, 1996—2 articles; Wiggins, 1996; Cutietta—4 articles) OOC Reaction paper #2 (D6) (Discipline).
Oct. 31	Assign day to peer-teach full lesson (D2) from Duling Unit (D3); Types of music technology for music educators.	In-class portion of midterm; Out-of-class due (D1).
Nov. 2	Readings and responses; Technology hands-on (Internet).	Rough draft of unit plan (D3); In-class reaction paper #3 (D6) (curriculum and methods).
Nov. 7	Resource lists, resource guidance, texts, other useful materials; Rough units back.	Skim pkt. 122–142 (Goodson & Duling, 1996). Read H 135–50. Various curricular configurations, pkt. 13; Read/skim H: 79–134.
Nov. 9	Technology hands-on (*Vision*).	
Nov. 14	Wrap-up and feedback on units; Final lesson and planning instruction; Interactive approaches outlined (obj. #10).	
Nov. 16	Music lessons using technology in school settings.	F6 due.
Nov. 21	Integrative approaches in general music and education: Collaboration as needed.	Rough draft of lesson plan (D2).
Nov. 23	THANKSGIVING BREAK	
Nov. 28	Needed qualities of general music teachers; Integration, cont.; Rough lessons back.	F7 due.
Nov. 30	An article by Bennett Reimer, pkt. 1a and H: 63–68; Start peer-teaching if necessary.	Collaboration project due (D7).

Dec. 5	Peer-teaching from unit w/lesson plan (D2)	Lesson plan due on day you teach (D2).
Dec. 7	Peer-teaching from unit w/lesson plan (D2)	
Dec. 12	Needed qualities of general music teachers; Integration, cont..	D3 due.
Dec. 14	Final instructions and integration of materials.	Notebook due (D4).

Final exam (D1)—as announced in University schedule: *do not* assume there is none!

MUED 341 PACKET

The packet for MUED 341 contains: (1) Selected readings from MENC, OMEA and other publications, all reproduced with permission; (2) handouts and materials created by the instructors (and others) to amplify the class's emphases—special learners, technology, multicultural teaching and learning, adolescent characteristics, classroom management, basic educational psychology applied to music teaching and learning, listening approaches to secondary music, curriculum in current state and national models, and lesson and unit planning and construction.

Handout Packet Reference List

Barry, N. H. (1996). Integrating the arts into the curriculum: A response from the author. *General Music Today, 10*(1), 10–12.

Barry, N. H. (1996). Integrating the arts into the curriculum, *General Music Today, 9*(2), 9–13.

Cutietta, R. A. (1996). Language and music programs. *General Music Today, 9*(2), 26–31.

Cutietta, R. A.(1996). Does music instruction aid academic skills? *General Music Today 10*(1), 24–27.

Cutietta, R. A.(1996). Does music instruction aid mathematic skills? *General Music Today, 9*(3), 28–30.

Cutietta, R. A. (1995). Does music instruction help a child learn to read? *General Music Today 9*(1), 26–31.

Dulling, E. (sic) (1992). The rote-note approach—A sample lesson. *TRIAD, 59*(5), 15. [General Music Insert].

Fallis, T. L. (1994). National standards: What's next? *Music Educators Journal, 81*(3), 26–28, 47.

Gerber, T. (1992). Meeting the challenge of middle school teaching. *Music Educators Journal, 78*(6), 37–41.

Goodson, C. A., & Duling, E. (1996). Integrating the four disciplines, *Music Educators Journal, 83*(2), 33–37.

Ullom, R. (1990). Should it be the end: General music, grade eight, and thirteen years young? *TRIAD, 57*(5), 26.

Wiggins, R. (1996) Integrating the arts into the curriculum is the wrong mind set. *General Music Today, 10*(1), 5–9.

COURSE REFERENCE LIST

This list contains articles, books, chapters of books, and other materials. Some of these may be used as readings for the class, while the others are for your reference or of historical interest. Supplemental lists will be found in your packet. Most of the material below may be found in the music library, in the curriculum lab, in the appropriate instructor's reserve box, office, or are available from the instructor.

Atterbury, B. (1989). Being involved in mainstreaming decisions. *Music Educators Journal, 75*(6).

Bennett, P. (1986). When 'method' becomes authority. *Music Educators Journal, 72*(9), 38–40.

Charles, C. M. (1986). Building classroom discipline: Twenty recurring themes. *General Music Journal, 5*(1), 20–22.

Coulter, D. J. (1984). The brain's timetable for developing music skills. *General Music Journal, 3*(1), 21–26. (This was a short-lived periodical published by OMEA in the late 1970s and early 1980s.)

Gerber, T., & Hughes, W. O. (1988). *Music in the high school: Current approaches to secondary general music instruction.* Reston, VA: MENC.

Gerber, T. (1994). Nurturing the young adolescent: High stakes for the school and social environment (Text, pp. 5–12).

Haack, P. (1994). Finding commonalties among the arts. (Text, pp. 79–82).

Haldeman, E. (1989). General music: What is it? *Readings in General Music.* Reston, VA: MENC.

Johns, S. B. (1996). Coping with middle school attitudes. *Choral Journal, 37*(1), 29–32.

Monsour, S. (1989). Problems facing general music today. *Readings in General Music*. Reston, VA: MENC.

Music Educators Journal, 83(2) September, 1996 (Entire issue on Discipline-Based Music Education.)

Myers, D. E. (1994). General music: Present and future. (Text, pp. 63–68).

Palmer, M., Hughes, W. O., Jothen, M., & March, H. C. (Eds.). (1989). *Promising practices: High school general music*. Reston, VA: MENC.

Shirey, K. F. (1991). Sound before symbol in general music classes. *TRIAD, 58*(6), 37–38.

Shull, S., & Berg, K. V. (1994). The middle school learner. (Text, pp. 13–17).

MENC. (1991). *Teaching general music: A course of study*. Reston, VA: MENC.

MENC. (1994). *The school music program: A new vision*. Reston, VA; MENC. (Music portion of National Standards with introduction and sequence chart.)

Welsbacher, B. (1989). Musical thinking in the special education classroom. In Eunice Boardman (Ed.), *Dimensions of musical thinking*. Reston, VA: MENC.

Woolfolk, A. E. (1993). *Educational psychology* (5th ed.). Boston: Allyn and Bacon.

Multicultural References

Anderson, W. M., & Campbell, P. S. (1996). *Multicultural perspectives in music education* (2nd ed.) Reston, VA: MENC. [in Curriculum Lab with CD]

Campbell, P. S., McCullough-Brabson, E., & Tucker, J. C. (1994). *Roots & branches: A legacy of multicultural music for children*. Danbury, CT: World Music Press. [in Curriculum Lab with CD]

Fowler, C. (1994). *Music! Its role and importance in our lives*. Mission Hills, CA: Glencoe Division, Macmillan/McGraw-Hill. [in Curriculum Lab with teacher's manual, video and CDs]

Fung, C. V. (1995). Rationales for teaching world musics. *Music Educators Journal, 82*(1), 36–40. [in course handout packet]

Fung, C. V. (1998). Mind opening through music: An internationalized music curriculum. In J. A. Mestenhauser & B. J. Ellingboe (Eds.), *Reforming the higher education curriculum: Internationalizing the campus* (pp. 118–124). Phoenix, Arizona: American Council on Education and Oryx Press. [in course handout packet]

Goetze, M. (2000). Challenges of performing diverse cultural music. *Music Educators Journal, 87*(1), 23–25, 48. [will be distributed in class]

International Society for Music Education. (1998). *Musics of the world's cultures: Policy and declaration of beliefs*. Reading, UK: International Society of Music Education. [in course handout packet]

Nettl, B. (Ed.). (1992). *Excursions in world music*. Englewood Cliffs, NJ: Prentice Hall. [in Curriculum Lab with cassette]

The JVC Video Anthology of World Music and Dance [in Music Library with 30 videos and accompanying booklets]

Titon, J. T. (Ed.). (1992). *Worlds of music*. New York: Schirmer Books. [in Curriculum Lab with CDs]

Technological References

Rudolph, T. E. (1996). *Teaching music with technology*. Chicago: GIA. [in Curriculum Lab]

Rudolph, T., Richmond, F., Mash, D., & Williams, D. (1997). *Technology strategies for music education*. Wyncote, PA: Technology Institute for Music Educators. [instructor's personal library]

Williams, D. B. & Webster, P. R. (1999). *Experiencing music technology* (2nd ed.). New York: Schirmer Books. [ML74 .W55 1999 in Music Library. Music Library also has 2 copies of the 1st ed.—1996.]

Various software and manuals in Music Lab and those in the Curriculum Lab.

Please read the entire Junior Methods Project Booklet, directing questions you may have to the department chair, Dr. Joyce E. Gromko.

Please remember that separate grades are given for the specific components of this course because it is taught by two members of the music education department. Students must receive a grade of "C" or better in both components for which a grade is given. Failure to do so will result in an incomplete and the repetition of that component, or other requirements as determined by the instructor. However, a grade of "C" for the entire course which results from an averaging of the grades from all components will be recorded as such.

MUSIC 321: TEACHING MUSIC IN THE SECONDARY SCHOOL
DR. SHARON DAVIS GRATTO
GETTYSBURG COLLEGE
FALL 2000

Class Meetings: Tues., Thurs., 10:00–11:15 p.m.; New Music Education Curriculum Library, First Floor
Instructor: Dr. Sharon Davis Gratto, Schmucker, Room 209, X-6135;
E-mail address: sgratto@gettysburg.edu
E-mail Alias: mus-321-a@gettysburg.edu
Office Hours: by appointment.

REQUIRED TEXTBOOKS AND MATERIALS

Barrett, J. R., McCoy, C. W., & Veblen, K. K. (1997). *Sound ways of knowing: Music in the interdisciplinary curriculum.* New York: Schirmer Books.

Burakoff, G., & Hettrick, W. E. (1980). *The sweet pipes recorder book* (Book I, soprano). Levittown, NY: Sweet Pipes, Inc.

Consortium of National Arts Education Associations. (1994). *National standards for arts education.* Reston, VA: MENC.

Fowler, C., Gerber, T., & Lawrence, V. (2000). *Music! Its role and importance in our lives* (2nd ed. student text). Woodland Hills, CA: Glencoe/McGraw-Hill.

Hinckley, J. M., & Shull, S. M. (Eds.). (1996). *Strategies for Teaching Middle-Level General Music.* Reston, VA: MENC.

MENC. (1996). *Music with a Sacred Text.* [Brochure]. Reston, VA: Author.

Thompson K. P., & Kiester, G. J. (Eds.). (1997). *Strategies for Teaching High School General Music.* Reston, VA: MENC.

Tuning fork (A=440) (also available for purchase in the music office)

Blank VHS Videotape to record peer and practicum teaching. One blank tape should be sufficient for two semesters of the elementary and secondary methods classes. *Five points will be subtracted from the letter grade for each lesson a student teaches without his or her own videotape, (including if another student's tape is used).*

Soprano recorder, Baroque fingering system (Aulos, Yamaha, or similar plastic brand preferred)

MENC/PMEA publications: the *Music Educators Journal, Teaching Music,* the *PMEA Journal;* other print materials, videotapes, CDs, and audio tapes related to the course that are available in the Music Department curriculum library or in the college library or that are distributed in class.

OBJECTIVES AND SCOPE

Students will study and evaluate methods, materials, and techniques related to teaching general music and performance classes in the middle, junior high, and high school, with emphasis on developing general music lessons. They will also begin to develop a personal philosophy of music education and examine current trends in education today that impact on the secondary school music program. Students will micro-teach lessons to their peers in class and to students in practicum settings as opportunities become available. The class will be taught using a combination of seminar-style lectures with discussion, peer-teaching, on-site observations, off-campus practicum teaching experiences, electronic dialogues, Internet searches, reading, writing, and materials and equipment for exploration.

By the time the course is completed, students should:
- be able to teach songs by rote and by note with and without accompaniment and to establish starting pitches using a tuning fork
- be able to accompany songs with simple piano and guitar parts
- be able to play soprano recorder well enough to teach a beginning recorder class; be familiar

with the instruments of the recorder family and related recorder teaching methods and materials

- be able to research, write, and prepare comprehensive secondary general music lesson plans and units, using a standardized format
- be familiar with and able to select and utilize quality age-appropriate materials and activities for general music, music theory, music history, and ensemble classes
- be able to use Kodály hand signs with corresponding pitch and rhythm syllables to teach music reading and song material
- be familiar with the instruments of the Orff-Schulwerk instrumentarium and other classroom instruments, including African percussion, simple dulcimers, and guitar
- be able to direct and sustain student attention to a piece of recorded music
- be able to plan and implement activities intended to encourage student creativity in the music class
- be familiar with the range of possibilities for using movement and dance in the secondary music class
- be familiar with a varied selection of secondary song, listening, and reading material, including selections from varied cultures within and outside the United States
- begin to understand ways to integrate music with other disciplines in the secondary curriculum
- begin to be familiar with ways to handle the inclusion of children with special needs into the secondary music class
- know the National and State Standards for Arts Education and how to apply the music standards to the secondary curriculum
- be familiar with ways to assess student progress in the secondary music classroom
- begin to form a personal philosophy of music education
- understand the importance of good oral and written communication with students and families

GENERAL REQUIREMENTS

(1) Punctual attendance at and participation in each class session. Attendance in this course should be treated as if you were working in a school music teaching position. One unexcused absence will be allowed. The final course grade will be lowered five points for each unexcused absence after the first. Students are responsible for all class work missed due to excused or unexcused absences. Since no senior recitals are scheduled for class meeting days, they will not be considered for excused absences. Students whose peer-teaching lessons are not ready on the assigned day may not be given another class day to teach that lesson.

(2) Observation of and participation in practicum classes.

(3) On-time completion of reading assignments and written work. Written assignments should reflect careful attention to spelling, grammar, and syntax, and must be prepared on a word processor. Late written assignments will receive a grade which is one level below the actual earned grade (i.e., A to A-, B- to C+, etc.). Peer-teaching assignments must be ready for presentation on the day scheduled, even if time does not allow the teaching to take place until the next class meeting. No written assignments will be accepted after the last day of classes, Friday, December 8.

(4) Because this is an upper-level class for music majors, students who take it are responsible for the information included in all assigned readings, whether or not they are discussed in class. Discussion of some readings will take place via e-mail dialogue.

(5) Timely and thoughtful responses to e-mail communications/dialogues.

(6) Attendance at monthly meetings (scheduled for Sundays at 6:15 p.m. with light supper!) of the Gettysburg CMENC chapter.

RESOURCE BIBLIOGRAPHY

Items included here represent a combination of required reading for this course and other materials to use as supplementary resources or future reference.

Abeles, H. F., Hoffer, C. R., & Klotman, R. H. (1984). *Foundations of music education* (2nd ed.). New York: Schirmer Books.

Anderson, W. M. (1991). *Teaching music with a multicultural approach.* Reston, VA.: MENC. (4 VHS tapes and a book)

Anderson, W. M., & Moore, M. C., (Eds.). (1998). *Making connections: Multicultural music and the national standards.* Reston, VA: MENC. (Includes recording)

Anderson, W. M., & Campbell, P. S., (Eds.). (1989). *Multicultural perspectives in music education* (2nd ed.). Reston, VA.: MENC. (includes recording)

Campbell, P. S. (1996). *Music in cultural context: Eight views on world music education.* Reston, VA: MENC.

Cooksey, J. M. (1992). *Working with the adolescent voice.* St. Louis, MO: Concordia Publishing House.

Elliott, D. J. (1995). *Music matters: A new philosophy of music education.* New York: Oxford University Press.

Erbes, R. L. (1992). *Certification practices and trends in music teacher education.* Reston, VA: MENC.

Gratto, S. D. (1994). *Performance-based arts education: A study of music in inter-arts programs for secondary students.* D.M.A. dissertation, Catholic University of America.

Hoffer, C. R. (1991). *Teaching music in the secondary schools* (4th ed.). Belmont, CA: Wadsworth Publishing.

Kaplan, P. R., & Stauffer, S. L. (1994). *Cooperative learning in music.* Reston, VA: MENC.

Mark, M. L., & Gary, C. L. (1999). *A history of American music education* (2nd ed.). Reston, VA: MENC.

MENC. (1995). *Scheduling time for music.* Reston, VA: MENC.

MENC Committee on Standards. (1986). *The school music program: Description and standards.* Reston, VA: MENC.

Palmer, M., Hughes, W. O., Jothen, M., & March, H. C., (Eds.). (1989). *Promising practices: High school general music.* Reston, VA: MENC.

Reimer, B. (1989). *A philosophy of music education* (2nd ed.). Englewood Cliffs, NJ: Prentice Hall.

Shmid, W. (1998). *World music drumming: A cross-cultural curriculum.* Milwaukee, WI: Hal Leonard Corporation. (Teacher's Edition, video, student and enrichment book)

Stauffer, S. L. (Ed.). (1995). *Toward tomorrow: New visions for general music.* Reston, VA: MENC.

Basal Music Series in the Curriculum Library, especially Silver Burdett Ginn's *World of Music* and *The Music Connection* and Glencoe/McGraw-Hill's *Music and You* and *Share the Music.*

Recordings and other audiovisual materials from the music department curriculum library or the college library.

Available music department computer software and equipment for teaching and music writing in the technology lab.

Current music education journals and current events materials available in the music department curriculum library or the college library.

ASSIGNMENT DETAILS

Observation Attendance and Reports. During the semester, each student will be responsible for observing and preparing a written report on three school music classes, one in a middle or junior high school, one in a high school, and one on a secondary grade level of the student's choice. At least one of these classes must be a general music class. Extra credit will be given for additional observations and reports and may include concert or assembly presentations. Written journal entries must be kept of all other observations not written up formally. Group observations and practicum experiences on Tuesdays and Thursdays will be scheduled beginning early morning before class, may include class time, and on one or two occasions will extend beyond 11:15 a.m. Students not involved in Tuesday rehearsals of the Women's Choir may use that time for off-campus independent observations. The Thursday time block from 11:15 a.m. to 1 p.m. is also available to be scheduled independently for observations and practicum experiences, except on Common Hour days. Check the Common Hour schedule carefully to avoid conflicts. Students need to make every effort to keep the time before class clear on days when school visits are scheduled. Adjustments will be made to accommodate individual course schedules.

Practical Experience. Peer-teaching assignments and accompanying lesson plans will be related to discussion topics. Plans are underway to provide each student with an opportunity for a general music teaching practicum experience at Gettysburg Middle and/or Biglerville Middle School.

Unit Outline. Outline of an integrated one-week unit plan around an assigned multicultural theme, grades 6–8. General music classes meet daily for four weeks in block or intensive scheduling periods of one hour and fifteen minutes each. The unit should last one week out of the four and incorporate a wide variety of music class activities. A detailed lesson plan for one class should be included with the unit outline. This unit may form the basis for one that you use during the student-teaching semester.

Comprehensive Musicianship Lesson. Select a choral, band, or orchestral score of your choice appropriate for use with a high school ensemble. Create a series of rehearsal plans designed both to teach the selection to your students and to guide them in the full understanding of the music and the composer. Include in your plans time for at least one related listening activity, ways to guide students to an understanding of the historical and cultural context of the piece, and techniques for using the piece as a tool to teach music reading and theory.

Collections of Materials and Resources. Each student will be expected to compile and submit the following by the last day of classes, Fri., 12/8:
- A large three-ring binder notebook sectioned off as follows to include:
  - Secondary Methods class notes
  - Articles handed out in class or collected independently
  - Three written observation reports; dated journal entries about other observations
  - Peer-teaching lesson plans, both yours and those of other students in the class
  - Basal series text evaluations in the form of general notes about series trends and changes over time and specific details about the most recent series of books from Silver Burdett Ginn and Glencoe/McGraw-Hill (considering layout, presentation/appeal, ease of use, index, content variety and quality, glossary, quantity of materials included, recordings, and other available supplementary materials)
  - A beginning list of your favorite general music song material, 6–8, and in which collection or basal series the songs are located (in order for you to locate them easily in the future
  - A beginning list of favorite choral and instrumental ensemble selections
  - A beginning list of recorder materials appropriate for middle and high school students
  - Copies of all written assignments and other work from this class, including the philosophy of music education and the back-to-school night letter
  - A beginning list of computer music software and equipment and music Internet sites appropriate for use with secondary students
- An inexpensive portable file box or milk crate containing
  - Secondary music programs, both for concerts personally attended and those collected
  - Music catalogs for vendors of secondary general, choral, and instrumental music materials and equipment

Examinations

Midterm Competency Evaluation on recorder, piano, and guitar. Individual appointments on October 17, 18, & 19.

In place of a written midterm examination, there will be four shorter tests on the readings during the semester. Missed tests will not be made up, but the lowest test grade for the semester will be dropped and not included in the semester average.

Final Competency Exams. Scheduled by individual appointment during the final examination period.

Written Final Examination. Friday, December 17, 8:30–11:30 a.m.

Extra Credit Assignments

• Attend a "Meet the Teacher" night at an area school (select from the Hanover, Gettysburg, Upper Adams, New Oxford, or Littlestown school districts) and report your experience back to the class via e-mail using the class alias. While this assignment is for extra credit, it is something that will be very helpful for you to observe. Your focus should be on what is happening schoolwide and what the music teacher's role in the event is. You should be present when the evening's events begin and should attend any large-group general meeting that takes place. An area PTA meeting or a Board meeting that includes a musical presentation may also be used for this assignment.

• Prepare and turn in a second unit plan for a middle school or high school instrumental or choral class modeled after the one you create for a general music class.

• Observe a full rehearsal (Monday nights from 6–7:15) of the Gettysburg College Children's Choir and record your observations about children's voices from ages seven through thirteen and between boys and girls.

GRADING

• Attendance/Participation, including school observations, CMENC Chapter Meetings and e-mail responses	5%
• Practicum teaching in a school setting	10%
• Peer micro-teaching (lessons taught in class)	15%
• Written assignments, including lesson plans, journal writing, philosophy, unit plan, back-to-school-night letter, and comprehensive musicianship lesson	15%
• Materials files and course notebook	5%
• Written observation reports (3)	15%
• Test average and midterm playing competency grade	15%
• Final exam and final playing competency grade	20%

SCHEDULE OF ASSIGNMENTS

Subject to change as observation and practicum teaching opportunities can be arranged; please bring all books and recorders to every class.

T-8/29   Class Introduction-syllabus and calendar review; lesson plan writing, including looking at plans in *Sound Ways of Knowing* text; National and State Arts Standards; curriculum library holdings; rote song teaching; philosophy of music education; visit piano lab
Assignment: prepare to teach the class an assigned song by rote (no lesson plan required); read National Standards Introduction and memorize the nine content standards for music in the order listed; Hoffer, pp. 1–21, 29–43, Ch. 11; *Sound Ways,* Ch. 9; begin work on written philosophy

R-8/31	Teach assigned songs by rote to class; recorder playing and discussion of recorder instrument family and secondary level recorder materials **Assignment:** Reimer, Ch. 1, 8, & 9; Elliott, Ch. 1 & 2; Hoffer, pp. 49–71
T-9/5	First guitar instruction day (subject to visiting instructor's availability) **Assignment:** Mark/Gary, Chs. 8 & 9 & pp. 311–14; Mark, *Contemporary Music Education*, pp. 38–48; Hoffer, pp. 390–92; prepare assigned Middle Level Strategies Lesson
R-9/7	Peer-teach Middle-Level Strategies Lessons in class **Assignment:** *Sound Ways*, Ch. 1–4; Hoffer, pp. 94–115
T-9/12	*Test #1; first draft of personal philosophy due;* introduction to World Music Drumming Curriculum **Assignment:** Hoffer, Ch. 15 & 16
R-9/14	Second guitar instruction day
Sunday, 9/17	*CMENC meeting, with light supper, 6:15–8. Special guest, Herbert Henke, Emeritus Professor, Oberlin Conservatory, and Dalcroze Eurhythmics specialist (note later ending time)*
T-9/19	*Visiting African Dance & Drum Ensemble class visit* **Assignment:** Select two listening examples from the Fowler CD collection to present to a secondary general music or music history/appreciation class, one from the Western European art tradition and one from a non-Western European culture; write lesson plans for each selection
R-9/21	*Second draft of personal philosophy due* Peer-teach the listening lesson for the non-Western recording in class **Assignment:** Prepare assigned High School Strategies lesson
T-9/26	*Draft of letter to parents on back-to-school night due* Peer-teach High School Strategies lesson
R-9/28	*Test #2* **Assignment:** Review Fowler units 1, 2, & 3; *Sound Ways*, Ch. 5 & 6
T-10/3	*Final version of letter to parents due* **Assignment:** Review Fowler units 4, 5, & 6; *Sound Ways*, Ch. 7; submit several choices of pieces for comprehensive musicianship lesson
R-10/5	**Assignment:** Review Fowler units 7, 8, & 9; *Sound Ways*, Ch. 8

W & R, 10/4 & 5 Midterm Competency check on recorder, piano, and guitar (sign up for appointments)
Reading Days, October 9 & 10

M-10/9	*PMEA District 7 Professional Development Day, hosted by Gettysburg College; extra credit available for attendance and assistance that day*
R-10/12	Peer-teach assigned Fowler lessons
T-10/17	**Assignment:** *Sound Ways*, pp. 226–36; Mark Contemp., pp. 161–66
R-10/19	**Assignment:** *Sound Ways*, Ch. 11; final choice of unit plan themes due today

Sunday, October 22, 6:15–7:30, CMENC meeting with light supper

T-10/24	Catch-up Day
R-10/26	*Test #3*
T-10/31	Comprehensive Musicianship Lessons Due (Hallowe'en!)
R-11/2	**Assignment:** *Sound Ways,* pp. 195–225
T-11/7	**Assignment:** *Sound Ways,* Ch. 12
R-11/9	*No class: Fall Convocation preparation* **Assignment:** *Sound Ways,* Ch. 13

Sunday, November 12, 6:15–7:30, CMENC meeting with light supper

T-11/14	Computer music software and Internet Web sites exploration day
R-11/16	Unit plans due
T-11/21	*Test #4*

Thanksgiving Holiday

T-11/28	Creative Movement and Folk Dance day
R-11/30	Backyard dulcimers exploration day
T-12/5	Orff instrumentarium exploration day
R-12/7	Final Class: Catch Up/Exam Review; *Observation reports and materials and resources files due, including class notes—all will be checked and returned in time to use to study for the final exam*

Recorder Ensemble Playing Sessions. Six sessions will be held on the following Friday afternoons: 9/8 (2–3 p.m.), 10/20 (2–3 and 3–4 p.m.), 11/3 (2–3 p.m.). Each student is required to attend two of these hour-long sessions or to make alternative arrangements in the event of a schedule conflict. Extra credit will be provided for students who attend more than two sessions. Meet in room 220 to receive your playing assignment for the day.

Written Final Exam. Thursday, December 14, 2000, 1:30–4:30. Individual instrument competency playing tests on piano, guitar, and soprano recorder will be scheduled during the examination period but prior to the written exam day.

INSTRUMENT COMPETENCIES

Piano. Play "The Star-Spangled Banner" in B-flat, "America" in F, and "America the Beautiful" in B-flat. Choose one accompaniment each to play from McGraw-Hill's *Share the Music* and Silver Burdett Ginn's *Music Connection* basal series texts in the Music Education Library, grades 5–8 (make an appointment early in the semester to see Mr. Matsinko for individual help with this assignment if you need it).

Guitar. Accompany yourself while singing "Where Have All the Flowers Gone?" Demonstrate your knowledge of how to tune the guitar and hold it correctly; choose a second song to play and sing from the *Burl Ives Guitar Method Book* in the Curriculum Library.

Recorder. *Toot Sweet* for Recorder, Level One, all three songs; Sweet Pipes recorder method, work through the book independently. Seniors in the class should be able to play anything in the book, and juniors should be able to play at least half of the book. "Suite on Three Notes:" be able to accompany each other on the piano while playing. This accompaniment may be simplified.

MUSIC 393: SECONDARY MUSIC METHODS
PROF. PAT KRUEGER
UNIVERSITY OF PUGET SOUND
FALL 2000

AIMS OF THE COURSE

- To gain understanding of the philosophical foundations of music and aesthetics in education and the role of music in society and in public schools
- To explore the personal and professional dimensions and possibilities of music education
- To develop skills in curriculum building, lesson planning, teaching methods and styles, and long-term goals in music education
- To develop an understanding of musical elements and concept-based teaching, and examine state and national standards/guidelines
- To begin developing a system for teaching music literacy skills
- To become familiar with resource materials in music education
- To acquire experience in written and oral communication
- To gain initial teaching experiences within multicultural school music classrooms
- To examine school music administrative components and skills including budgeting, music library organization, scheduling, recruiting, and performance programming
- To develop experience with music evaluation processes, audition techniques, music group organization, and repertoire selection appropriate for schools
- To gain experience with technology in music education
- To explore the production of high school music theater, jazz ensembles, jazz choir, and marching band

COURSE OUTLINE
Readings are due the day they are listed.

Week 1: August 28/30
Introduction: What is my role as a music educator? Developing a philosophy of music education and teaching: Becoming an activist and advocate for arts education. Arts video. Library visit: Electronic music education resources. Group school visit.
Read Wolfgang, Ch. 1; Hoffer, Ch. 2.
Assignment: Interview question preparation.

Week 2: September 6
Interviewing for my first teaching position; What is my philosophy? Developing a personal teaching style for classroom discipline and student responsibility. Teacher/student interaction. Group school visit.
Read Wolfgang, Ch. 1; Hoffer, Ch. 2.

Week 3: September 11
The elements of music and concept-based teaching in music: What is a spiral curriculum and how do I build one? Lesson planning, curriculum building, and music programming. Developmental learning theory. National and state standards. Gordon: Teacher Effectiveness Training.
Classroom observation techniques: What am I looking for? Conducting sectionals and small-group lessons. Visit/observe your assigned public school classroom each week. Write and report in class upon reactions and teaching experiences. Due each Monday. Discuss lesson plan assignment.
Read Hoffer, Ch. 5; Wolfgang, Ch. 2. MENC Software: Ch. 1–5, 7

Week 4: September 18
Lesson plan assignment and presentation due.
Individual differences of students, learning styles, and alternative teaching approaches. Multicultural music: Why and how should I include multicultural music in my curriculum?
Read Hoffer, Ch. 8. (Use Hoffer, Ch. 9 & 10 and *Essential Elements* texts as resources for lesson planning.)

Week 5: September 25
Teaching techniques for sight-reading and skill-building in music ensembles and classes. Developing a system for teaching music literacy. Glasser: Reality Therapy. Discuss Assignment—Sight-reading.
Read Wolfgang, Ch. 5.

Week 6: October 2
Sight-reading assignments due; work on long-term plans. Writing your resume. Begin jazz observations.
Read MENC Software: Ch. 5.

Week 7 & 8: October 9/16
Elementary/Secondary Instrumental Methods. Repertoire building, music selection, philosophy. Concert planning, music literature, and instrumentation. Group school visit.
Assignment: Examine school music library/visit local music store for literature. Discuss literature/eight-week assignment.
Read Hoffer, Ch 12.

Week 9: October 23
Jazz Band/Choir (Jazz observation assignment due.) Group school visit.
Skim Wolfgang, Ch. 6 & 7.

Week 10: October 30
Choral Music Methods and changing voice. Bring in and discuss parent/student beginning-of-the-year letters from your practicum teacher. (Bring copies for each member of the class.) Check progress on literature assignment. Work on eight-week plan in class. Resume due.
Read Hoffer, Ch. 11.

Week 11: November 6
Computer technology workshop in secondary music education, electronic computer/keyboard lab, Rm 215.
Read Wolfgang, Ch. 10.

Week 12: November 13
Literature Collection due. Assertive Discipline, Canter. State teacher certification.
Read Wolfgang, Ch. 10 & 13. MENC Software, Chpts. 8, 16, 17.
Assignment: Budget plan and grading policy.

Week 13: November 20
Videotapes due (last day to turn in). Budget, contests and clinics, concert planning. Grading systems and evaluation in music. Recruiting and retention of music students. Cooperative learning vs. competition. Complete grading policy and budget. Possible conferences.
Read Hoffer, Ch. 13.

Week 14: November 27
Long-term planning: Long-term/eight-week plan final draft due in individual conferences.
Read Hoffer, Ch. 17. MENC Software: Chs. 3, 8.

Week 15: December 4
Practicum self-evaluation, discipline plan, philosophy assignment, in class. All practicum reports, checklists due. Last day to turn in written work.

ASSIGNMENTS

All written assignments should be typewritten.

• Read, think about, and discuss assigned readings.

• Attendance and participation in class activities and discussions, and in-class written assignments. Attendance is required at each class session and practicum weekly. Points will be lost for all unexcused absences. (25%)

• Sight-reading lesson assignment and presentation. (5%)

• Visit/observe public school settings; choose teaching site. Weekly practicum teaching in schools: Musicianship Skills (10%), Professional responsibility and written reactions from school observations, lesson plans, and evaluations (20%). (30% total)

• Begin resource file for teaching and music education notebook, including a bibliography and repertoire list for Jr. and Sr. High music ensembles. Literature assignment. (5%)

• Jazz Band or Choir, marching band, or musical theater observation and assignment. (5%)

• Budget plan and grading policy assignment (in class). (5%)

• Lesson plan assignment and presentation. (5%)

• Discipline plan/philosophy assignment. (5%)

• Videotape of practicum teaching and written analysis. (10%)

• Long-term/eight-week curriculum plan (include framework of state or national standards). (5%).

TEXTS

Hoffer, C. R. (2000). *Teaching Music in the Secondary Schools.* (required)

Wolfgang, C. H. (1999). *Solving Discipline Problems* (4th ed.). (recommended).

Music Educators' Journal (required, purchased through MENC application)

Software: *Teacher Success Kit: Music Education.* (1998). MENC. (required)

Essential Elements. (1995). Hal Leonard Pub. (Available for Choir, Band, or Strings. Choose your primary area: required).

MUSE 332: Secondary Music Methods
Dr. Margaret Schmidt
St. Cloud State University
Spring 2001

Instructor: Dr. Margaret Schmidt
Office: PAC 238
e-mail: mschmidt@stcloudstate.edu
Phone: 255-3223 (Music Dept. Office)
Office hours: as posted, and by appointment
Class meeting times: Mondays 12:30–1:20, Wednesdays 12:00–12:50, Fridays 9:00–9:50
Benton-Stearns Educational Cooperative, Pat Zimmerman, teacher: 253-8940.
Best times to call: 8:00–8:30 a.m., 3:00–3:15 p.m.

Texts

Abrahams, F., & Head, P. (1998). *Case studies in music education.* Chicago: GIA Publications, Inc.
Student membership in MENC, includes subscriptions to *Teaching Music* and *Music Educators Journal.* ($21)

Other useful resources

The Write Place at SCSU offers all kinds of writing help. Riverview 118, http://leo.stcloudstate.edu
Music education and advocacy materials are available through the MENC Web site: www.menc.org
You may wish to access the complete MENC *Strategies for Teaching* series free at: www.NotationStation.net
Career Services offers help with resumes, job searches, etc.: AS 102, http://condor.stcloudstate.edu/~careersv/
Notebook: Advocacy. SMF 069
Notebook: Philosophy. SMF 070

Course Objectives

- To develop a concept of teaching as making informed decisions among a variety of options
- To develop individual professional goals and to refine a personal philosophy of music education
- To develop a repertoire of teaching strategies appropriate to the developmental characteristics and learning styles of adolescents
- To develop observational skills to analyze the effectiveness of interactions within teaching-learning situations
- To develop rationale and curricular goals for general music and performance classes in the secondary school
- To develop a file of resources for use in designing and teaching a variety of secondary school music classes

Assignments

(1) Complete assigned readings, writing a brief (2–4 paragraph) response to each reading. Topics will be assigned. (5 points each)

(2) Select three pieces appropriate for sixth-grade chorus, band, or orchestra. Develop a list of concepts and skills students would need to perform the pieces successfully in a concert. (20)

(3) Given a list of ideas for a concert for middle-level general music, develop a list of the concepts and skills students would need to perform the pieces successfully in a concert. (20)

(4) Develop a long-range plan, showing what skills and activities you would include in each lesson for a 10-week trimester to prepare the students to be successful in a concert. Activities should address a wide range of abilities and learning needs. Include at least one activity incorporating music from a non-Western culture and one activity incorporating American folk or popular music. Include at least one

activity asking students to improvise or compose and one activity focused on listening to music. (50)

(5) Develop two 30-minute lessons appropriate to several aspects of the music you selected in Assignment 2. Teach your lesson to the students at Benton-Stearns Educational Cooperative, and complete a self-evaluation for each lesson. (50 each)

(6) Assist with presentation of a concert at Benton-Stearns Educational Cooperative, and write a reflective paper on what you learned in preparing and presenting the concert. (50)

(7) Attend at least two sessions at the MMEA Midwinter Clinic in Minneapolis, Thursday, Friday and Saturday, Feb. 15–17. Write a summary of the sessions you attend, attaching any relevant materials. (50)

(8) Arrange or compose a piece (at least 32 bars in length) for seventh or eighth grade vocal or instrumental trio or quartet. Using a computer program (*Finale* is recommended), save your arrangement on disk and print a score and parts. Create and print one part transposed for a vocal range or instrument different from your original score. (25)

(9) Demonstrate guitar performance skills appropriate for teaching a three-week guitar unit in middle school general music class. A specific list of skills will be provided. (50)

(10) Using a word-processing program, create a home page for a school music program, including grading policies, concert dates, and other relevant information. Save your work as HTML. For an example, see Sartell bands: www.cloudnet.com/~trains/bmain.html (25)

(11) Using a word processor, create a resume, appropriate as an application for a position as a music teacher. Attach a one-page statement of your beliefs about the value of music education and/or a position paper appropriate for a student-teaching application. Save your work on a disk. (25)

(12) Develop annotated bibliographic references for selected materials for teaching secondary school music. To create a class file of references, send your annotations to the instructor by e-mail: mschmidt@stcloudstate.edu. In class, give an oral presentation to your colleagues. (20)

(13) Observe at least two different secondary music classes or a non-school-based middle-level group. Report on your observations, in assigned formats. Your observations should include a general music class and a middle school or junior high performance group. (50 each)

(14) Develop a file of resources for teaching secondary school general music and performance classes. Completed course assignments and class notes will form the basis of your file. Additional materials are welcome, including information from other courses you have taken at SCSU. These may be organized in any format that makes sense to you. (20)

(15) Participate fully in all class discussions and activities, including additional writing assignments and quizzes. For an excused absence, leave a message at 255-2295 or speak with the instructor in advance. You will lose five points for each absence from class or for consistent tardiness. Points lost through an excused absence may be made up with the consent of the instructor (15 points maximum). (150)

GRADING

All points earned for assignments throughout the semester will be totaled for your final grade:

> 90% of the total needed to earn an A
> 80% needed to earn a B
> 70% needed to earn a C

You must earn a C or better in this course (and finish your piano proficiency) to qualify to student teach.

A professional attitude toward attendance and assignments is expected. All assignments are due at the beginning of class on the day specified. Late assignments will receive a proportion of the points otherwise earned:

Same or next school day	90%
Within one week	70%
More than one week	50%
After class final	0

Habits such as good spelling, appropriate grammar, organized writing, and neatness are essential for teachers, as is the ability to read and follow instructions. On all assignments, points earned depend on attention to these details.

Should you receive less than 80% on an assignment, you may be given an opportunity to redo the assignment. Points to be made up must be completed within three school days of the returned graded assignment to receive credit. Extra-credit assignments may be arranged only to replace points lost through an excused absence.

Class final: Friday, May 11, Informance Concert at Benton-Stearns Educational Cooperative, 10:15–12:45

SCHEDULE OF ASSIGNMENTS DUE

Monday	Wednesday	Friday
	1/17: Introduction. Seconday school music.	1/19: Read text, pp. 50–60. From concerts to curriculum development.
1/22: Assignment 3, first draft. Integrating music in the curriculum.	1/24: Curriculum development.	1/26: Read text, pp. 37–49. Planning lessons.
1/29: The relationship between curriculum and classroom management.	1/31: Read text, pp. 69–85. Planning lessons.	2/2: Assignment 3 due. Curriculum development.
2/5: Teaching class guitar. Rote methods.	2/7: Guitar proficiencies. Teaching guitar. Rote methods.	2/9: Guitar proficiences. Teaching composition and improvisation.
2/12: Assignment 4 plan due. Guitar—Teaching composition and improvisation.	2/14: Guitar worksheets due. Teaching class guitar.	2/16: No class. Attend MMEA
2/19: Guitar proficiencies. Materials and methods.	2/7: Guitar proficiencies. Teaching class guitar.	2/23: Letter to principal due. Complete guitar proficiences (Assignment 9).
2/26: Assignment 7 (MMEA summary) due. Effective rehearsals.	2/28: Read Lenzini, Moyer, or Williamson. Effective rehearsals.	3/2: Teaching movement and dance.
3/5: Read text, pp. 118–130. Teaching desired student behavior.	3/7: Read text, pp. 106–117. Assessment of learning. Mn. Profile of Learning.	3/9: Observation 1 due. Teaching listening lessons.
3/19: Read text, pp. 151–163. Contests, festivals, and your philosophy of teaching.	3/21: Read text, pp. 61–68. Contests and your philosophy of teaching.	3/23: Expressing your philosophy of teaching.
3/26: Read text, pp. 164–175. Copyright issues. Selecting and arranging music.	3/28: Arranging music. Meet in PA 163. Bring headphones and disk.	3/30: Arranging music. Meet in PA 163. Bring headphones and disk.
4/2: Arranging music. Meet in PA 163. Bring headphones and disk.	4/4: No class.	4/6: Assignment 8 due. Resumes and job hunting.

4/9: Read text, pp. 131–139. Communicating with parents.

4/11: Read text, pp. 141–150. Communication with parents.

4/13: Assignment 11 due.

4/16: Developing a Web site. Meet in PA 163. Bring disk.

4/18: See below.* Developing a Web site. Meet in PA 163. Bring disk.

4/20: Assignment 10 due. Materials for teaching.

4/23: Read text, pp. 18–29. Schedules and budgets.

4/25: Assignment 12 due. Materials for teaching.

4/27: Observation 2 due.

4/30: Read text, pp. 96–105. Starting a new job.

5/2: Music in the curriculum.

5/4: Course summary.

Student-teaching applications are due Wed., April 18, to the Clinical Experiences Office.
Final exam, Friday, May 11, 10:1–12:45: Assignment 6, Assignment 14

CITATIONS FOR READINGS

Abrahams, F., & Head, P. (1998). *Case studies in music education.* Chicago: GIA Publications.

Lenzini, C. S. (2000). Having fun in middle school: An interview with music director Deborah Shofner. *The Instrumentalist, 54*(6), 10–14.

Moyer, R. (1997). Directing middle school orchestras: An interview with Terry Shade. *The Instrumentalist, 52*(1), 12–15.

Williamson, S. (2000). Positively adolescent. *Music Educators Journal, 86*(4), 29–32.

RESOURCES FOR SECONDARY MUSIC

Bailey, W. (1994). *The complete marching band resource manual.* Philadelphia: University of Pennsylvania Press. (MT733.4 .B35)

Casey, J. L. (1991). *Teaching techniques and insights for instrumental music educators.* Chicago: GIA. Publications, Inc.

Colwell, R. J., & Goolsby, T. (1992). *The teaching of instrumental music* (2nd ed.). Englewood Cliffs, NJ: Prentice Hall, Inc.

Dillon, J. A., & Kriechbaum, C. B. (1978). *How to design and teach a successful string and orchestra program.* San Diego, CA: Kjos West.

Farnan, L., & Johnson, F. (1988). *Music is for everyone: A handbook for providing music to people with special needs.* Milwaukee: Hal Leonard Publishing Co.

Fowler, C. (1994). *Music! Its role and importance in our lives.* Mission Hills, CA: GLENCOE DIVISION, Macmillan/McGraw-Hill.

Haritun, R. (1994). *Music teacher's survival guide.* Weest Nyack, NY: Parker Publishing Co.

The Instrumentalist. (1996). *New director's handbook.* Northfield, IL: Author.

Lavender, C. (1987). *Help! I'm a substitute music teacher.* Milwaukee: Hal Leonard Publishing.

Miles, R. B., & Blocher, L. R. (1996). *Block scheduling: Implications for music education.* Springfield, IL: Focus on Excellence, Inc.

Mitchell, L. (1992). *The music teacher's almanac.* West Nyack, NY: Parker Publishing Co.

Phillips, K. H. (1992). *Teaching kids to sing.* New York: Schirmer Books.

Sheldon, D. A., & Sheldon, R. (1996). *The complete woodwind instructor.* Oskaloosa, IA: C. L. Barnhouse Company.

Spanko, Jean. (1985). *Taming the anthill.* Memphis, TN: Memphis Musicraft Publications.

Walker, D. E. (1989). *Teaching music: Managing the successful music program* (2nd ed.). New York: Schirmer Books. (MT1 W28)

Weikart, P. S. (1989). *Teaching movement and dance* (3rd ed.). Ypsilanti, MI: The High/Scope Press. Text and recordings. (GV1753.5 .W45)

Wise, P. C. (1996). *So... you're the new band director: Now what?* Needham Heights, MA: Simon & Schuster Custom Publishing.

MUSIC 57-376, 876: MUSIC IN THE SECONDARY SCHOOLS
LEWIS H. STROUSE, D.A.
CARNEGIE MELLON UNIVERSITY, COLLEGE OF FINE ARTS
SPRING 2000

Instructor: Lewis H. Strouse, D.A.
Office: CFA 162, x8-1432   **E-mail:** Strouse+@Andrew.CMU.Edu
Course Focus: A comprehensive view of the secondary school music program
Description: This course is intended to develop a detailed understanding of music curricula, instructional practice, and administrative procedures at the secondary school level.

TEXTS AND MATERIALS
Required
> Hoffer, C. (1991). *Teaching Music in the Secondary Schools.*
> Strouse. *Course Packet for Music in the Secondary Schools.*

Reference
> Ryan & Cooper (1998). *Those Who Can, Teach.* (8th ed.).
> Strouse. Course Packet for Principles of Education: (Pedagogy, Section G)

Reserve
> See "Reserve Listing for Spring 2000." Additional readings may be provided in class or placed on library reserve during the semester.

Materials
> 2-1/2" notebook (suggest slant-ring binder); enough sets of notebook index sheets/dividers to satisfactorily index your course notebook (see below).

DETAILED STATEMENT OF INTENT
The main purpose of the course is to bring students to a satisfactory level of competency in regard to
- a personal philosophy of music education and its relationship to educational practice
- implementing general music (non-performance) courses
- implementing performance classes
- aligning instructional practice with the National Standards in Music Education
- a proactive approach to preventive discipline
- a working knowledge of administrative procedures which attend the development and maintenance of a well-founded secondary music program

EVALUATION
The final evaluation estimate will comprise seven projects (70 pts) and the final evaluation interview (30 pts).
Grade scheme: A (9–10 pts), B (8 pts), C (7 pts), D (6 pts), R (0–6 pts).
Late work: See below.

STATEMENT OF PROFESSIONAL STANDARDS
Evaluation Criteria
(1) *Class Attendance.* Discussions with colleagues concerning professional matters add immensely to your professional knowledge. To that end, class attendance is of paramount importance. Each absence beyond a limit of one will lower the next project grade by one full letter grade. Excused absences are defined as personal/family emergencies or absences sanctioned by the Head of the School of Music. The attendance policy is strictly adhered to. Students anticipating a problem with regular class attendance should speak with Dr. Strouse.

(2) *Projects.*
- All course projects are to be typewritten, unless otherwise noted. In cases where a specific format has not been prescribed for the project, the student is to create a format that gives a well-ordered and professional appearance.

- Each project submitted on time may be resubmitted, once, for re-evaluation. Resubmissions must occur on or before the class following the original due date. The grade for the resubmission will be the final grade for the project.
- Late work. Because an important part of class instruction is derived from the discussion of projects, projects submitted late will be accepted within 48 hours of the due date, minus two full letter grades. Projects will not be accepted beyond this 48-hour extension.
- Course projects are designed to focus on the professional application of course information. It is expected that considerable care will be taken in the preparation and presentation of each project. Further, it is expected that as concerns arise in class preparations, you will make an appointment with Dr. Strouse to discuss your plans. Plan ahead—panic at the beginning!!!

(3) *Course Notebook.* As well as being a key reference for you as you begin your teaching career, your course notebook will serve as the basis for the organization of your continuing education information—a volume to which additional material may be added. The regular and systematic updating of your professional knowledge is key to your best instructional practice—the best care of your students. Continuing education is a fact of life for educators who exemplify the highest standards of educational practice. The organization of continuing education information, be it from reading journals, attending meetings and conferences, or personal creative activity, is a component of every professional's library.

Divide and label your notebook into the following sections using a set of notebook index dividers:
- Syllabus and Course Schedule
- Course Packet subdivided according to Table of Contents sections for easy reference
- Weekly notes and handouts exclusive of course packet material
- Course project completions
- A minimum of five journal articles, personalized (underlined/highlighted portions), concerning secondary music education
- Sections of personal interest may be added
- Secondary Guided Teaching Section: Include materials pertaining to your Secondary Guided Teaching field experience.

(4) *Final Evaluation Interview.* An oral exam intended to simulate a professional job interview. Interview questions will require you to synthesize various components of course content into concise, articulate responses. You will be required to present (a) a professional resume (10%), (b) a teaching portfolio (including five samples of your best work from certification courses taken (10%), (c) course notebook (10%), and (d) the quality of your verbal responses (70%). You will receive feedback immediately following the interview.

Instruction. Class instruction will derive from a mixture of lecture, the discussion of assigned readings, and the presentation of course projects. Class activities and discussion are intended to clarify and reinforce course content and enable individuals to contribute experiential knowledge. It is expected that you will reference excerpts from assigned readings to support your view of issues.

Journal Review. As a regular part of continuing professional education, it is expected that educators will keep abreast of the latest developments in their primary and cognate fields through (1) regular reading of selected professional journals, (2) contributing research or writings to professional journals, (3) membership and regular attendance of professional society meetings, and (4) regular attendance at local, state, regional, or national conferences. The following journals are suggested: *Music Educators Journal* and the related state journal *J. of the Pennsylvania Music Educators Association, The Instrumentalist, J. of the American Choral Directors' Association.* Additional journals should be read in cognate areas of specialization (e.g., *J. of the International Trombone Association, J. of Counseling and Development,* etc.).

Article Review. As you read articles, it is useful to (1) identify the article's essential content—the important themes, components of the article, (2) consider how you can best apply the content of the article in your educational practice, and (3) consider whether the article is sufficient in detail to realize its practical application.

Professional Society Memberships. You should be active in at least two professional societies: (1) MENC, which represents all phases of music education at all academic levels, and (2) a professional society representing a cognate field (e.g., American Choral Directors' Association).

COURSE SCHEDULE

See "Project Description" sheets for explanation of projects identified on this course schedule. Where requested, prepare study-guide questions presented in the course packet for each Hoffer text chapter assignment. Class discussion will include the study-guide questions. Questions marked as "Issues" in the study guide need not be prepared for this course.

1/18 **Course Introduction, Overview of Secondary School Music Curriculum**
   (1) Course overview
   (2) Review of goal and basic structure of general education
   (3) A view of teaching assignment possibilities for the secondary music educator (B1)
   (4) Review of course content sources in secondary school music (see bibliography)
   (5) Developing conviction through a philosophy of music education
   (6) Sampling of school district and parental views of music education (A10)
   (7) Assignment due 2/1
       (a) Project #1: Formulating a personal philosophy of music education
       (b) Hoffer, Ch. 3, "The Reasons for Music in the Schools"

1/25 Analysis of student-teaching videos

2/1 **Philosophy of Music Education**
   (1) Individual presentations of Project #1
   (2) Hoffer, Ch. 3: Study guide questions
   (3) Advocacy: Review of research in support of music in K–12 curriculum
   (4) Assignment due 2/8:
       (a) Project #2: Text review for general music.
       (b) Prepare Hoffer, Ch. 6, "Teaching General Music."

2/8 **General Music: Middle School and High School**
   (1) Individual presentations of Project #2
   (2) Discussion of Hoffer, Ch. 6
   (3) Assignment due 2/22:
       (a) Course packet section D: "Middle School General Music"
       (b) Complete course packet p. D18

2/15 **Web-Based Instruction**
   (1) Purpose and instructional strategies
   (2) Design Software
   (3) Web-based resources

2/22 **Middle School General Music**
   (1) Review of middle school general music course material using whole-class approach via discussion of CP p. D18 worksheet.
   (2) Assignment due 3/7:
       (a) Project #3: Preparing a middle school general music unit
       (b) Hoffer, Ch. 7, "Teaching Music Appreciation, Fine Arts, and Theory"
       (c) Course packet section E: "Music Appreciation"

2/29 School Visit

3/7 **General Music: Middle School and High School**
   (1) Individual presentations of Project #3

3/7   (2) Course packet section E: Topic-specific instructional approaches in general music
(cont.) (3) Hoffer, Ch. 7.
         (4) Assignment due 3/14: Course packet section I: "Discipline"

3/14   **Preventive Discipline**
       (1) Approaching classroom management through "preventive discipline" (Section I)
       (2) Assignment due 3/21
               (a) Project #5: Reactive discipline
               (b) Prepare Hoffer, Ch. 16: "Music Teaching and Student Discipline"

3/21   **Student Motivation, Reactive and Proactive (Preventive) Discipline**
       (1) Individual presentations of Project #5
       (2) Hoffer, Ch. 16
       (3) Assignment due 4/4.
               (a) Project #6: Comprehensive musicianship in rehearsal
               (b) Prepare Hoffer, Ch. 4, "The Music Curriculum," pp. 64–66, 161–66
                   ("Performing Groups" and "Enriching the Rehearsal")

4/4   **Comprehensive Musicianship in Rehearsal**
       (1) Individual presentations of Project #6
       (2) Hoffer, Ch. 4, "The Music Curriculum," pp. 64–66 ("Performing Groups" and "Enriching the Rehearsal")
       (3) Assignment due 4/11:
               (a) Prepare Hoffer, Ch. 8, "Teaching Performing Groups"
               (b) Course packet section G: "Performance Classes"

4/11   **Performance Classes**
       (1) Hoffer, Ch. 8
       (2) Selecting repertoire
       (3) Introducing new pieces
       (4) Assignment due 4/18: Course packet section J: "Preliminary Administrative Planning"

4/18   **Administration: Preliminary Planning**
       (1) Review and clarify administrative procedures of preliminary planning
       (2) Preparing a five-year budget plan
       (3) Assignment due 4/25:
               (a) Project #7, Composing a budget proposal
               (b) Course packet section K: "Internal Administrative Planning"

4/25   **Administration: Internal Planning**
       (1) Discussion of Project #7
       (2) Review and clarify administrative procedures of internal planning
       (3) Assignment due 5/2: Course packet section L: "External Administrative Planning"

5/2   **Administration: External Planning**
       (1) Review and clarify administrative procedures of external planning.
       (2) Discussion of Final Evaluation Interview.

TBA   **Final Evaluation Interview (Oral)**

COURSE PACKET DESCRIPTION

It is incumbent upon teacher education faculty to present a large base of instructional materials as a foundation from which their students may craft future course content and instructional practices. The content of the course packet serves this purpose.

The majority of course packet material consists of original work developed during the course of my educational practice in secondary school. Other material includes items collected from school entities, such as unpublished forms for organizing trips, letters and processes related to student recruitment, and samples of in-service teacher evaluation forms.

The course packet is organized into three broad categories and each category is divided into lettered sections, with the pages of each section numbered consecutively. Organizing the packet in this way allows adding and deleting pages in a section without having to renumber the pages of the entire packet.

The following is an outline of the course packet content with a basic description of each section:

I. Foundation

    A. Philosophy of Music Education

        1. References to current professional philosophy

        2. Worksheet for developing a personal professional philosophy

        3. Printed materials concerning the advocacy efforts of local schools

II. Music Curriculum Content and Pedagogy

    B. Curriculum Components

- Listing of typical music course offerings
- Sample teacher schedules

    C. Course Structure

- Parameters of overall course design
- Primary approach to instruction
- Composing a course assessment package

    D. Middle School General Music

- Sample general music unit (contributed by Patricia Bauer, North Allegheny School District)
- Worksheet review of unit concerning format, pacing, integration of National Standards, learning styles
- Method of formulating a general music unit

    E. Music Appreciation

- Complete course packet (Strouse) for high school "Introduction to Music" course
- Active learning projects that model the musician's critical thinking and creative processes
- Various methods of assessment
- Ways of organizing essential information about elements of music and musical styles for effective learning
- Ways of connecting course content to student life experiences

    F. Music Theory

- Outline of topics to be addressed
- Ways of structuring theory worksheets
- Practical application of music theory skills
- Sequence for teaching aural skills in rhythmic, melodic, and harmonic dictation

    G. Performance Classes

- Instrumental and choral audition forms
- Sources and ways of selecting performance literature
- Method for introducing pieces
- Rehearsal format
- Concert programming
- Score analysis protocol
- Typical problems and correctives in instrumental and vocal ensembles

    H. Course Evaluation

- Tools for course evaluation by students
- Reporting student grades to parents
- Weekly practice slips

I. Discipline
- Motivating students in performance classes
- Motivating students in general music, non-performance classes
- Approach to preventive discipline
- Approach to reactive discipline
- Maintaining emotional balance in the face of discipline problems

III. Administration of the Secondary School Music Program
J. Preliminary Planning
- Elements of a strong music program
- Preparing for your first year
- Budget planning and preparation
- Preparing a student-teaching portfolio
- Technology recommendations for office and classroom

K. Internal Planning
- Developing a music department handbook
- Planning the yearly performance calendar
- Sample constitutions for performance groups and adult booster groups
- Sample processes for student recruitment and class scheduling

L. External Planning
- Logistics of organizing concert performances
- Details of travel preparations
- Organizing summer camps for band, chorus, orchestra

M. Study Guide for Current Text
- Focus student reading on selected topics

PROJECT DESCRIPTIONS

I. Formulating a Personal Philosophy of Music Education. From your educational philosophy stems your firm conviction for the position of music education in the school curriculum. Your educational philosophy also defines your approach to instructional practice. Your views on both of these issues will guide your decisions concerning what to teach (selection of course content), how to teach (selection of delivery options), and how to evaluate student learning (selection of assessment options).

The following publications concerning music education philosophy are widely respected by music educators. Prepare formal written responses to the readings, as requested. Minimum length per response is one page, typewritten. Responses will be evaluated in terms of the quality of grammar and clarity of content. Inform your views by referencing specific quotes in the readings, (i.e., place the quote in quotation marks followed by the page number in parentheses).

A. Respond to *one* of the following readings. These readings are on the Hunt reserve.
1) Leonhard (1985). *A realistic rationale for teaching music* [781.1 F78M]. Do you believe Leonhard presents arguments that would convince a school board to continue its support of music education? Why, why not?
2) Lehman (1995), "What Students Should Learn In The Arts", in A. A. Glatthorn (Ed.), *Content of the Curriculum* (pp. 1–22) [Personal Copy Reserve]. Dr. Lehman, former director of the school of music at the University of Michigan and past president of MENC, presents a current view of music education in this respected publication by the Association for Supervision and Curriculum Development. Respond to this article.

B. *Personal philosophy of music education.* Complete the form titled "Components of Your Philosophy of Music Education." This form asks you to address the principal components of a professional philosophy statement. In the future, your views of these components will lead you to formulate the philosophical essay usually required as a part of your application for a professional position.

    C. The following questions reflect contemporary issues in music education. They could be posed to you at a job interview or by a parent, student, or taxpayer-at-large. You need not prepare written responses to these questions, but be prepared to say how you would respond if any of these questions were posed to you.

        1) Do you believe solo and ensemble competition has a place in music education?

        2) What is the place of the marching band in the music curriculum?

        3) My daughter studies voice privately, sings in the church choir and high school chorus, and wants to be a business major in college. Does she *really* need to be in the high school chorus when she could be taking other courses that would better prepare her for the rigors of her college major?

        4) How will studying general music benefit my son in middle school?

        5) How will participating in band and choir help my daughter do well on the SAT?

II. Text Review for General Music. Review the text *Music! Its Role and Importance in Our Lives* on library reserve and evaluate its appropriateness for a general music class. You will be assigned a specific unit of the text to evaluate. Select one chapter of the unit and evaluate the chapter in terms of each of the following: (a) writing style (clear, understandable?), (b) the amount of material covered on particular topics (too much, too little, just right?), (c) degree of emphasis on musical qualities, (d) presentation of material that is interesting for the student who is not a musician, and (e) variety of delivery and assessment options for use by the teacher. Reference at least two specific examples from the text to support your evaluation in each of the five areas by quoting the excerpt and placing the page location in parentheses.

III. Preparing a Middle School General Music Unit.

    A. Complete and submit the following on sheets separate from your unit project.

        1) Identify the theme of the unit and present three outcomes to be realized by the unit. (Assume it will take two class periods to realize the three outcomes.)

        2) Explain the students' readiness level for this unit, (i.e., what background knowledge do the students need to begin work on this unit?) Be specific here. Do not simply say "students must understand notation." What notation must they understand?—whole, half, quarter, eighth notes?

        3) Include a unit objective check-off sheet that the teacher can use to mark the exercises completed by the student.

    B. Include the following in your unit project:

        1) Interactive Modes: A combination of individual learning and formal cooperative learning

        2) Recall exercises to test the students' knowledge base prior to completing creative/authentic activities

        3) Include at least two creative activities: One intrapersonal activity and one two-person group

        4) Include enough worksheets to realize each outcome (usually 1–3 sheets is suffcient); make two copies of your worksheets: one with answers and one without answers

        5) You may prepare your unit in a style and format similar to the Bauer model

        6) Number the pages of your unit

        7) Compose worksheets that utilize two or more content standards on the way to realizing a particular outcome (e.g., notating intervals followed by performing the intervals on a bell set)

        8) Be certain to include instructions on all worksheets

    C. Title each of your worksheets and indicate their relationship to Outcomes 1, 2, or 3 in the upper right-hand corner.

IV. Learning Assessments. As a way of developing a frame of reference for our discussion of learning assessment, identify four different courses you took in high school (two music and two non-music) and respond to the following questions in terms of each course:

    A. Describe the methods of assessment used to determine course grades, and categorize the assessment method in terms of the assessment categories contained on the Principles of Education form, "Assessment Options." If you can recall the grade weight given to each assessment, indicate it.

  B. Do you believe each method of assessment was effective in accurately measuring student ability? If not, how would you change the assessment to more accurately measure the students' ability?

V. Reactive Discipline.

  A. Complete "Case Study Report On Discipline" (in CP) describing a familiar experience. (I12)

  B. Complete the worksheet "Case Studies in Discipline" (in CP). (I13)

VI. Comprehensive Musicianship in Rehearsal. In simplest terms, "comprehensive musicianship" refers to learning about features of the music, in addition to note-reading skills, that enhance student understanding of the music, raise interest in the music, and improve performance skill. A "comprehensive musicianship approach" to instruction reinforces learning by providing a broader context to the piece being performed. The class time devoted to teaching about these additional features of context, or learning components, is often very limited (e.g., 3–5 minutes). However, experiential observations by music educators indicate that learning about musical works in this broad context actually improves the students' ability to perform the work effectively. [Consider this: Viewed another way, in the absence of a comprehensive musicianship approach to music learning, what type of intelligence(s) is necessary to perform music, i.e., in playing or singing the notes from the page, at which Bloom or Taba cognitive level is the student operating?]

Comprehensive musicianship components derive their content from four discipline-based approaches reflected in the National Standards, e.g., (1) *production* (analysis, composition, improvisation, performance, and interpretive decisions—relates to Standards 1–5), (2) *history* (the historical and cultural contexts of a musical work—relates to Standards 8–9), (3) *aesthetics* (dealing with criteria for responding to works emotionally—relates to Standards 6–7), and (4) *criticism* (evaluating the compositional quality of the work or the performance quality—relates to Standards 6–7).

  A. Review two ensemble works (the choral piece, and the band or orchestra piece) contained in the reserve file "Music for Analysis." For each work, identify four learning components, one for each of the areas identified above, give the content of the component to be taught, and indicate the usefulness of this information for the performer or the listener that you would discuss in class.

  B. On a separate paper, respond to the following: High schools frequently offer non-performance courses such as music history and music theory. From your perspective as a performance major, how does the study of music history and music theory impact your performance of music?

VII. Composing a Budget Proposal. Prepare a budget request for equipment and instruments as assigned. Refer to "Budget Proposal Description" in course packet for the structure of the proposal. Attire, music, and equipment catalogs have been placed on reserve. Consult the reserve text *Teaching Music* by D. Walker, pp. 82–107, for ideas on formulating rationales in support of the items being requested.

MUSIC EDUCATION SELECTED BIBLIOGRAPHY

Catalog numbers are listed for those books available in Hunt Library.

General Application at Secondary Level

Bessom, M. E., Tatarunis, A. M., & Forcucci, S. L. (1980). *Teaching music in today's secondary schools* (2nd ed.). New York: Holt Rinehart & Winston. (hard) [780.72 B55t2]

Canter, L. (1994). *Assertive discipline teacher's plan book plus #1.* Santa Monica, CA: Lee Canter & Associates. [Ovrsz Q 371.102 H78T]

Hoffer, C. (1991). *Teaching music in the secondary schools* (4th ed.). Belmont, CA: Wadsworth. (hard) [780.72 H69t4]

Mark, M. L. (1996). *Contemporary music education.* New York: Schirmer. (hard)

Mitchell, L. (1985). *A practical handbook for musical theater* (2nd ed.). Fort Dodge, IA: Comedia. The book analyzes 65 popular musicals suitable for high school performance.

The following paperback publications are available from MENC, Reston, VA

Davidson, J. (1994). *TIPS: Thinking skills in the music classroom.*

Fleming, L. (1994). *Getting started with jazz band.*

Lehr, M. R. (1998). *Getting started with elementary-level band.*

MENC. (1989). *Music booster manual.* (1989).

MENC Committee on Standards. (1989). *Guidelines for performance of school music groups.* [780.7 M9873g]

Michelson, S. K. (1994). *Getting started with high school choir.*

Rossman, R. L. (Ed.). (1989). *Tips: Discipline in the music classroom.* [780.7 R83d]

Schaberg, G. (1995). *Tips: Teaching music to special learners.*

Zerull, D. S. (1994). *Getting started with high school band.*

General Music

Bennett, M. D. (1978). *Surviving in general music.* Memphis, TN: Pop Hits. (2 vol. set and accessories). Presents a variety of lesson activities.

Campbell, P. S. (1991). *Lessons from the world: A cross cultural guide to music teaching and learning.* New York: Schirmer. [780.7 C18L]

Fowler, C. (1994). *Music! Its role and importance in our lives.* Mission Hills, CA: Glencoe.

Gerber, T., & Hughes, W. (Eds.). (1988). *Music in the high school: Current approaches to secondary general music instruction.* Reston, VA: MENC. Proceedings of the National Conference on Music/Arts for the High School General Student, June 25–28, 1986, Orlando, Florida.

Magazines: *Music Alive* (P.O. Box 904, Rochester, VT 05767, 1-800-435-5003); *Music K–8.*

Metz, Donald. (1980). *Teaching general music in grades 6–9.* Columbus, OH: Charles E. Merrill. (paper) Offers information on philosophy, organization and discipline, sample lesson plans. [780.72 M59t]

Regelski, T. A. (1981). *Teaching general music.* New York: Schirmer. (hard) [780.72 R33t]

Schafer, R. M. (1992). *A sound education: 100 exercises in listening and soundmaking.* Indian River, Ontario, CND: Arcana Editing. [153.6 S29s]

Schafer, R. M. (1976). *Creative music education.* New York: Schirmer. (paper) [780.72 S39c]

Willoughby, D. (1993). *The world of music.* [781.1 W73W2]

Music Appreciation

Machlis, J. (1990). *The enjoyment of music* (6th ed.). New York: W.W. Norton. (hard) [780.2 M14e3; recordings to 3rd edition, #2985]

Music Education: Foundations

Boyle, J. D. (Ed.). (1974). *Instructional objectives in music.* Reston, VA: MENC.

Colwell, R. (Ed.). (1992). *Handbook of research on music teaching and learning.* New York: Schirmer. [780.7 H236]

Cutietta, R., Hamann, D. L., & Walker, L. M. (1995). *Spin-offs: The extra-musical advantages of a musical education.* Elkhart, IN: United Musical Instruments.

Gardner, H. (1983). *Frames of mind: Theory of multiple intelligences.* New York: Basic Books. (See the section on musical intelligence.)

Lehman, P. R. (1987). *Music in today's schools: Rationale and commentary.* Reston, VA: MENC.

Leonhard, C., & House, R. W. (1972). *Foundations and principles of music education.* New York: McGraw-Hill. [780.72 L58f2]

Leonhard, C. (1985). *A realistic rationale for teaching music.* Reston, VA: MENC.

Reimer, B. (1989). *A philosophy of music education* (2nd ed.). Englewood Cliffs, NJ: Prentice Hall.

Robinson, R. L. (Ed.). (1993). *Preparing to teach music in today's schools.* Reston, VA: MENC.

Music History

Grout, D. J., & Palisca, C. V. (2001). *A history of western music* (6th ed.). New York: W.W. Norton.

Wold, M., Martin, G., Miller, J., & Cykler, E. (1994). *An outline history of western music.* (8th ed.). Madison, WI: Brown & Benchmark.

Music Theory

Arlin, M. I., Lord, C. H., Ostrander, A. S., & Porterfield, M. S. (1989). *Music sources.* Englewood Cliffs, NJ: Prentice Hall. (paper) A collection of excerpts and complete movements. Compositions are sectioned according to particular harmonic illustrations and type of form demonstrated.

Duckworth, W. (2001). *A creative approach to music fundamentals* (7th ed.). Belmont, CA: Wadsworth. (paper) Ideas on introducing music fundamentals that are adaptable to elementary and secondary school students.

Harder, P. O., & Steinke, G. (1991). *Basic materials in music theory* (7th ed.). Boston: Allyn & Bacon. (paper) A programmed course in fundamentals. [5th ed. (1982) available: 781.07 H25b5]

Ottman, R. W. (2001). *Music for sight singing* (5th ed.). Pearson Publications.

Music Theory (PNMN faculty recommendations)

Jones, G. (1974). *Music theory.* Barnes & Noble Outline Series.

Manoff, T., Miller, J., & Hestermann, P. (2000). *The music kit.*

Turek, R. (1992). *Analytical anthology of music.* [780.9 A5322a2]

EDUCATION AND EDUCATION-RELATED SELECTED BIBLIOGRAPHY

Boyer, E. L. (1983). *High school: A report on secondary education in America.* New York: Harper & Row. (paper) An excellent evaluative review of the social atmosphere and academic setting of schools.

Buscaglia, L. (1982). *Living, loving, and learning.* New York: Holt, Rinehart, and Winston. (hard) A wonderful insight into people relationships and the full enjoyment of life. You will probably find yourself many times in the pages of this book.

Carnegie, D., & Pell, A. (1998). *How to win friends and influence people.* New York: Simon & Schuster. (paper).

Cohen, H. (1980). *You can negotiate anything.* New York: Bantam Books. (paper) Comments on the temperament and thought processes necessary for negotiation—persuading others to your point of view.

Gallwey, W. T. (1974). *The inner game of tennis.* New York: Bantam Books. (paper) Discussion of a successful style of teaching tennis—applicable to teaching practically anything.

Hamachek, D. E. (1974). *Psychology in teaching, learning, and growth* (2nd ed.). Boston: Allyn and Bacon. A very good text on experiential practices.

McCormack, M. H. (1986). *What they don't teach you at Harvard business school.* New York: Bantam Books. (paper) Being successful in high pressure professional environments—the importance of being highly sensitive to people's feelings no matter how difficult the circumstances.

Schwartz, D. J. (1981). *The magic of thinking big.* New York: Simon & Schuster. (paper) Successful personal development through positive self-concept; motivating others.

Stanton, H. E. (1978). *Helping students learn.* Washington, DC: University Press of America. (paper) Successful teaching approaches by faculty at the University of Tasmania.

Watson, G. (1996). *Teacher smart!* West Nyack, NY: Simon & Schuster. (paper) 125 tested techniques for classroom management, control, and subject-specific learning activities for K thru 12.

Music 57-355: Secondary Guided Teaching
Lewis H. Strouse, D.A.
Carnegie Mellon University
Spring 2000

Instructor: Lewis H. Strouse, D.A.
Office: CFA 162 (x8-1432)
E-mail: Strouse+@Andrew.CMU.Edu
Course Focus: Seminar and Internship in Secondary School Music.

Required Materials
- Hoffer. *Teaching Music in the Secondary Schools* (4th ed.)
- Strouse. *Course Packet for Music in the Secondary Schools*
- Police background checks and medical test to be submitted to host school:
    - Two background checks: Child Abuse Clearance and Criminal Clearance from PA State Police.
    - TB Test (Test is free through CMU Student Health Service.)
- One good-quality videotape

Reference Material
Strouse. Course packet for *Principles of Education* "Pedagogy," Section G.

Description
This offering is a pre-student-teaching seminar and field experience intended to familiarize the student with current educational practices in the secondary school.

Detailed Statement of Intent
The main purpose of the course is to bring students to a satisfactory level of competence in regard to
- understanding and application of appropriate and effective instructional practices in line with the National Standards in Music Education
- an acquired repertoire of effective instructional practices in classroom and rehearsal settings
- the continued formulation of a nascent educational philosophy, in preparation for the application of effective instructional practices in the student-teaching experience.

Evaluation
- Seminar (50%): Grade average obtained from two projects (10%), Midterm Exam (40%).
- Internship (50%): Four LPs (5%), two videotape submissions (30%), six "Daily Field Experience Reports," and journal entries (5%), Cooperating Teacher Evaluation (10%).

Grade scheme: A = 90–100, B = 80–89, C = 70–79, D = 60–69, F = 0–59.

Subjective grading: A+(100), A(95), A-(91); B+(89), B(85), B-(81); C+(79), C(75), C-(71); D+(69), D(65), D-(61); F (0–59)

Seminar Guidelines
Weeks of 1/18 thru 3/7

Instruction. Seminar instruction will derive primarily from the discussion of assigned readings and projects. This portion of the course will offer the opportunity for in-depth discussion of the instructional application of assigned material, a discussion of current issues with invited educators, and discussion of your concerns as a prospective music educator.

Class Participation. It is expected that each student will actively contribute to the discussion of assigned readings and chapter questions. It is important to develop your ability to present informed discussion. It is expected that you will reference excerpts from assigned readings in order to support your view of issues.

Class Attendance. Regular and prompt attendance is expected. Each absence from seminar beyond the limit of one will lower your seminar grade by a full letter. The class attendance policy is strictly adhered to. Students anticipating some problem with regular class attendance must see the instructor immediately.

INTERNSHIP
Weeks of 3/14 thru 5/2

Internship Placement. You will be placed in a secondary school field experience in an area of music education other than your forte. For example, an instrument major would be placed in either a general music or a choral setting. Furthermore, an effort is made to place you in a middle school setting, since your student-teaching placement will most likely be in elementary school and high school.

Every effort is made to locate you at a school that is as near as possible to the location of your local residence. See the sheet titled "Field Experience Guidelines for Interns" for detailed instructions concerning your Secondary Guided Teaching field placement.

Evaluation Criteria

Lesson plans. Lesson plans (LP) may be completed using the lesson plan form of your choice. A sheet containing three "Lesson Plan Preliminaries" strips has been attached to this syllabus. Please attach one of these strips to your lesson plan and complete the strip as requested. In the event you are able to teach an entire class period, refer to the appropriate class format found in the *Principles of Education* course packet to assist you in sequencing class activity.

Teaching Videotapes. You will receive very valuable feedback from a videotape review of your teaching. Selected portions of your teaching videotapes may be presented to the secondary methods class. You may retain your videotapes following completion of Secondary Guided Teaching. Your VHS tapes will be evaluated in terms of the "General Instruction Protocol." Do not submit your next VHS recording until you have received feedback from Dr. Strouse on your previous submission.

Daily Field Experience Report. A Daily Field Experience Report is to be completed for each day of field experience. These reports are intended to be a general summary of your day's activity in the school. Reflective journal comments (see Journal description below) are to be made on the back of each Daily Field Experience Report. Additional sheets may be attached if needed.

Journal. The purpose of making reflective journal comments is to focus attention on the importance of reflective thought as a means of evaluating one's professional practices, on a daily basis. A journal entry should be made for each of your internship days. Your comments should include reactions to lesson planning, classroom/rehearsal teaching, and the complementary experiences of teaching, (e.g., observations of individual students, relationship with the cooperating teacher, relationships with other teachers and administrators, and the overall social environment of the school.) The writing style of journal entries may be conversational and informal in nature. Journals will serve as a means of personal communication between you and Dr. Strouse. Journal writing will be evaluated in terms of content quality and quantity.

Cooperating Teacher Evaluations. The cooperating teacher will submit a written evaluation of your work following completion of your internship. It is intended that the evaluation reflect a summary of feedback previously received from your cooperating teacher.

COURSE SCHEDULE
Seminar: January 18–March 7

1/18   (1) Course overview and distribution of child abuse and criminal clearance forms, as needed

        (2) Pedagogy Review

                (a) "General Instruction Protocol" and related materials, as needed

                (b) "Topic Introduction Plan"

                (c) Delivery options and assessment options

        (3) *Graded Assignment #1* (Due date: Monday, Jan. 24, Noon. Bring to CFA 162): Structure one topic introduction plan for a secondary general music class based on a lesson plan selected from *Teaching Examples,* on Hunt reserve. Your plan should reflect the elements of an effective LP described by the "General Instruction Protocol," and should include the following parts: (a) Anticipatory Set, (b) Hunter I, (c) Hunter II, and (d) Hunter III.

1/25   (1) Discussion of LP assignment

        (2) Review Classroom LP vs. Rehearsal LP

        (3) Review other pedagogical materials, as needed

2/1   Hoffer, Ch. 5: "Psychology and Music Teaching:" Study guide questions

2/8   (1) Hoffer, Ch. 15: "Teenagers and Music:" Study guide questions

        (2) Internship assignments

        (3) "Music in the Secondary School" Project #4: Learning Assessments. Due: 2/22.

2/15   Web-based instruction: (1) Review of model programs, (2) Integrating instructional software, (3) Composing instructional units

2/22   (1) Discussion of Project #4

        (2) Composing an assessment package for performance classes

        (3) Hoffer, Ch. 17: "Planning and Assessing Music Teaching:" Study guide questions

        (4) Graded Assignment #2 (Due: 2/29): Using the sheet "Composing an Assessment Package" as a guide, prepare an assessment package that you believe would accurately measure student learning in band, chorus, or orchestra (your choice of ensemble), at the middle school or high school level (your choice), over the course of one semester.

2/29   School Visit

3/7   *Midterm Examination* (Covers Hoffer study guides for Ch. 5, 15, and 17 only.)

Field Internship: Weeks of 3/14 thru 5/2
See "Field Experience Guidelines for Interns."

FIELD EXPERIENCE GUIDELINES FOR INTERNS
Internship Preparation
- Contact your cooperating teacher and discuss the class schedule prior to your first visit.
- Confirm directions to the school.
- Ask your cooperating teacher how you should proceed with submitting proof of both police clearances and the TB Test.
- Arrange a minimum of one contact hour per week.
- Actual teaching practice will begin for the intern at a time selected in consultation with the cooperating teacher. It is expected that a minimum of four teaching hours will be completed by the intern.
- Arrive at the host school on time, preferably early.
- Dress appropriately for an educator at the host school.
- In the professional setting offered by the field experience, the intern represents not only herself

or himself, but also the School of Music, the College of Fine Arts, and the University. A professional demeanor is expected at all times.

- When the intern must deviate from the regular schedule, the cooperating teacher must be informed at least 48 hours in advance of the schedule change to allow for alternative planning.

Lesson Planning and Documentation

- Complete a Daily Field Experience Report for each day of the field experience. Reflective journal comments are to be made on the back of this form.
- Complete a lesson plan for each class, or portion of a class, taught. Typically, this would include general music classes, large and small ensemble classes, and ensemble sectionals. Lesson Plan forms will be provided to you.
- Lesson plan objectives are to be in concert with the objectives of the cooperating teacher.
- All ancillary materials for lesson planning should be included with the regular LP submissions, and all lesson plan materials are to be filed in the intern's course notebook for Music in the Secondary School.
- When not teaching, observations should be made of other host school experiences, agreed to by the cooperating teacher, and students should enter their comments into the field experience journal.
- It is expected that the student teacher and cooperating teacher will meet regularly for evaluative discussions.

Internship Evaluation Sequence

Lesson plans and VHS materials should be submitted twice before the last week of the semester. These submissions would occur on or about the fourth week and the sixth week of your internship. This schedule will enable Dr. Strouse to give you feedback that you can implement before your field experience is completed. Do not make VHS tape #2 until you have received feedback from Dr. Strouse on VHS tape #1.

If your host school cannot provide you with a camcorder and tripod for videotaping, you may check out this equipment from CMU's IST (Instructional Systems Technology) office located in Hunt Library. Simply provide the IST office with your CMU ID and the course number. Reservations are required—plan your videotaping at least one week ahead.

First Submission: Accumulated "Daily Field Experience Reports," lesson plans, and VHS tape with accompanying lesson plan.

Second Submission: Accumulated "Daily Field Experience Reports," lesson plans, and VHS tape with accompanying lesson plan.

Any remaining "Daily Field Experience Reports" and lesson plans may be submitted on or before your final evaluation interview for Music in the Secondary School.

GUIDELINES FOR THE COOPERATING TEACHER

- Please review the *Secondary Guided Teaching* syllabus and "Field Experience Guidelines" so that you are aware of the intern's requirements.
- The interns are required to complete an appropriate lesson plan for every class, or portion of a class, taught. I will analyze student lesson plans for particular components; however, the lesson plan format is left to the discretion of the intern. Please feel free to share your lesson plan format with your intern.
- Please arrange regular evaluative discussions with your intern. Be candid with your appraisal of strengths and weaknesses. Secondary Guided Teaching is not an "automatic A" nor is it simply a "formality" course that all students pass despite the quality of their work. This course may be a crossroads for some students.
- Interns are expected to conduct themselves in a manner befitting professional educators. If you are concerned about any aspect of your intern's work, please notify Dr. Strouse immediately: Office (412) 268-1432.

• Please complete the "Cooperating Teacher Evaluation" form and return it to me as requested in the memo to cooperating teachers. As stated in the syllabus, your grade will be computed in the intern's final grade in Secondary Guided Teaching.

DAILY FIELD EXPERIENCE REPORT

Intern _____ Date _____

Cooperating Teacher _____ School _____
Instruction: Complete this report for each school visit. Mark the items you completed under each category.

1. Category I: Experiences in which you were primarily an observer, e.g.,
   _____ a. Observing different styles and methods of teaching
   _____ b. Observing individual differences among pupils
   _____ c. Observing various aspects of classroom organization and management
   _____ d. Observing outside the principal assignment area
   _____ e. Other_____
Comments:

2. Category II: Pre-teaching activities that required you to be more involved than Category I activities, e.g.
   _____ a. Interacting with individual students during seatwork
   _____ b. Engaging in discussions about specific classroom events with the teacher(s)
   _____ c. Engaging in social interaction with teacher(s) within the school
   _____ d. Engaging in social interaction with students(s) within the school
   _____ e. Engaging in social interaction with support staff within the school
   _____ f. Preparing instructional materials
   _____ g. Operating audiovisual equipment
   _____ h. Reading pupils' written work
   _____ i. Other _____
Comments:

3. Category III: Teaching, activities that required you to prepare for particular instructional tasks, e.g.,
   _____ a. Planning for teaching
   _____ b. Tutoring individual pupils
   _____ c. Teaching small groups of pupils
   _____ d. Teaching whole classes
   _____ e. Involvement in cocurricular activities
   _____ f. Other _____
Comments:

MUSIC FOR THE
CLASSROOM TEACHER

MUED 245: MUSIC TEACHING SKILLS
FOR THE MIDDLE CHILDHOOD TEACHER
DR. ED DULING
BOWLING GREEN STATE UNIVERSITY
FALL 2000

Description: Development of skills for planning and implementing children's musical experiences with emphasis on middle childhood grades (4–9); focus upon thematic integration with other subject areas

Instructor: Dr. Ed Duling
TA: Carrie Chalfin

Location and Times: All sections meet *together* on Mondays, 8:30 AM
Room 1040 of MMAC
All other days the sections meet *separately* in 2121
Call # 71968 meets Tuesdays at 8:30
Call # 87612 meets Wednesdays at 8:30
Call # 82941 meets Thursdays at 8:30
Call # 84486 meets Fridays at 8:30

Office Hours: By appointment in Room 2161, or at class time. Check hours posted on 2161.
Carrie is in room 3156.

Phones: 2-0281 (Office)   e-mail: eduling@bgnet.bgsu.edu
Carrie has no phone; her e-mail is frandle@bgnet.bgsu.edu

Prerequisite: Eng 112 and EDCI/EDFI 202; see me if there are problems

TEXT/MATERIALS
• Anderson, W. M., & Lawrence, J. E. (1998). *Integrating music into the elementary classroom* (4th ed.). Belmont, CA: Wadsworth Publishing. ISBN: 0-543-52596-2. (Code: A & L)
• Cornett, C. E. (1999). *The arts as meaning makers: Integrating literature and the arts throughout the curriculum.* Upper Saddle River, NJ: Prentice Hall. ISBN: 0-13-792920-X. (Code: CC)
• Obtain a soprano recorder and MUED 245 Handout Packet (Code: "Pkt.") at the Bookstore
• You will need a three-ring notebook for maintaining packet and creating a resource file/notebook

Please see me if you are graduating or have special needs!!!

GOALS OF THE COURSE
(1) To synthesize a basic understanding of the elements of music and musical activities (as taught and used by classroom teachers rather than music specialists)
(2) To review/learn general principles of educational psychology involved in teaching, with emphasis upon those directly related to music and arts integration by classroom teachers in grades 4–9

(3) To construct knowledge about how music can be used with the other arts (visual art, dance, theatre) and other school subjects through several integrative frameworks (vs. what passes for "integration" in some schools)

(4) To collaborate with MUED 341 (Music Ed. Majors) in constructing integrated units of study for grades 4–9

(5) To review and apply connections among current standards (e.g., State of Ohio CAE Model and the National Standards for Arts Education) as well as interfaces between integrative frameworks outlined in #3 above and Standards

STUDENT LEARNING OUTCOMES

Given all the learning activities within the course, the student will, to the satisfaction of the instructor do the following:

(1) Demonstrate through playing, singing, and writing an understanding of the basic elements of music

(2) State the value of music, both as a school subject in and of itself and as an art integrated with other arts and subjects

(3) State and apply physical, emotional, intellectual, social, and musical developmental characteristics of students in grades 4 through 9 to the planning and teaching of music lessons

(4) Demonstrate, through peer teaching, an integrated lesson at proper developmental levels for students in grades 4–9

(5) Utilize principles of educational psychology as they pertain to planning music and integrated lessons

(6) Identify and demonstrate proper integration of music with other curricular areas through application of at least one integrative model and one or more of the National Standards in a unit plan using ideas generated in collaboration with MUED 341 students

EVALUATION

Evaluation of the activities supporting the student learning outcomes will be accomplished by the awarding of points based on the following outline:

Activities	Points	Final Grades
Midterm Exam	75	A = 400–360
Notebook	30*	B = 359–320
Participation	30	C = 319–280
Peer-teaching		D = 279–240
Presentation	20	E = 239 > oops!
Peer-teaching plan	20	
Unit Plan	70*	
MUED 341 Collaboration	20	
Rough drafts (10 each)	20	
Basic skills assessments		
Recorder/piano(15 each)	30	
Quizzes on elements (3)	30	
Arts statement	20	
Arts Integration model	15	
Ed. Psych check	20	
Total possible	**400**	

* = includes 10 points for exam day attendance and exchange

You may miss class once without penalty. Save this for when you *really* need it. After this one time, you will lose your participation points for that class. Please keep in touch regarding your absences, and provide me with any written medical excuses you may collect.

EXPLANATIONS OF TOPICS AND ACTIVITIES ABOVE

Midterm Exam. Given during class time on a mid-semester day. Tentatively Oct. 24–27.

Final Exam Day. Per campus schedule when announced by registrar's office. A portion will be your unit plan outline, and a portion will be given to in-class activities. See caveat at end of syllabus.

Class Materials Notebook. This will be a notebook, preferably three-ring. It is due on exam day. (It will be returned before you leave the exam). It will contain the following:
- Materials from any MUED 245 packet, arranged as you see fit (Some of these may have to be copied as assigned from reserve materials.)
- Daily dated class notes
- Your peer-teaching lesson plan and unit plan/outline
- Additional handouts given in class
- Any graded classwork
- Copies of peer plans and materials from classmates
- Additional materials you may wish to add

Participation. There are points for participating in class. You have to be here to participate in the activities listed below. Attendance at class is important as we only meet twice per week. You may miss once. Keep me informed about absences by calling or e-mailing. When I know you are out for a good reason, I take off fewer points for absenses past the first. I reserve the right to ask for an excuse from an M.D. Please inform me of "University Absences" *in advance* (field trips, teams, etc.).

Class-participation activities in MUED 245. Musical participation and learning, as related to integrative and music teaching, will include:
- Singing
- Movement: primarily directed toward singing games, play parties, response-oriented demonstrations, and as related in integrative possibilities
- Listening: creative and physical responses; organization of, reasons for; listening as a start to integrative possibilities
- Playing instruments: primarily for accompaniment purposes with emphasis on recorder and piano
- Use of musical participation in all its forms in relation to integration of music, the arts, and other subject areas

Pedagogical participation and learning
- Instruction in and application of understandings about children's development to music, arts, and integrative teaching
- Instruction about planning, organizing, adapting, and presenting musical, artistic, and integrated materials to elementary students
- Opportunities for peer collaboration on integrated units of study

Peer-teaching. This is a 3–5 minute in-class lesson segment presented to classmates as per the schedule on the outline. The instructor reserves right to assign materials and other parameters. This lesson is to illustrate one of the integrative approaches covered and must identify applicable State and National Standards.

Peer-teaching Lesson Plans. Plans for the above lesson following the outline in the handout packet. Dates as noted below. A portion of points is for the rough draft.

Peer-teaching allows 245 students: (1) a chance to develop confidence in their teaching potential in the discipline of music as integrated with other subjects and the other arts, (2) a chance to share any creative integrative ideas or musical content that they develop or discover, (3) a chance to plan and organize instruction and presentation. Evaluation of peer-teaching is by the instructor and includes constructive feedback provided via a form and the grading of the written plan.

Unit Plan. This is an integrated unit using music and/or other arts. The unit will include the peer-teaching lesson. A rough draft is part of the course points. It is due the next-to-last day of class. Instructions on how to do this unit are in the course packet.

Note: This semester, as a result of a grant from PICT (Preservice Infusion of Computer Technology) we will be pilot-testing an alternative method of recording and saving our unit plans and related materials. The instructor will outline procedures for doing so using a G4 laptop and a CD writer ("burner") to create a disc to save the text of your unit and such art, music, dance, and theatre as can be legally stored on the disc from the World Wide Web and other external sources. You will need a Mac-formatted "Zip" disc and two CD-R or CD-RW discs.

Collaboration. This is defined as a one-hour meeting with MUED 341 students—music education majors—for purposes of collaboration on ideas for integrated units.

Basic Skills Assessments

Recorder/Piano Proficiencies. These consist of playing two or three tunes on the recorder for one of the instructors, as well as finding pitches and playing very simple tunes on the piano. Do not write in finger numbers for either of these!! Due as outlined below.

Three Quizzes/worksheets on Elements. On days noted in the outline below.

"Checks." The instructor reserves the right to assign these as either in- or out-of-class activities.

- Arts Statement: A short writing assignment that will challenge you to summarize the importance of inclusion of the arts in the middle level curriculum
- Integration Model: An assignment that will require you to synthesize basic principles of integrated teaching that honors each subject included
- Ed Psych: A quiz or other assignment that will ask you to synthesize the principles of educational psychology germane to this course

Tentative Outline of Activities

Expect some changes! Assignments are noted on the day they are due.

Aug. 28	Syllabus distributed. Discussion of class, materials, procedures. Life Histories of Music. Musical elements illustrated; advocacy, Pkt., 1–2 (Phillips: "Rationale…"), 144 (Ullom: "Should it be the end…").
Aug. 29, 30, 31, Sept.1	Basics of educational psychology—Read A & L, 1–18. Pkt., 159. Music Elements, Pkt., 3–6, 11–13. Skim A & L, 39–84 (note bold headings).
Sept. 4	**No Class. Labor Day**
Sept 5, 6, 7, 8	Applying elements using ed. psych. principles. What Students will be like, Pkt., 39–44 (Coulter: "The Brain's Timetable…"), 139–43, 145 (John: "Coping with…," and Caissey: "Characteristics…"). **Element def. quiz.**
Sept. 11	Have recorders by today. Applying music elements to recorder. A & L, 233–43. Pkt., 177. **Note names quiz.**
Sept. 12, 13, 14, 15	Further recorder work, very basic piano. A & L, 221–27, inside back cover (Don't tear it out!), and Pkt., 176. Piano lab.
Sept. 18	Sound before symbol and other principles revisited. Review A & L, 1–18 and Pkt., 14–17 (Duling: "More than Gems…," and Shirey: "Sound before Symbol…"). Apply using recorder. **Rhythms/meter quiz.**
Sept. 19, 20, 21, 22	Listening lessons. Pkt., 145–57 (Flowers: "Listening…," Sims: "Sound Approaches…," and Yokers, "Fast Food…"). A & L, 271–330.

Sept. 25	Basic methodological approaches in music. A & L, 112–17, 377–84, 338–39, and Pkt., 18–25 (Bennett: "When 'Method'...").
Sept. 26, 27, 28, 29	Catch-up day—information not covered in Ed. Psych. and Music. Integrating songs. A & L, skim 143–220.
Oct. 2	Basic lesson planning and objectives. Pkt., 50–53 (Duling: "The Rote-Note..."), and A & L, 19–38.
Oct. 3, 4, 5, 6	Further information and planning background. Pkt., 54–68. **Recorder and piano tests as scheduled—outside of class.**
Oct 9	The arts and music in the middle-level curriculum. Read CC, v–33, 398–404.
Oct. 10, 11, 12, 13	Explanation of Unit Plan/outline (handout). Ideas of A & L for integration. Skim 405–55. **Ed. Psych/planning quiz.**
Oct. 16/17	**Fall Break.** Tuesday class will have alternate information. All sections have written directives on material below.
Oct. 18, 19, 20	Sue Snyder's, Jackie Wiggins's, and Sharon Nelson's basic approaches. DBME. Pkt., 69–77h and 77–88 (Goodson and Duling: "Integrating...," Barry: two "Integrating..." articles, and Wiggins: "Integrating..."). What's on the exam.
Oct 23	Cornett's Ideas. Read CC, 34–75. Exam Review. Unit ideas.
Oct 24, 25, 26, 27	**Midterm Exam.**
Oct. 30	Midterm returned and reviewed. Ideas of A & L for Integration. Skim 457–502.
Oct. 31, Nov. 1, 2, 3	Music-specific ideas of Cornett, 325–66 (Ch. 11 & 12). List unit topics.
Nov.6	Strategies of Cornett, CC, 367–82. Sorting strategies for units.
Nov. 7, 8, 9, 10	**Rough draft unit plan due.** Arts with arts strategies. CC, 383–97. Pkt., 178–79 (Duling: "Agalina...," and "Blues Ruler...").
Nov. 13	Unit drafts returned. Comments for improvement. **Integration models and arts statement assignments due.**
Nov. 14,15,16,17	Teaching a song. A & L, read/skim 85–142 and Pkt., 7–9 (compare). **Peer-teaching rough drafts due.**
Nov. 20	Mozart Effect and what music "helps." Pkt., 113–38 (Cutietta: all four articles, and Reimer: "Facing..."). **Teaching days assigned.** Rough drafts returned. Comments for improvement.
Nov. 21,22,23,24	Thankgiving Break
Nov. 27	Special learners. Pkt., 45–49c (Atterbury: "Being Involved...," and Thompson: "Challenges of..."). National and State standards.
Nov. 28,29,30, Dec. 1	**Peer-teaching lessons.**
Dec. 4	M. O. for exam day. Classroom Management. CC, 433–34.
Dec. 5,6,7,8	**Peer-teaching lessons**
Dec. 11	Advanced application of National and State standards with other school subjects' standards
Dec. 12,13,14,15	**Unit plan due.** Final considerations and review. Final Exam time will be per university schedule! **Notebooks due** (to be taken at the end of the final). Units returned; units exchanged.

You are responsible for the time of the final exam! Do not plan to leave early! Plane tickets are no excuse!!

More questions arise in this class because students do not read this syllabus thoroughly at the start of the semester and throughout the semester than for any other reason. *Read it, please; it contains almost everything you need to know.*

MUED 245 PACKET

The packet for MUED 245 contains: (1) Selected readings from MENC, OMEA and other publications, all reproduced with permission; (2) handouts and other materials created by the instructors (and others) to amplify the class's emphases—basic approaches to traditional music literacy (reading) through recorder and basic piano, a review of educational psychology pertaining to middle-level (grades 4–9) teaching of music and related arts, a grounding in models of integration involving music, the arts and other school subjects, and coverage of unit and lesson planning and creation relating to music, the arts, and other subjects areas as integrated content.

Reference List of Handout Packet Articles

Atterbury, B. (1989). Being involved in mainstreaming decisions. *Music Educators Journal, 75*(6), 32–35.

Barry, N. H. (1996). Integrating the arts into the curriculum: A response from the author. *General Music Today,10*(1), 10–12.

Barry, N. H. (1996). Integrating the arts into the curriculum. *General Music Today, 9*(2), 9–13.

Bennett, P. (1986). When 'method' becomes authority. *Music Educators Journal, 72*(9), 38–40.

Caissy, G. A. (1985). Characteristics of Middle-level Students and Resultant Programming Considerations. [Figure only]. *Music Educators Journal, 71*(7), 39.

Coulter, D. J. (1984). The Brain's timetable for developing music skills. *General Music Journal, 3*(1), 21–26. [This was a short-lived periodical published by the Ohio Music Education Association in the late 1970s into the 1980s.]

Cutietta, R. A. (1996). Language and music programs. *General Music Today, 9*(2), 26–31.

Cutietta, R. A.(1996). Does music instruction aid academic skills? *General Music Today 10*(1), 24–27.

Cutietta, R. A.(1996). Does music instruction aid mathematic skills? *General Music Today, 9*(3), 28–30.

Cutietta, R. A. (1995). Does music instruction help a child learn to read? *General Music Today 9*(1), 26–31.

Duling, E. (1990). Agalina Hagalina. *TRIAD, 57*(5), 10 [General Music insert].

Duling, E. (1991). The blues ruler: A lesson strategy. *TRIAD, 58*(5), 15. [General Music insert].

Duling, E. (1996/7). More than "gems:" What Mrs. Hilyard knew. *TRIAD, 64*(3), 9–10.

Dulling, E. (sic) (1992). The rote-note approach—A sample lesson. *TRIAD, 59*(5), 15. [General Music Insert].

Flowers, P. J. (1990). Listening: the key to describing music. *Music Educators Journal, 77*(4), 21–23.

Goodson, C. A., & Duling, E. (1996). Integrating the four disciplines. *Music Educators Journal, 83*(2), 33–37.

John, S. B. (1996). Coping with middle school attitudes. *Choral Journal, 37*(1), 29–32.

Phillips, K. H. (1998). A rationale for music education. [Readers Comment]. *Music Educators Journal, 84*(5), 10.

Reimer, B. (1999), Facing the risks of the "Mozart Effect." *Music Educators Journal 86*(1), 37–43.

Shirey, K. (1991). Sound before symbol in general music classes. *TRIAD, 58*(6), 37–38.

Sims, W. L. (1990). Sound approaches to elementary music listening. *Music Educators Journal, 77*(4), 38–42.

Thompson, K. P. (1999). Challenges of inclusion for the general music teacher. *General Music Today, 12*(3), 7–9.

Ullom, R. (1990). Should it be the end: General music, grade eight, and thirteen years young? *TRIAD, 57*(5), 26.

Wiggins, R. (1996) Integrating the arts into the curriculum is the wrong mind set. *General Music Today, 10*(1), 5–9.

Yokers, M. (1989). Fast food. *TRIAD, 56*(5), 24–26. [General Music Insert].

MUS 261: MUSIC IN THE ELEMENTARY CLASSROOM
DR. CAROLINE PERKINS
DEPAUW UNIVERSITY
SPRING 2000

Instructor: Dr. Caroline Perkins
Office: 658-4503, Room 225E
E-mail: ckperkins@depauw.edu
Class Hours: 10:00–11:50 Tues., Thurs.
Location: Room 17 PAC
Office Hours: 11–12 Mon., Wed.; 2:30–4 Mon., Wed., and by appointment

COURSE DESCRIPTION

The fundamentals of music and methods of teaching general music to children in grades kindergarten through six. Includes a survey of materials and observations in the Putnam County School Districts.

COURSE TOPICS

- Child Development
- Musical Development of Children
- Lesson Planning and Sequencing
- Fundamentals of Music
- Experiences with Music
- Music and Materials Selection
- Music Materials and Basal Series
- Diverse Student Population
- Integration of Music into the General Education Curriculum
- Evaluation of Music Learning
- Technology for Music Instruction
- Curriculum Design and Evaluation

COURSE OBJECTIVES

Through a variety of in-class activities and outside assignments, the students will do the following:
- increase their musical skills and understanding
- establish a foundation for continued development of the following skills: singing, playing instruments, listening, moving to music, creating music, and music reading
- become aware of the musical characteristics of children at various developmental stages
- become aware of musical understandings or concepts which are appropriate for elementary students
- demonstrate knowledge of materials that may be used in planning music activities such as children's literature, singing games, folk songs, recordings, and technology
- select music and plan music lessons appropriate for elementary students
- gain skills needed for leading musical experiences with children

COURSE MATERIALS
Required Materials

- Anderson, W. M., & Lawrence, J. E. (1998). *Integrating music into the elementary classroom* (4th ed.). Cincinnati: Wadsworth Publishing Company.
- Soprano Recorder
- *Ed Sueta Recorder Method,* Book One
- VHS tape
- Binder for Class Materials

Materials on Reserve in Music Library
- *Music in the Elementary School* by Nye et al.
- *Music in Childhood: From Preschool through the Elementary Grades* by Campbell and Scott-Kassner

Relevant Periodicals in the Music Library
- *General Music Today*
- *Journal of Research in Music Education*
- *Music Educators Journal*
- *Teaching Music*
- *Update: Applications of Research in Music Education*

GRADING SCALE

A+ = 98–100	A = 94–97	A- = 90–93
B+ = 88–89	B = 84–87	B- = 80–83
C+ = 78–79	C = 74–77	C- = 70–73
D+ = 68–69	D = 64–67	D- = 60–63
F = 59 and below		

EVALUATION

Grading will be based upon data obtained from the following sources and will be weighted as indicated.

10% Field Experience. Field experience will take place in the local public schools. A write-up for each observation and a reflective self-evaluation for each teaching episode are required. There will be a total of six school visitations.

Components of Grade: Attendance, evaluation by cooperating teacher(s), write-ups, and self-reflections.

25% Teaching Episodes. There will be four peer-teaching episodes: (1) rote song, (2) song with accompaniment (Autoharp, guitar, pitched instrument, or piano), (3) music activity of choice, and (4) integrated lesson.

Songs must be memorized. Do not teach with your lesson plan in hand. Properly give pitch and tempo. Model appropriate vocal quality for children. On the day of your peer-teaching, arrive early to locate and organize all of the materials required for your lesson so that we may begin class promptly.

20% Lesson Plans. Four lesson plans will be required. These plans correspond to your peer-teaching episodes. For one lesson, you are required to create an original visual aid.

5% Reflection Papers. These are reflections or self-evaluations of your peer-teaching episodes. Consider the things you did well and the things you need to improve on. Careful and thoughtful reflection is expected. Watch the video of your peer-teaching episode before writing your paper.

10% Evaluation of Music Series. Review and evaluate the following music series:
- *Share the Music* by McGraw-Hill
- *The Music Connection* by Silver Burdett Ginn

10% Evaluation of Music Software. Select *five* of the following sixteen software packages for review and evaluation:

A Little Kidmusic	*Making Music*
Alice's Adventures in Musicland	*Menlo the Frog*
Allie's Playhouse	*Music Ace*
Beethoven Lives Upstairs	*Music Ace II*
Children's Song Book	*Music Lessons*
Early Music Skills	*Music Time*
Instruments of the Symphony	*Musical World of Professor Piccolo*
Juilliard Music Adventure	*Rock, Rap, and Roll*

5% Playing Exams. There will be a total of five playing exams: Autoharp, guitar, piano, pitched instrument, and recorder.

5% Story. Integrate music into the children's story of your choice. Student participation in the story is suggested.

10% Lesson or Story Presentation. This presentation will be for elementary students. You may choose to teach any of the lessons from your peer-teaching episodes, teach a new lesson, or present your children's story. This assignment includes observation of the class for which the presentation is designed, discussion of plan with classroom teacher, presentation of lesson or story, evaluation by classroom teacher, and self-evaluation of presentation. You are responsible for arranging this presentation. If you need my assistance in locating a site, preparing your presentation, etc., please do not hesitate to contact me. *I strongly suggest that you complete this presentation prior to May 1.*

Other Expectations
- Assigned readings
- In-class activities
- Individual practice with instruments
- Organized binder containing class notes, notes on readings, handouts, peer evaluations, and assignments. Consider putting class notes and notes from your readings on computer.

Written work is to be word processed. Any work turned in otherwise will be returned to you ungraded. All assignments are due at the beginning of class on the assigned day. Grades for late work will be lowered one letter grade for each day late. This policy is designed to help keep you on schedule.

DUE DATES

Keep in mind that many of the due dates are scheduled for the second portion of the semester. *I strongly recommend that you begin your assignments early and allow ample time for completion.* It is perfectly acceptable to turn in assignments prior to their due dates.

Peer-Teaching and Lesson Plans
Rote Song: March 2
Song with Accompaniment: April 13
Music Activity of Choice: April 25
Integrated Lesson: May 4

Self-Reflections on Peer-Teaching
Rote Song: March 7
Song with Accompaniment: April 18
Music Activity of Choice: April 27
Integrated Lesson: May 9

Playing Exams
Guitar and Autoharp: April 6
Pitched Instrument and Piano: April 11
Recorder: May 9

Observation Write-Ups and Self-Reflections on Micro-Teaching
Class period after each visit. A total of six write-ups or self-evaluations should be submitted.
You are responsible for rescheduling observations if cancellations or absences are encountered.

Series Evaluation. February 17
Please Note: This assignment will take some time to complete.

Story. April 20

Lesson/Story Presentation. prior to May 1

Technology Evaluation. May 2
Please Note: This assignment will take some time to complete.

ATTENDANCE POLICY

Attendance, preparation, and participation are expected and required. Each student is responsible for contacting the instructor if and when an absence is unavoidable. Each student is responsible for checking with the instructor or a classmate when an absence occurs in order to stay on schedule with class assignments, readings, etc.

Excused absences include family emergency, illness, and university approved activities. Unexcused absences include other classes, vacation plans, computer problems, sleep deprivation, Greek activities, etc.

One point will be subtracted from your final grade for each unexcused absence and for each unreported absence. Absences prior to and following school recesses (i.e., leaving early for and/or returning late from break) will be counted as two absences.

Punctuality is a professional courtesy and allows for the smooth start of each class session. Three tardies will equal one absence.

This course is designed to be a seminar which requires active participation by everyone. Thus, the success of the course depends on the contributions made by each of you. It takes all of us working together to form an effective learning community.

PROFESSIONAL RESPONSIBILITIES FOR SCHOOL OBSERVATIONS

Attendance. If you must be absent from any of your school visitations due to illness or emergency, you must inform the people affected by your absence (i.e., placement teacher and carpool members, if applicable). You are expected to reschedule missed visitations with your placement teacher.

Privacy Issues. We need to be cognizant of the importance of respecting the privacy of the children observed. Do not discuss classroom scenarios that might be embarrassing to teachers, parents, or children or that might include sensitive information about a child or family. During class discussions, use pseudonyms. Use professional judgement when discussing students, situations, etc., at your field experience site.

Deportment. You will be viewed and judged as an adult by students, parents, and teachers. Dress appropriately. Do not wear jeans or hats. Do not chew gum. Be polite and considerate to everyone you encounter, including the principal, secretaries, custodians, teacher assistants, parents, etc. Arrive a few minutes prior to your scheduled observation. Please continue the tradition of representing yourself and DePauw in a professional manner.

Please Note. If you have a disability and require auxiliary aids, services, or accommodations, please contact me in my office so that we may discuss your particular needs.

Please do not hesitate to ask questions or contact me if you are unclear about assignments, readings, etc. I am looking forward to a GREAT semester, I hope you are too!!

TENTATIVE SCHEDULE OF CLASS TOPICS

February 1   **Introduction**
                    10:30 Visit the Technology Lab (Julianne Miranda)
                    What Does a Classroom Teacher Need to Know about Teaching Music?

February 3   **Fundamentals of Music**
                    Read Ch. 3.

February 8   **Fundamentals of Music**
                    Review Ch. 3.

February 10   **Child Development and Musical Development**
                    Read pp. 21–33, 234–40, *Music in the Elementary School.*
                    How Children Learn
                    Read Ch. 1.

February 15	**Selection of Music and Materials**
	Guidelines for Teaching Music
	Read Ch. 2.
February 17	***Share the Music* (Macmillan) and *The Music Connection* (Silver Burdett Ginn)**
	Read preface/introduction in the teachers edition (any grade level between K–6) of the two basal series texts.
	Familiarize yourself with each series.
	Series Evaluation Due.
	Planning—The Parts of a Lesson Plan
February 22	**Planning Music Lessons**
February 24	**Sharing, Discussion, and Critiquing of Student Plans**
	Lesson Plan Due.
	Planning and Sequencing Music Lessons
	In-class planning activity.
February 29	**Teaching Music through Singing**
	Vocal Development
	Read Ch. 4.
	Demonstration of Singing Lessons
March 2	**Peer-teaching: Rote Song**
	Time Limit: 10 minutes.
	Lesson Plan Due.
	Teaching Music through Playing Classroom Instruments
	Read Ch. 6.
March 7	**Guitar: D chord**
	Self-Evaluation of Peer-teaching Due.
	Teaching Music through Movement
	Read Ch. 8.
March 9	**No Class (MENC National Conference)**
March 14	**Guitar: D and A7 chords.**
	Teaching Music through Listening
	Read Ch. 7.
March 16	**Autoharp**
	Creative Experiences with Music
	Read Ch. 9.
March 21	**Piano**
	Music and Children's Literature
March 23	**Pitched Instruments**
	Music and Children's Literature
April 4	**Unpitched Instruments**
	Practice Session for Playing Exams
April 6	**Playing Exams: Autoharp and Guitar**
	Students with Disabilities
	Read Ch. 14, *Music in Childhood.*

April 11	**Playing Exams: Piano and Pitched Instrument** **Students in the Inner City**
April 13	**Peer-Teaching: Song with Accompaniment** Time Limit: 10 minutes. Lesson Plan Due. **Review of Music Reading: Recorder**
April 18	**Curriculum Design and Evaluation** Read Ch. 11, *Music in Childhood.* **Evaluation and Assessment** Read Ch. 4, *Music in the Elementary School.* Self-Evaluation of Peer-teaching Due.
April 20	**Story Presentations** **Integrating Songs with Other Subjects and Activities** Read Ch. 5.
April 25	**Peer-Teaching: Music Activity of Choice** Time Limit: 15 minutes. Lesson Plan Due. **Integrating Music with the Study of Peoples, Places, and Cultures** Read Ch. 10.
April 27	**Experiences with Music and Other Arts** Read Ch. 11. Self-Evaluation of Peer-teaching Due. **Integrated Thematic Lessons and Units**
May 2	**Technology for Music Instruction** Read Ch. 12, *Music in Childhood.* Music Software Reviews Due. **Music to Enhance the Learning Environment**
May 4	**Peer-teaching: Integrated Lesson** Time Limit: 15 minutes. Lesson Plan Due. **Music to Enhance the Learning Environment**
May 9	**Playing Exam: Recorder** **Discussion of Lesson/Story Presentation and Observations** Self-Evaluation of Peer-teaching Due.
May 11	**What Does a Classroom Teacher Need to Know about Teaching Music?** **Why Is Music Important in the Elementary Classroom?** **Wrap-up** Self-Evaluation of Peer-teaching Due.

MUSC 2361: Music in the Interdisciplinary Curriculum
Dr. Diane Persellin
Trinity University
Fall 2000

CATALOG STATEMENT

Strategies for teaching are presented by connecting music with other areas of the elementary curriculum in valid and imaginative ways. Emphasis is given to how the study of music can enhance the understanding of expression, history, and culture. Students will acquire basic music skills in order to provide music leadership in the classroom. Prerequisite: EDUC 2107 or 2108.

CLASS MEETINGS

Tuesdays and Thursdays from 9:55–11:10 a.m.; Ruth Taylor Music Center Room 113.

OFFICE HOURS

Tuesdays and Thursdays 11:10–12:00 noon
Monday and Wednesday 1:30–2:20; Fridays by appointment.

INSTRUCTOR

Dr. Diane Persellin
Ruth Taylor Music Center Room 104
999-265 office phone
dpersell@ trinity.edu

TEXTBOOK

Barrett, J., McCoy, C., & Veblen, K. (1997). *Sound ways of knowing: Music in the interdisciplinary curriculum.* New York: Schirmer.

SUPPLEMENTARY MATERIALS

Nylon string guitars will be used in this class. You may borrow a school guitar, if needed.

COURSE OBJECTIVES

Knowledge. As the student, you will demonstrate knowledge
  • in singing, moving, listening, describing, and creating in the elementary classroom
  • about the child's voice and how to select appropriate music for children
  • in the rudimentary reading of music
  • in planning music activities for all children, including children with special needs
  • of recent research related to music and child development, learning theory, and modalities
  • of materials that may be used in planning music activities such as children's literature, singing games, folk songs from other cultures, recordings, and technology (Music of Mexico and Zimbabwe will be presented as examples in class. Resources are available to find quality music in other cultures, as well.)
  • of the National Standards in Music Education

Skills. As the student, you will demonstrate skill in
  • singing with a class and leading classroom singing
  • playing a minimum of three chords and three strums on the guitar
  • playing simple accompaniments on an Orff tonebar instrument
  • leading children in expressive movement, patterned movement, action songs, and singing games
  • utilizing music to teach other subjects with an emphasis on language arts, social science, art, and drama

- utilizing music to create a positive and welcoming atmosphere and to assist in behavior management in the classroom

Values. As the student, you will gain an awareness of
- the importance of music for all children
- your own musical growth
- your own creativity

SUGGESTED READINGS

Andress, B. (1989, October). Music for every stage: How much? What kind? How soon? *Music Educators Journal, 22–27.*

Bartholomew, D. (1993, November). Effective strategies for praising students. *Music Educators Journal,* 40–43.

Bennett, P. (1988, September). The perils and profits of praise. *Music Educators Journal,* 22–24.

Bridges, M. (1993, Fall). The benefits of vocal exploration. *General Music Today,* 30–34.

Cutietta, R. (1995, Fall) Does music instruction help a child learn to read? *General Music Today.* 26–31.

Darrow, A. (1990). Research on mainstreaming in music education. *Update, 9*(1), 35–37.

Gromko, J. E. (1995, Spring). A sound project in composition for young children. *General Music Today,* 27–30.

Feierabend, J. (1995, Summer). Music and intelligence in the early years. *Early Childhood Connections,* 5–13.

Lewis, B. (1989). The research literature in movement-based instruction with children: Implications for music teaching and learning. *Update, 7*(2), 13–17.

Malin, S. (1988, November). Classroom teachers: Elementary to music education. *Music Educators Journal,* 30–33.

Masterson, M. (1994, May). Moving beyond "It's got a good beat." *Music Educators Journal,* 24–28.

McCoy, C. (1994, Spring). Music and children's literature: Natural partners. *General Music Today,* 15–19.

Persellin, D., Pautz, M., Feierabend, J., Kenney, S., & Andress, B. (1994, August). Finding quality literature for young children. *Teaching Music,* 19+.

Shehan, P. (1987). Stretching the potential of music: Can it help reduce prejudices? *Update, 5*(2), 17–20.

Single, N. A. (1991). Summary of research-based principles of effective teaching. *Update, 2*(9), 3–10.

Snyder, S. (1994, Spring). Language, movement, and music—Process connections. *General Music Today,* 4–9.

Stuessy, J. (1994, January). When the music teacher meets Metallica. *Music Educators Journal,* 28–32.

Upitis, R. (1995, Spring). Fostering children's compositions: Activities for the classroom. *General Music Today,* 16–19.

Walker, D. (1989, Fall). Using instruments in today's general music classroom. *General Music Today,* 14–17.

Webster, P., & Hickey, M. (1995). Challenging children to think creatively. *General Music Today,* 4–10.

Wiggins, J. (1995, Spring). Learning through creative interaction with music. *General Music Today,* 11–15.

ASSESSMENT

Teaching Children   15–20%

At Hawthorne Elementary School and University Presbyterian Children's Center. Includes all written teaching strategies, teaching of the children, and the reflective assessment of the teaching and learning.

Three Observations (due 12/4)   10–15%

Can include one Orff workshop on Saturday morning. September 15. I am pleased to set these up for you according to your schedule.

Term Paper or Web Site (8–10 pages)   0–10%
    Topic due 9/28. Outline due 10/20. Paper due 11/20.
    Must include two lesson plans.

In-class Participation   10–15%
    Includes in-class presentations and discussions. Energetic attendance is required.
    After two absences, your grade will be lowered from an A to an A-, A- to a B+, etc.
    Unusual and extenuating circumstances will be dealt with on an individual basis.

Service Learning Project   10–15%
    Develop a collection of songs and activities that you can share with children at
    the Battered Women's Shelter or the San Antonio, Children's Shelter. Share your
    plans and experiences in class and write your personal reflections on the project.
    (Minimum of four visits; I am pleased to make these contacts for you.)

Guitar Proficiency   10–15%
    Tested in groups of four, but with individual grades (11/3)

Optional Final Exam during final exam period   0–10%

Journals   0–5%
    Minimum of eight; minimum of one-half page in length

Elementary Portfolio Notebook or Files   5–10%
    Due the last day of class

Written Assignments not addressed by other projects   10–15%

    Rubrics will be used for all assignments to provide structure and to help you meet your goals. These will be provided in class. The teaching assignments will be modeled using a rubric. You will have some leeway in how you wish some of the projects to be weighted in this class. At mid-semester you will be asked to evaluate your progress and give a tentative weighting to completed or uncompleted projects. These percentages can be modified during the final self-assessment due on the last day of class.

INITIAL AGENDA

Date	Topic	Reading	Due
8/24	Course introduction.		
8/29	Music in our lives.	pp. 1–8, (Barrett).	Bring "the Circles Exercise" (p. 2) to class.

Project I: Music in Early Childhood

Date	Topic	Reading	Due
8/31	Experiencing music through singing (#1).* The child's voice. Songs, materials, and music activities for young children (#1, 2, & 3).	Singing handout	
9/5	Introduction to playing the guitar (#2 & 5). Encouraging children to sing (#1). Songs, materials, and music acitivtes for young children (#1, 2, & 3).	Guitar handout. Persellin, D., Pautz, M., Feierabend, J., Kenney, S., & Andress, B. (1994, August). Finding quality literature for young children. *Teaching Music,* (19+).	Practice playing songs with D and A7 chords.

9/7	Guitar: Learning to play the G chord (#2 & 5). Understanding music through listening and moving (#6). Songs, materials, and music activities for young children (#1, 2, & 3).	Achilles, E., Andress, B., Custodero, L., Hanna, N., Jarjisian, C., Kenney, S., Levinowitz, L., McGrath, B., Persellin D., Roebuck, E., & Sims, W. (1999, Oct.) What's happening in early childhood music education. *Teaching Music,* 30–37.	Practice playing three-chord songs. Highlight chord changes in your music.
9/12	Guitar: Learning to play a new strum (#2 & 5). The Mozart Effect: Does music make you smarter? The effect of music on other areas of learning.	Flohr, J., Miller, D., & Persellin, D. (1999, June). Recent brain research on young children. *Teaching Music,* 41–43.	Practice playing with two strums.
9/14	Guitar: Learning to lead songs using a guitar (#2). Songs, materials, and music activities for young children (#1 & 2).	Turner, M. (1999, July). Child-centered learning and music programs. *Music Educators Journal,* 30–33.	Practice starting three-chord songs.
9/19	Guitar: Learning to transpose music to D Major (#2). Songs, materials, and music activities for young children (#1 & 2).		Practice guitar with your small group.
9/21	Meet at the University Presbyterian Children's Center at 10 a.m. I will teach a class of three-year-olds (#7).	Stauffer, S. (1999, Sept.). Beginning assessment in elementary general music. *Music Educators Journal,* 25–30.	
9/26	Bring your guitar to University Presbyterian Children's Center at 10 a.m. We will all play and sing with the children with each of you leading a song.(#1 & 2).		E-mail journal entry on your class observation. E-mail your teaching strategy for 9/28. Schedule an appointment with partner and instructor to discuss teaching strategy.
9/28	Meet at University Presbyterian Children's Center at 10:00 a.m. Teach a small group of three- or four-year-olds with your teaching partner (#1, 2 3, 7).		E-mail your assessment of your teaching and of the children's learning (Use the rubric as a guideline).
10/3	Guitar proficiency with your small group(#1, 2, & 3).		Come prepared to play and sing five three-chord songs with confidence and pizzazz. Complete a guitar proficiency rubric.

Project II: Preparing to Teach Music to First and Second Graders in an Integrated Classroom

10/5   Music and the interdisciplinary curriculum (#8 & 9). The National Standards in Music Education.

     pp. 9–34 (Barrett).

10/10   Integrity in the interdisciplinary curriculum (#8 & 9) Using music to teach other subjects.

     pp. 35–48 (Barrett). Cutierra, R., Hamann, D., & Walker, L. (1995). Does music instruction aid reading skills? *Spin-Offs: The Extra-Musical Advantages of a Musical Education.* United Musical Instruments. 7–14.

10/12   Writing a lesson plan for an integrated music lesson (#8 & 9). State-adopted primary music textbooks and materials.

10/17   Getting to know a work of art (#6). Authentic assessment in the arts.

     pp. 49–68 (Barrett).

     Your lesson plan for the first- or second-grade class is due. Schedule an appointment to review your plan with your partner and your instructor.

10/19   Meet at Hawthorne Elementary School at 10:00. I will teach a first-grade class modeling an integrated lesson plan.

     Revise your plan based on this observation.

10/24   Teaching partners teach first or second graders at Hawthorne Elementary School for first time.

     E-mail a journal entry on your assessment of teaching, of the children's learning, and your teaching strategy for 10/26.

10/26   Teaching partners teach first or second graders for second time at Hawthorne Elementary.

     Assessment of teaching due. Next teaching strategy due.

10/31   Teaching partners teach first or second graders for third time at Hawthorne Elementary School.

     Assessment is due.

Project III: Preparing to Teach Music to Fourth and Fifth Graders in an Integrated Classroom.

11/2   Exploring relationships among the arts (#8). Theme and variations in music.

     pp. 69–84 (Barrett). McCoy, C. (2000, July) The excitement of collaboration. *Music Educators Journal,* 37–44.

11/7   Perceptions, patterns, and processes. Elements of music (#5 & 6).

     pp. 85–108 (Barrett).

     Analyze a lesson plan in the state-adopted textbooks that explore a relationship among the arts.

11/9	Planning interdisciplinary arts experiences for students (#8 & 9).	pp. 109–34 (Barrett).	
11/14	Music in Context. Expression of Culture: Mexico (#9)	pp. 135–56 (Barrett).	In the fourth and fifth grade state-adopted music textbooks, analyze a multicultural lesson and an interdisciplinary arts lesson. Be prepared to share your analysis in class.
11/16	Meet at Hawthorne Elementary at 10:00. I will teach a demonstration class of fifth-graders to model an integrated lesson for you. Exchange your analysis of a teaching strategy found in the state-adopted textbooks. Discuss strengths and weaknesses of each lesson with peer.	pp. 271–305 (Barrett).	Teaching strategy for first class is due.
11/21	Teaching partners will teach fourth or fifth graders for first time at Hawthorne Elementary.		Assessment is due. Teaching strategy for first class is due.
11/23	Thanksgiving.		
11/28	Teaching partners will teach fourth or fifth graders for second time at Hawthorne Elementary.		Assessment is due. Teaching strategy is due.
11/30	Teaching partners will teach fourth or fifth graders for third time at Hawthorne Elementary.		Assessment is due.
12/5	Closure and final evaluations.		Self-evaluation due.

**The National Standards that are addressed specifically are indicated with the topics.

CHORAL METHODS

Music 155: Seminar in Music Education
Jazz Choir/Show Choir
Dr. Virginia C. Bennett
Drake University
Fall 2000

Meetings: Class meets in FAC 304. Wednesdays 2:00 p.m. until 2:50 p.m.
Instructor: Dr. Virginia C. Bennett, Ph.D.
Office: 425 Harmon Fine Arts Center
Phone: 271-2823
E-mail: virginia.bennett@drake.edu
Office Hours: Mon.–Thurs. 1:00–1:50 p.m.; Fri. 10:00–10:50 a.m. Other times by appointment.
Prerequisites: Students must have completed all theory classes and be of senior status on the choral/general track in music education to be eligible to take this seminar.
Credits: Two

COURSE GOALS
To become familiar with selected aspects of
- Jazz choir literature
- Jazz choir techniques, procedures, and performance
- Show choir literature
- Show choir techniques, procedures, and performance
- Rehearsal techniques in the secondary choral program
- Management techniques in the secondary choral program
- The National Standards for Music Education, as they relate to jazz and show choir genres
- Rehearsal and management strategies appropriate to a secondary choral program

PROCEDURE
This course is a senior-level seminar which will require the full participation of all students in discussion, observation, and the compilation of ideas. The success of this seminar rests largely with the students who will set plans for learning about the jazz choir and show choir genres. Requirements are listed as follows:

Observe Jazz and Show Choir Rehearsals. This will include a minimum of fourteen one-hour observations of secondary choral jazz choir and show choir rehearsals, divided as follows: a minimum of seven hours observing jazz choir rehearsals and a minimum of seven hours observing show choir rehearsals. One of your observations for each kind of choir may be a public concert. Recommended observation sites and a form to guide your review of each observation are attached to this document.
Procedures for Observation Visits
(1) A copy of the observation validation form located in this document should be initialed by the director when you attend a rehearsal. You should plan to stay a minimum of fifty minutes, or the full length of the rehearsal, for validation as one hour of observation. You may stay up to a maximum of two hours in one rehearsal and receive two hours of observation credit. *You should observe a minimum of three different sites for each kind of choir.* Each observation should be reviewed in writing, according to the form located in this document, and kept

in your notebook. Your observation validation form should be submitted in your notebook.

    (2) You should plan to utilize a business-casual style of dress and assume a positive, attentive attitude. You should plan to take notes.

    (3) If the instructor asks you to assist in some way during the rehearsal, you should do so. If, after providing the assistance, you find that you did not feel comfortable in that role, please visit with that instructor about it, or talk with me.

Review Information on Jazz and Show Choirs.

    (1) A minimum of three articles/videos for each specialized kind of choir should be investigated, reviewed in writing, and kept in your log. These should not be materials reviewed in class.

    (2) A bibliography is attached. If you locate other materials of interest, please discuss them with me prior to including them.

Attend Seminar Meetings. Fifty minutes per week to share experiences and update your colleagues on your learning. You should plan to take notes for inclusion in your notebook.

    (1) Guest speakers will attend occasionally.

    (2) Videos and CDs will be shared.

    (3) You should plan to take notes for inclusion in your notebook.

Notebook. Compile a notebook of your materials from the course, which should include the following four main sections:

    (1) observation reports

    (2) summaries of at least six readings/videos on various aspects of jazz and show choir (three for each)

    (3) your typed notes/observations on information presented by guest speakers

    (4) a summary of your learning in this seminar which should be presented in writing and orally during the final exam period. You should make specific reference to the National Standards as related to all aspects of your learning.

How to Get the Most Out of This Course

- Take active responsibility for your own learning.
- Fulfill the requirements of the seminar accurately and punctually.
- Work diligently to discover new information to share.
- Reflect sincerely and personally about your learning.
- Participate regularly in class discussions, activities, and projects.
- Visit with the instructor and other students in the class if you have questions.
- Develop your own standards for judging the quality of your work.
- Reflect on your personal growth and development as a teacher.

Required Membership

Collegiate Music Educators National Conference (CMENC)

Class Attendance Policy

This course is vital to your professional preparation as a music educator. Regular and punctual attendance is crucial to your success. You are required to notify the instructor immediately of all absences and provide appropriate documentation upon your return. Provisions for making up work related to an excused absence must be made immediately upon return to class in a written contract with the instructor which will specify exact deadlines and will include written dated signatures of the student and the instructor.

Special Considerations

If you need course adaptations or accommodations because of a disability, if you have emergency medical information to share with me, or if you need special arrangements in case the building must be evacuated, please make an appointment with me as soon as possible.

Please: no eating or drinking in class.

ASSESSMENT

Final Grades will be based on the following scale of points received in the course:

A	90–100%	B	80–89.9%
C	70–79.9%	D	60–69.9%

Grade Distribution

Midterm Essay:	20%
Final Essay:	20%
Notebook Presentation (Oral & Written):	30%
Class Work:	30%

CALENDAR

Unit I: Jazz Choir

Week 1	Introduction—Distribution of syllabus and discussion of class goals. Set specific goals for the jazz choir unit.
Week 2	Discussion of the National Standards as they relate to the jazz choir genre.
Week 3	Listen to and sing jazz.
Week 4	Equipment for the jazz choir: Linda Vanderpool, Hoover HS.
Week 5	Guest speaker: Mike Malloy, SW Community College.
Week 6	Guest speaker: Mike Malloy.
Week 7	Seminar review of articles on jazz choir unit.
Week 8	Midterm essay on jazz choir.

Unit II: Show Choir

Week 9	Introduction to show choir. Set specific goals for the show choir unit. Discuss the National Standards as they relate to the show choir genre.
Week 10	Watch show choir videos.
Week 11	Sing show choir music.
Week 12	Guest speaker: Ms. Mary Anne Sims, Roosevelt HS.
Week 13	Guest speaker: Ms. Jody White, Urbandale HS.
Week 14	Seminar review of articles.
Week 15	Final essay on show choir.

Final Exam. This time will be utilized for the presentation of your notebooks. You should plan to provide handouts of your major points. The time scheduled is Tuesday, December 19th, 9:30–11:20 AM.

When planning to make an observation, please remember to call ahead to the director to receive permission and to verify the dates and times of the rehearsal.

Following is a schedule of rehearsals at which you may observe:
Unit 1: Jazz Choir
Valley High School. Until the end of October, jazz choir rehearsals are scheduled for Tuesday evenings, 5:00–8:00 p.m. Beginning November 1, jazz choir rehearsals are scheduled for Monday evenings, from 5:00–8:00 p.m. The director is Mr. Jim Cacciatore, 226-2638.

Hoover High School. Harmony jazz choir will meet daily at approximately 9:30–10:30 a.m. Contact Ms. Linda Vanderpool, 242-7262

Waukee High School. Jazz choir rehearsals are on Tuesday and Thursday, 7:00–7:45 a.m. Contact Mr. Ryan Beeken, 987-5163.

Unit 2 Show Choir

Johnston High School. Show choir rehearsals are every other school day. Varsity: 10:22–11:07 (Ms. White). Junior Varsity: 11:11–11:56 (Brenton Brown). Monday evenings, 7:00–10:00. Contact Ms. Jody White, 278-0449.

Lincoln High School. Call Ms. Dina Else at 242-7500.

Roosevelt High School. Varsity show choir rehearsals are scheduled for 9:36–10:29 every school day. Junior Varsity show choir rehearsals are scheduled for 11:32–12:22 every school day. Contact Mrs. Mary Ann Sims, 242-7348.

Urbandale High School. Varsity show choir rehearses on Monday evenings, 7:00–9:00 p.m., and Thursday evenings, 7:30–9:00 p.m. Prep show choir rehearses on Tuesday evenings, 7:00–9:00 p.m. and Thursday evenings, 6:00–7:30. Contact Mr. Steve Woodin, 457-6872.

Waukee High School. Show choir rehearses Monday evenings, 7:00–10:00 p.m. Contact Mr. Ryan Beeken, 987-5163.

Waukee Middle School. Seventh and eighth grade show choir rehearsals are on Thursdays at 7:00 a.m. Contact Mr. Brent Peterson, 987-5177.

OBSERVATION VALIDATION FORM: FIRST HALF OF FALL SEMESTER, 1999

Name _____

Dates Observed _____

Date	Location	Time spent Arrival and Departure	Instructor Initials
Date	Location	Time spent Arrival and Departure	Instructor Initials
Date	Location	Time spent Arrival and Departure	Instructor Initials
Date	Location	Time spent Arrival and Departure	Instructor Initials
Date	Location	Time spent Arrival and Departure	Instructor Initials
Date	Location	Time spent Arrival and Departure	Instructor Initials
Date	Location	Time spent Arrival and Departure	Instructor Initials

OBSERVATION REPORT

Your observation report should include comments regarding the following:

(A) Logistical Considerations
(1) Name of the school
(2) Name of the choral instructor
(3) Type of choir (Jazz or Show)
(4) Level of the choir (advanced or beginning group)
(5) Length of your visit (time in/time out)

(B) Students
(1) Approximate number
(2) Grade level of the majority
(3) Maturity level
(4) Interest level
(5) Ability level

(C) Instructor
(1) Manner
(2) Organization
(3) Pacing

(D) Learning Environment
(1) Space
(2) Temperature
(3) Lighting
(4) Equipment

(E) Your reaction/comments/questions

BIBLIOGRAPHY ON JAZZ CHOIR AND SHOW CHOIR

The reading in this course is selected by each student from this bibliography.

Albrecht, S. K. (1984). *Choral music in motion: Adding movement to your choral program.* Van Nuys, CA: Alfred Publishing.

Albrecht, S. K. (1989). *Choral music in motion (vol. 2): Movement for larger groups.* Van Nuys, CA: Alfred Publishing.

Grier, G., & Sharar, T. (1986, September). Room for all, and eyes of the beholder. *Music Educators Journal,* 15–17.

Itkin, D. (1986, April). Dissolving the myths of the show choir. *Music Educators Journal,* 41.

Jacobson, J. (1993). *Gotta sing, gotta dance: Basics of choreography and staging.* Milwaukee, WI: Hal Leonard Publishing Corporation. (Book and four videos.)

MENC. (1994). *The school music program: A new vision.* Reston, VA: MENC.

MENC Committee on Performance Standards. (1996). *Performance standards for music: Strategies and benchmarks for assessing progress toward the national standards, grades PreK–12.* Reston, VA: MENC.

Madura, P. D. (1999). *Getting started with vocal improvisation.* Reston, VA: MENC

Mattson, P. (1995). *Vocal jazz: The art and the technique.* Video featuring VoicesIowa. Southwestern Community College, Creston, Iowa.

Morgan, J., & Burrows, B. (1981, April). Sharpen your edge on choral competition. *Music Educators Journal,* 44–47.

Robinson, R. (Ed.). (1994). *Getting started with jazz/show choir.* Reston, VA: MENC.

Web sites: Yahoo.com
showchoirs.com
info@iaje.org, or www.iaje.org
(IAJE is the acronym for the International Association of Jazz Educators)

CDs

Mattson, P. (1994). *You must believe in spring.* VoicesIowa, Phil Mattson, Conductor. SMV Records, Southwestern Community College, Creston, IA 50801.

Mattson, P. (1996). *Night in the city.* Phil Mattson and the P.M. Singers. SRH Records.

Mattson, P. (1996). *Jubilee.* Phil Mattson and the P.M. Singers. SRH Records.

Mattson, P. (1998). *An evening of vocal jazz.* Featuring the 1998 Iowa All State Jazz Choir and VoicesIowa. Comprehensive Sound Services, 11168 Lodge Avenue., Greene, IA 50636. 515/823-4831.

Mattson, P.(1999). *Is God a three-letter word for love.* Phil Mattson and Vocalogy. SMV Records, School for Music Vocations, Southwestern Community College, Creston, IA 50801.

Salucka, R. (1998). *Waltz for Debby.* Jazz Transit and R.S.V.P. Kirkwood Community College, Cedar Rapids, Iowa. Comprehensive Sound Services, 11168 Lodge Avneue. Greene, IA 50636. 515/823-4831.

Salucka, R. (1999). *I hear music.* Jazz Transit and R.S.V.P. Kirkwood Community College, Cedar Rapids, IA. Comprehensive Sound Services, 11168 Lodge Avenue. Greene, IA 50636. 515/823-4831.

Videos

Cabaret '99 (May 14 & 15, 1999). Onalaska High School's Choral Music Department. Comprehensive Sound Services, 11168 Lodge Avenue. Greene, IA 50636. 515/823-4831.

1997 Urbandale Show Choir Jamboree Evening Final Competition. (February 15, 1997). Comprehensive Sound Services, 11168 Lodge Avenue, Greene, IA 50636. 515/823-4831.

1999 Heelan High School Show Choir Invitational. (March 13, 1999). Bishop Heelan Catholic High School, Sioux City, Iowa. Comprehensive Sound Services, 11168 Lodge Avenue. Greene, IA 50636. 515/823-4831.

1999 Urbandale Show Choir Jamboree Evening Final Competition. (February 13, 1999). Comprehensive Sound Services, 11168 Lodge Avenue, Greene, IA 50636. 515/823-4831.

Mattson, P. (1995). *Vocal jazz: The art and the technique.* Featuring VoicesIowa. School for Music Vocations, Southwestern Community College, Creston, IA 50801. 515-782-7081.

MUS 352: Secondary Vocal Music Methods, Materials, and Curricula
Dr. Caroline Perkins
DePauw University
Spring 2000

Instructor: Dr. Caroline Perkins
Office: 658-4503, Room 225E
E-mail: ckperkins@depauw.edu
Class Hours: 2:00–3:50 Tues., Thurs.
Location: Room 17 PAC
Office Hours: 11:00–12:00 Mon., Wed.; 2:30–4:00 Mon., Wed.; and by appointment

Course Description

Methods and materials appropriate for teaching vocal music at the middle and high school levels. General survey of middle and high school curricula and study of philosophical bases of curriculum design. Includes an analysis of texts, literature, and representative materials outlining related responsibilities of the vocal music teacher. Provides detailed consideration of organization, development, maintenance, and evaluation of comprehensive choral programs in secondary schools. Observation of music teaching and participation in music teaching are included in the coursework.

Course Objectives

Through a variety of in-class activities and outside assignments, the students will
- become familiar with the characteristics of middle and high school students
- become familiar with appropriate materials for teaching musicianship within the choral rehearsal
- establish criteria for the selection of appropriate repertoire, texts, materials, and vocalises for use in middle and high school vocal music classrooms
- develop a working knowledge of the National Standards for Music Education
- develop the ability to plan for comprehensive vocal music instruction
- develop part-reading skills
- develop a set of goals for the choral program
- develop knowledge of effective administrative techniques for grading, auditioning, recruiting, and seating chorus members
- become familiar with methods of organizing, developing, and maintaining a comprehensive vocal music program in secondary schools
- exhibit knowledge of and familiarity with current professional issues
- gain an understanding of the teacher's educational and professional responsibilities to students, the choral program, the school, the community, and the profession

Course Topics
- National Standards for Music Education
- Rehearsal Planning and Techniques
- Vocal Pedagogy
- Adolescent Voice
- Repertoire and Materials Selection
- Organization and Administration of a Vocal Music Education Program
- Programming Music
- Evaluation of Music Students
- Behavior Management

- Ensembles
- Festivals and Contests
- Professional Ethics
- Process of Securing a Teaching Position
- Role of a Music Educator
- Incorporation of Music Concepts in the Choral Rehearsal
- Curriculum Design
- Curriculum Models
- Goals and Objectives

In brief, MUS 352 focuses on

Philosophy: Why teach choral music?
Students: Who will we teach? What are the basic traits and abilities of these students?
Subject: What should be taught?
Methods: How do we teach it? What materials do we use to teach it?
Evaluation: Has any learning taken place in the choral classroom?

MATERIALS

Required Texts

Consortium of National Arts Education Associations. (1994). *National standards for arts education.* Reston, VA: MENC.

Brinson, B. A. (1996). *Choral music methods and materials: Developing successful choral programs (Grades 5–12).* New York: Schirmer Books.

Relevant Periodicals in the Music Library

- *Choral Journal*
- *Journal of Research in Music Education*
- *Journal of Research in Singing*
- *Journal of Research in Singing and Applied Vocal Pedagogy*
- *Journal of Singing*
- *Music Educators Journal*
- *NATS Bulletin*
- *NATS Journal*
- *Teaching Music*
- *Update: Applications of Research in Music Education*

Materials on Reserve in Music Library

Sight Singing

- *The Sight Singer (Vol. 1)* by Snyder (2 & 3 part mixed)
- *The Sight Singer, (Vol. 1)* by Snyder (unison & 2 part treble)
- *Sight Singing for SSA* by Eilers and Crocker
- *Songs for Sight Singing* (JH and HS, SATB) by Henry and Jones
- *Sight Singing for Young Teens (Vols. 1–3)* by Elliott
- *Sight Singing Made Simple* by Banguess
- *Sing Choral Music at Sight* by Anderson
- *Teaching Choral Sight-Reading* by Boyd
- *Successful Sight Singing (Book 1 & 2)* by Telfer

Warm-Ups

- *Warm-Ups and Workouts for the Developing Choir (Vol. 1 & 2)* by Crocker
- *Successful Warm-Ups (Books 1 and 2)* by Telfer
- *Complete Choral Warm-Up Book. A Sourcebook for Choral Directors* by Robinson and Althouse

Curriculum/Repertoire Books
- *Sing!* by Schott, Land, Monsour, Rao, and Whitlock
- *We Will Sing! Choral Music Experience for Classroom Choirs* by Rao
- *Essential Musicianship: A Comprehensive Choral Method* by Crocker and Leavitt
- *Essential Repertoire for the Young Choir (Vol. 1 & 2)* by Crocker
- *Essential Repertoire for the Concert Choir (Vol. 1–4)* by Crocker
- *Essential Repertoire for the Developing Choir* by Killian
- *Choral Connections* by Tower (8 vol., mixed, treble, tenor-bass)
- *World of Choral Music* by Hausmann

Books
- *Comprehensive Choral Music Education* by John Hylton
- *Choral Techniques* by Gordon Lamb
- *Teaching Music: Managing the Successful Music Program* by Darwin Walker
- *Dimensions of Musical Thinking* by MENC
- *Teaching Music in the Secondary Schools* by Charles Hoffer
- *The Choral Experience: Literature, Materials, and Methods* by Robinson and Winold
- *Choral Techniques: Beyond the Basics* by Johnson

Other Repertoire Books
- *The A Cappella Singer* by Chough-Leighter
- *Second Concord Anthem Book* by Davison and Foote
- *Five Centuries of Choral Music* by Hartshorn
- *Carols for Choirs* by Jacques and Willcocks

Miscellaneous
- *Action Kit for Music Education* by MENC
- *Music for a Sound Education: A Tool Kit for Implementing the Standards* by National Coalition for Music Education

GRADING SCALE

A+ = 98–100	A = 94–97	A- = 90–93
B+ = 88–89	B = 84–87	B- = 80–83
C+ = 78–79	C = 74–77	C- = 70–73
D+ = 68–69	D = 64–67	D- = 60–63
F = 59 and below		

EVALUATION

Grading will be based upon data obtained from the following sources and will be weighted as indicated.

10% Field Experience. This will take place in local public schools. It includes a write-up for each observation and a reflective self-evaluation for each teaching episode. A total of six school visitations is required.
Components of Grade: Attendance, evaluation(s) by cooperating teacher(s), write-ups, and self-reflections.

25% Teaching Activities and Plans
- Audition middle and/or high school students for choir (5%)
- Lead a sight-reading/singing and warm-up segment (5%)
  Warm-up session (5–7 minutes)
  Introductory sight-singing lesson (8–10 minutes)
  A warm-up to work on trouble spots of a selection.
- Introduce a new piece to middle and/or high school students (15%)

For all presentations, a lesson plan containing a description of the class being taught, objectives, procedures, and means of evaluation must be submitted.

20% Tests. Midterm and Final—10% each

15% Assignments
- Audition card (10%)
- Based on given criteria for selecting music, justify the inclusion of five songs in your music program (20%)
- Score analysis (20%)
- Original warm-up using *Finale,* or other notation program, for selected piece which focuses on expected trouble spots (i.e., difficult interval(s), harmony, melodic pattern, articulation, etc.) (5%)
- Set of rules and consequences appropriate for your music classroom (10%)
- Grading policy for your music classes (10%). Your policy should reflect your decisions as to what criteria will be assessed, the method of assessment, the relevance of each criteria, and the overall grading standard. Be prepared to defend your grading policy.
- Evaluations of curricula, sight singing and warm-up materials (10%). Include bibliographic information, a description of contents (theory, history, composers, performance literature, sight-reading materials, vocal pedagogy, listening examples, lesson plans/guides, age level, assessment ideas), a synopsis, and comments.
- Mock interview (10%)
- Rehearsal critique (5%)

10% Lesson Plan. Design a plan for a comprehensive vocal music class. Choose either middle school or high school.

5% Goals and Objectives. Develop a set of broad philosophical goals for use in the choral program. Develop a hypothetical choral program by class level and purpose. Construct a detailed set of instructional objectives for one level of these classes.

5% Score Reading. Parts and accompaniment. You will be asked to play any two parts together, any three parts together, all four parts together, reduce the accompaniment, and play the accompaniment as written.

5% Budget. You have $45,000 to start a new program. Spend it as you see fit. Be able to justify your purchases. Consider that your budget in subsequent years will be $1,000 per year. Prepare your budget in a spreadsheet package such as *Excel.*

5% Sample Program. Describe a hypothetical school ensemble in terms of its community, student body, and prior musical achievements. Develop a concert program of fifteen selections designed for a public school concert by your hypothetical group. Assume that you have approximately six weeks to prepare the ensemble for the performance.

Other Activities
- (1) Assigned readings
- (2) In-class activities
- (3) Active participation in student chapter of MENC

Due Dates
Teaching Activities and Plans
- Audition: February 17
- Sight-singing and warm-up: March 2
- Rehearsal of new piece: April 18

Tests
- Midterm: March 14
- Final: May 15

Assignments
- Audition card: February 15
- Evaluations
    - Curriculum: February 22
    - Warm-up materials: February 22
    - Sight-singing materials: February 24
- Original warm-up: February 29
- Rules and consequences: March 7
- Grading policy: March 23
- Rehearsal critique: April 4
- Justification of song choices: April 6
- Score analysis: April 11
- Mock interview: May 9

Lesson Plan. March 14

Goals and Objectives. March 21

Part Reading and Accompaniment Performance. April 13

Sample Program. April 18

Budget. May 2

Observation Write-up and Self-reflections. Class session after each visitation

Written work is to be word processed. Any work turned in otherwise will be returned to you ungraded. All assignments are due at the beginning of class on the assigned day. Grades for late work will be lowered one letter grade for each day late. This policy is designed to help keep you on schedule.

ATTENDANCE POLICY

Attendance, preparation, and participation are expected and required. Each student is responsible for contacting the instructor if and when an absence is unavoidable. Each student is responsible for checking with the instructor or a classmate when an absence occurs in order to stay on schedule with class assignments, readings, etc.

Excused absences include family emergency, illness, and university-approved activities. Unexcused absences include other classes, vacation plans, computer problems, sleep deprivation, Greek activities, etc.

One point will be subtracted from your final grade for each unexcused absence and for each unreported absence. Absences prior to and following school recesses (i.e., leaving early for and/or returning late from break) will be counted as two absences.

Punctuality is a professional courtesy and allows for the smooth start of each class session. Three tardies will equal one absence.

This course is designed to be a seminar which requires active participation by everyone. Thus, the success of the course depends on the contributions made by each of you. It takes all of us working together to form an effective learning community.

PROFESSIONAL RESPONSIBILITIES FOR SCHOOL OBSERVATIONS

Attendance. If you must be absent from any of your school visitations due to illness or emergency, you must inform the people affected by your absence (i.e., placement teacher and carpool members, if applicable). You are expected to reschedule missed visitations with your placement teacher.

Privacy Issues. We need to be cognizant of the importance of respecting the privacy of the students observed. Do not discuss classroom scenarios that might be embarrassing to teachers, parents, or children, or that might include sensitive information about a child or family. During class discussions, use pseudonyms. Use professional judgement when discussing students, situations, etc. at your field experience site.

Deportment. You will be viewed and judged as an adult by students, parents, and teachers. Dress appropriately. Do not wear jeans or hats. Do not chew gum. Be polite and considerate to everyone you encounter, including the principal, secretaries, custodians, teacher assistants, parents, etc. Arrive a few minutes prior to your scheduled observation. Please continue the tradition of representing yourself and DePauw in a professional manner.

Please Note: If you have a disability and require auxiliary aids, services, or accommodations, please contact me in my office so that we may discuss your particular needs.

Please do not hesitate to ask questions or contact me if you are unclear about assignments, readings, etc. I am looking forward to a GREAT semester, I hope you are too!!

TENTATIVE SCHEDULE OF CLASS TOPICS

February 1   **Introduction**
                Case Study: In the Thick of It
                Religious Music in the Schools

February 3   **Philosophical Foundations**
                Read Ch. 1, Brinson.
                Look at *Action Kit for Music Education.*
                The Role of the Music Educator
                Read Ch. 1, *Teaching Music.*

February 8   **Recruitment and Retention of Singers**
                Read Ch. 2, Brinson.
                Case Study: Solitude of Success

February 10   **Auditioning Singers**
                Read pp. 29–43, Brinson.
                Read pp. 159–67, *Choral Techniques.*
                Read pp. 74–79, *The Choral Experience.*
                Placement of Voices and Seating Arrangements
                Read pp. 43–53, Brinson.
                Read pp. 167–71, *Choral Techniques.*
                Read pp. 162–65, *The Choral Experience.*
                Read pp. 22–26, *Choral Techniques: Beyond the Basics.*

February 15   **In-Class Activity: Mock Auditions and Voice Placement**
                Audition card due.
                Be prepared to conduct a mock audition and place voices.
                Development of a Choral Curriculum
                Read pp. 55–61, Brinson.
                Look at *National Standards* (introduction and 9–12 standards).
                Look at sample curricula.
                Look at *Music for a Sound Education: A Tool Kit for Implementing the Standards.*

February 17   **Mock Auditions at Greencastle Middle or High School**
                Be prepared to audition GMS or GHS students.
                Curricula
                Become familiar with the following materials:
                    • *Sing!*
                    • *We Will Sing! Choral Music Experience for Classroom Choirs*
                    • *World of Choral Music*

February 22	**Curricula**

February 22   **Curricula**
Become familiar with the following materials:
- *Essential Musicianship: A Comprehensive Choral Method*
- *Essential Repertoire for the Young Choir*
- *Essential Repertoire for the Concert Choir*
- *Essential Repertoire for the Developing Choir*
- *Choral Connections* (mixed, treble, tenor-bass)

Evaluation of curricula due.
Warm-Up Materials
Become familiar with the following materials:
- *Warm-ups and Workouts for the Developing Choir*
- *Successful Warm-ups*
- *Complete Choral Warm-Up Book: A Sourcebook for Choral Directors*

Evaluation of warm-up materials due.

February 24   **Sight-Reading Materials**
Read p. 42, *Choral Techniques: Beyond the Basics.*
Become familiar with the following materials:
- *The Sight Singer*, two- and three-part mixed, and unison and two-part
- *Sight Singing for SSA*
- *Songs for Sight Singing*
- *Sight Singing for Young Teens*
- *Sight Singing Made Simple*
- *Sing Choral Music at Sight*
- *Successful Sight Singing,* Books 1 and 2
- *Teaching Choral Sight-Reading*

Evaluation of sight-reading materials due.
Rehearsal Planning
Read pp. 127–41, Brinson.
Watch video 3 from *Choral Triad Video Series.*

February 29   **Sight-Reading and Warm-Up Demonstrations in class**
Original warm-up due.
Goals and Objectives for the Choral Program

March 2   **Lead Sight-Reading and Warm-Up Activities at GMS/GHS**
Teaching Music Concepts within the Choral Rehearsal
Watch video 4 from *Choral Triad Video Series.*

March 7   **Planning**
In-class activity.
Behavior Management in Rehearsal
Read Ch. 9, Brinson.
Rules and Consequences due.

March 9   **No Class (MENC National Conference)**

March 14   **Planning**
Lesson Plan due.
Class discussion of plans.
Provide a copy for the instructor and each class member.
Test

March 16	**The Rehearsal**
	Read pp. 141–51, Brinson.
	Read pp. 37–39, *Choral Techniques: Beyond the Basics.*
	Read pp. 154–62, *The Choral Experience.*
	Watch video 1 from *Choral Triad Video Series.*
	The Rehearsal/Common Rehearsal Problems
	Read Ch. 8, *Dimensions of Musical Thinking.*
	Read pp. 165–69, *The Choral Experience.*
March 21	**Daily Rehearsals**
	Read Ch. 9, *Choral Techniques.*
	Goals and Objectives due.
	Final Rehearsals and Concert Preparation
	Read Ch. 10, *Choral Techniques.*
March 23	**Critique Choir Rehearsal at GMS or GHS**
	Evaluation/Writing Test Questions/Portfolio
	Read pp. 62–71, Brinson.
	Read pp. 370–379, *Teaching Music in the Secondary Schools.*
	Personal Grading Policy due.
April 4	**Repertoire**
	Read Ch. 5, Brinson.
	Read Ch. 7, *Choral Techniques.*
	Programming Music
	Read Ch. 6, Brinson.
	Rehearsal Critique due.
April 6	**Repertoire**
	Justification of five songs due.
	Programming Music
	In-class activity.
April 11	**Musical Analysis and Score Preparation**
	Read Ch. 7, Brinson.
	Read pp. 91–93, *Choral Techniques.*
	Watch videos 5 and 6 from *Choral Triad Video Series.*
	Score analysis due.
	Vocal Techniques and Musicianship Skills
	Read Ch.10, Brinson.
	Watch video 2 from *Choral Triad Video Series.*
April 13	**The Changing Voice**
	Read Ch. 11, Brinson.
	Read "The Adolescent Female Voice" in March 1991 *Choral Journal.*
	Watch video: *Baressi on Adolescent Voice.*
	Part-Reading and Accompaniment Performances
April 18	**Rehearse Piece at Greencastle Middle or High School**
	Organizing Small Ensembles
	Read Ch. 12, *Choral Techniques.*
	Sample Program due.

April 20	**Discussion of Rehearsal Experience at GMS or GHS**
	Pop Ensembles and Musical Productions
	Read Ch. 12, Brinson.
	Read pp. 244–51, *Comprehensive Choral Music Education.*
April 25	**Planning for Special Events**
	Read pp. 231–44, *Comprehensive Choral Music Education.*
	Management of a Choral Program
	Read Ch. 13, Brinson.
April 27	**Budget**
	Read pp. 248–59, *Choral Techniques.*
May 2	**Budget**
	Budget due.
	Case Study: The Right Choice
May 4	**The Choral Profession**
	Read Ch. 10, *Comprehensive Choral Music Education.*
	Professional Ethics and Teacher Relationships
	Read Ch. 16, *Choral Techniques.*
May 9	**Finding a Job**
	Read Ch. 15, *Choral Techniques.*
	Mock Interview.
May 11	**Discussion of Field Experience and GMS/GHS Activities**
	Wrap-Up
May 15	**Final (6–9 p.m.)**

MUSC 372: Secondary Choral Music Methods
Dr. Sandra Frey Stegman
Northern Illinois University

Class Schedule: Tues., Thurs. 9–10:50 a.m.; Rm. 202

Course Description

Secondary Choral Music Methods is designed to facilitate the development of skills, techniques, under-standings, and professional dispositions which are: (a) important to working with young people in choral music-making and learning, and (b) necessary to the successful planning and implementation of a choral music education program for junior high and high school students. In addition, this course encourages students to understand themselves better as persons and educators in relationship to their future students and the greater profession. In Secondary Choral Music Methods, students will explore topics of vocal pedagogy, literature selection, educational considerations, rehearsal techniques and strategies, program planning and development, musical literacy, learning environments, musical assessment and evaluation, personal practical knowledge and related teacher images, and professionalism. In addition, students will have experience in planning a secondary choral program, writing lesson plans, implementing teaching strategies and techniques, selecting and evaluating literature, considering greater educational issues, and making critical assessments of musical and teaching observations.

Course Outcomes

Upon completion of Secondary Choral Music Methods, students will know and be able to apply peda-gogical knowledge and skills appropriate to choral music education. This will be demonstrated by the student in the following ways:
- articulating logical rationales and supporting philosophy of music education for the role of music in the school curriculum
- identifying and applying teaching methods for secondary choral music education, incorporat-ing strategies for diverse learners and the inclusion of musical technology
- identifying and applying teaching methods for integrating music into other areas of the curriculum
- identifying and describing characteristics of appropriate music education materials and litera-ture (traditional and multicultural) for a variety of music education settings
- identifying and describing vocal classifications and ranges and the stages of vocal maturation from childhood through late adolescence
- applying the techniques of accompanying classroom and performing ensembles
- describing and applying principles of Comprehensive Musicianship and National Standards-based instruction in choral music classrooms
- identifying and applying techniques for assessing student aptitude and achievement, appropri-ate to the school music program
- designing, developing, and implementing sequential curriculum appropriate to the school com-munity
- reflecting on and revising practice towards enhanced music-making and learning

Expectations

It is expected that
- students will actively participate in the learning process and the construction of meaning relat-ed to themselves as a person, educator, and musician
- students will come to class having read the assigned readings and prepared to participate, pre-sent, etc., accordingly
- assignments will be submitted on the due date in appropriate format

- assignments will be word-processed and double-spaced unless indicated otherwise
- students will attend all class sessions (absences for illness require notification of the instructor; absences for special circumstances must be approved in advance)
- students will look ahead to future readings and assignments to ensure adequate planning and preparation time
- appointments with the instructor are arranged in a timely manner (i.e., plan ahead)

GRADING

60% Class Assignments and Attendance. Written, class discussion, presentations, reviews and reflections, quizzes, notebook, journals, technology mini-project, etc.

Technology Mini-Project. (1) Expansion of a project from MS/JH Methods, or (2) involvement in Web-based school composition project, or (3) continuation/extension of instructional technology used in DeKalb HS Choral Classrooms. (Include in upcoming teaching episode(s).)

20% Midterm Project. Propose and complete a project designed to further a special interest or to address an underdeveloped area of skill, knowledge, and/or practice.

20% Final Project. A curriculum project facilitating the integration of educational and musical thinking. It should include educational objectives, programming, musical and learning outcomes, assessment procedures, and a relationship to the National Standards. (A detailed description will be provided.)

Each unexcused absence will result in a one-half letter grade reduction in attendance.

A=Outstanding   B=Very Good   C=Minimum/Average   D=Poor/Weak   F=Not completed/submitted

WEEKLY SCHEDULE

A weekly schedule of assignments and activities will be provided periodically. Due dates and more specific information regarding assignments and presentations will also be provided. Because of the interactive nature of this course, adjustments within the weekly schedule may be necessary.

REQUIREMENTS

Required Texts

Brinson, B. A. (1996). *Choral music methods and materials.* New York: Schirmer Books.
Consortium of National Arts Education Associations. (1994). *National standards for arts education.*
    Reston, VA: MENC.

Supplemental Text

Roe, P. F. (1996). *Choral music education.* Prospect Heights, IL: Waveland Press, Inc.

Additional Materials

Videotape, large three-ring binder

Clinical Hours.

Thirty clinical hours are required for completion of this course. Fifteen of these are incorporated into the course.

Course Notebook

- Music Education "Credo"
- Resume
- Course Notes
- Essential Articles and Materials
- Other Pertinent Information
- Assignments, Presentations. Observations. Reflections. etc.

Professional Folio.
See separate criteria sheet.

Dekalb High School Chorus Schedule

| 8:45–9:35 | Treble Chorus | M–F |
| 9:40–10:30 | Mixed Chorus | M–F |

Important Additional Dates

1/27	Dr. R. Bastian; Vocal Health and Concerns
1/28–29	IMEA Conference; Peoria
3/4	Solo and Ensemble Festival; Sycamore High School
4/8	Large Group Contest; Harvard High School

RESOURCES

Course Readings, Videos, Materials. (On Reserve)

The Arts PROPEL Video Handbook. Cambridge: Harvard Project Zero.

Apfelstadt, H. (1989). Musical thinking in the choral classroom. In Eunice Boardman (Ed.). *Dimensions of musical thinking.* (pp. 73–81.) Reston, VA: MENC.

Barresi, A. *Barresi on the adolescent voice.* Madison: University of Wisconsin. Video.

Bogar, T. (1983, September). From the drama director's chair. *Music Educators Journal,* 41–48.

Consortium of National Arts Education Associations. (1995, November). Setting the record straight: Give and take on the National Standards for Arts Education, Part 1. *Choral Journal,* 17–24. Reprinted from *Music for a sound education: A tool kit for implementing the standards.* 1994. Reston, VA: MENC.

Gilbert, N. (1993, December). Sacred music in the public schools. *Choral Journal,* 4–5.

Lee, M. (1983, September). Selecting, staging, and singing a show. *Music Educators Journal,* 41–48.

Religious Music in the Schools: MENC Policy Statement. (1996) Reston, VA: MENC.

Renolds, C. (1984, November). Sacred music: How to avoid cooking your goose. *Music Educators Journal,* 29–33.

Sekulow, J. A. (1993, December). Christmas observations in public schools: A legal opinion. *Choral Journal,* 52–54.

Smith, A. (1994, February). Letter to the editor. *Choral Journal,* 4.

Additional Materials and Resources. (On Reserve)

Adams, C. (1991). *Daily workout for a beautiful voice.* Santa Barbara, CA: Santa Barbara Music Publishing. Video.

Anderson, W. (Ed.). (1991). *Teaching music with a multicultural approach.* Reston, VA: MENC.

Anderson, W., & Campbell, P. S. (Eds.). (1989). *Multicultural Perspectives in Music Education.* Reston, VA: MENC.

Bartle, J. A. (1988). *Lifeline for children's chorus.* Toronto: Gordon V. Thompson Music.

Campbell, P. S. (1991). *Lessons from the world: A cross-cultural guide to music teaching and learning.* New York. Schirmer Books.

Choksy, L., Abramson, R. A., Gillespie, A. E., & Woods, D. (1986). *Teaching music in the twentieth century.* Englewood Cliffs, NJ: Prentice Hall, Inc.

Crocker, E. (Ed.). (1995). *Essential musicianship.* Milwaukee, WI: Hal Leonard Corporation. (Various levels of teacher and student editions.)

Crocker, E. (Ed.). (1995). *Essential repertoire.* Milwaukee, WI: Hal Leonard Corporation. (Equal and mixed voices, teacher and student editions).

Ehmann, W., & Haasemann, F. (1981). *Voice building for choirs.* Chapel Hill, NC: Hinshaw Music.

Haasemann, F., & Jordan, J. (1999). *Group vocal technique: Book and vocalise cards.* Chapel Hill, NC: Hinshaw Music.

Nesheim, P. (1995). *Building beautiful voices*. Dayton, OH: Roger Dean Publishing.

Phillips, K. H. (1992). *Teaching kids to sing*. New York: Schirmer Books.

Rao, D. (Ed.). (1990). *Choral music for children*. Reston, VA: MENC.

Telfer, N. (1995). *Successful sight singing*. San Diego: Neil A. Kjos Music Company.

Telfer, N. *Successful sight singing performance selections:* Equal and Mixed Voices. San Diego: Neil A. Kjos Music Company.

Webb, G. B. (Ed.). (1993). *Up front!* Boston: E.C. Schirmer Music Company Inc.

Miscellaneous.

Curriculum Guides, Repertoire Lists, Octavos, etc.

CALENDAR

January

T-18   Questions and Critical Issues; Philosophical, Educational, Personal
        Midterm Project (Due March 7)
        Assigned Reading: Brinson, Ch. 7
        Tues. Assignment: Past, Present, and Future

Th-20   Music Education in the Choral Classroom
        The National Standards within a Comprehensive Musicianship Approach
        Discuss and Apply: Brinson, Ch. 7; Roe, pp. 54–56.
        Assigned Reading: Brinson, Ch. 11

T-25   The Adolescent Singer; Boys' and Girls' Changing Voices
        In-Class: View and Discuss Barresi Video
        Discuss and Apply: Brinson, Ch. 11
        Due: Past, Present, Future

Th-27   The Adolescent Singer; Literature Selection and Learning Strategies
        Quiz: Adolescent Singer
        Assigned Reading: Brinson, Ch. 3, pp. 29–43
        Special Guest: R. Bastian; 5:30–8 p.m., Rm. 173. *Attendance Required.*

February

T-1   Students as Individuals; Voice Checks
        Discuss and Apply: Brinson, Ch. 3, pp. 29–43
        In-Class: Peer Voice Checks, Using vocalises from reading and video
        Due: Midterm Proposal, First Literature Perusal Form

Th-3   Students as Individuals; In-School Voice Checks and Observation at DeKalb High School
        In-School Presentations: Administer Voice Checks, Journal Writing
        Assigned Reading: Brinson, Ch. 5

T-8   Music Education in the Choral Classroom
        Reflection and Discussion: Voice Checks and Observation at DeKalb HS
        Materials and Resources; Library Reserves
        Discuss and Apply: Brinson, Ch. 5
        Assigned Reading: Brinson, Ch. 10

Th-10   Vocal and Choral Fundamentals: Preparation to Sing, to Listen, to Learn
        Discuss and Apply: Brinson, Ch. 10
        In-Class: Present Single Warm-up, Using Piano
        Tues. Assignment: Written Warm-up Plan and Presentation. Design ten-minute warm-up

Th-10
(cont.)
sequence to prepare students to sing, to listen, to learn. Provide connection to DeKalb piece and initiation of rehearsal/learning process.

T-15　Vocal and Choral Fundamentals in Educational Context
Due: Written Warm-up Plan with Connection to Literature
In-Class Presentations: Warm-up Plan and Beginning of Rehearsal; Videotape. Presentation must incorporate National Achievement Standard(s) and methods of engaging the students in the learning process.
Assigned Reading: Brinson, Ch. 8, pp. 141–54

Th-17　Music Education in the Choral Classroom; Instructional Technology
In-Class: Individual/Small Group Work on Technology Mini Projects
Due: Literature Collection 1; In-Class and DeKalb Chorus Selections

T-22　Vocal and Choral Fundamentals and Solo/Ensemble Preparation
In-School Presentation: Present Warm-up Sequence and Videotape or Rehearse Solo/Ensemble Students. *Journal* throughout this process!

Th-24　Vocal and Choral Fundamentals and Solo/Ensemble Preparation
In-School Presentation: Present Warm-up Sequence and Videotape or Rehearse Solo/Ensemble Students. *Journal* throughout this process!
Due: Video Review and Reflection (In-School Teaching)

T-29　*In-School Presentation:* Present Warm-up Sequence and Videotape or Rehearse Solo/Ensemble Students. *Journal* throughout this process!
Due: Video Review and Reflection (In-School Teaching)

March
Th-2　Vocal and Choral Fundamentals and Solo/Ensemble Preparation
In-School Assignment: Adjudicate Solo and Ensemble Presentations
Due: Video Review and Reflection (In-School Teaching)
Assigned Reading: Brinson, Ch. 5 and 6

Sat-4　Solo and Ensemble Festival; Sycamore High School—*Attendance Required*

T-7　Music Education in the Choral Classroom; Repertoire and Programming
Discuss and Apply: Brinson, Ch. 6
Due: Midterm Projects

Th-9　Music Education in the Choral Classroom; Crone Middle School
Special Guests: Crone Middle School Chorus and Anne Pugliese, educator
In-class: Questions and Discussion
Journal during and after this special presentation!

Spring Break

T-21　Music Education in the Choral Classroom; Repertoire, Programming, Curriculum
Discuss: Brinson, Ch. 5 and 6
Apply: Final Project

Th-23　Music Education in the Choral Classroom; Musical Literacy
Review: Brinson, Ch. 10, pp. 197–208
In-Class: Discuss, Apply, and Generate Ideas from Comprehensive Musicianship Perspective
Due: Literature Collection 2; Selections for Final Project
Assigned Reading: Brinson, Ch. 4

T-28   Music Education in the Choral Classroom; Authentic and Portfolio Assessment
        Discuss and Apply: Brinson, Ch. 4
        In-class: View and discuss Arts PROPEL video (excerpts)

Th-30   Vocal and Choral Fundamentals and Large Group Contest Preparation
        In-School Presentation: Present Warm-up Sequence and Videotape or Rehearse sectional.
                        Journal throughout this process!

April
T-4   Vocal and Choral Fundamentals and Large Group Contest Preparation
        In-School Presentation: Present Warm-up Sequence and Videotape or Rehearse sectional.
                        Journal throughout this process!
        Due: Video Review and Reflection (In-School Teaching)
        Assigned Reading: "Religious Music in the Schools;"
                        Reynolds, "Sacred Music" in *MEJ*, Nov. 1984, pp. 29–33.
                        Gilbert, "Sacred Music in Public Schools," "ACDA Policy Statement,"
                        Sekulow, "Christmas Observations in Public Schools," in ACDA *Choral
                        Journal*, Dec. 1993, pp. 4–5 & 52–54.
                        Smith, "Letter to the Editor" in ACDA *Choral Journal*, Feb. 1994, p. 4.

Th-6   Music Education in the Choral Classroom; Plurality, Sacred Music, and Other Critical Values
        Discuss: Assigned Readings Above (First hour)
        Vocal and Choral Fundamentals and Large-Group Contest Preparation
        In-School Assignment: Present Warm-up Sequence and Videotape. Adjudicate Large-Group
                        Presentations (Second hour)
        Due: Video Review and Reflection (In-School Teaching)
        Assigned Reading: Brinson, Ch. 2

Sat-8: IMEA Large-Group Contest; Harvard High School

T-11   Music Education in the Choral Classroom; Recruitment and Retention
        Discuss: Brinson, Ch. 2
        Due: Video Review and Reflection (In-School Teaching)
        Assigned Readings: Brinson, Ch. 9
                        Apfelstadt; "Musical Thinking in the Choral Rehearsal" in *Dimensions of
                        Musical Thinking* (Ch. 8) (Reserve)

Th-13   Music Education in the Choral Classroom; Learning Environments and Educational Priorities
        Discuss and Apply Assigned Readings Above
        Due: Literature Collection 3; Selections for Final Project

T-18   Music Education in the Choral Classroom; Learning Environments and Educational Priorities
        Focus: Planning; Strategies and Procedures; Instructional Representations
        In-Class Presentation: Rehearsal/Learning Sequence.
                        Prepare and present fifteen-minute rehearsal sequence (typed).
                        • explicitly incorporate National Achievement Standard(s) within com-
                          prehensive Musicianship Approach, including ideas from Brinson and
                          Apfelstadt
                        • facilitate engaged learning
                        • videotape for self-assessment

Th-20   Music Education in the Choral Classroom; Learning Environments and Educational Priorities
        Focus: Planning; Strategies and Procedures; Instructional Representations

Th-20   *In-Class Presentation:* Rehearsal/Learning Sequence
(cont.)   Prepare and present fifteen-minute rehearsal sequence (typed).
                                           • explicitly incorporate National Achievement Standard(s) within com-
                                             prehensive Musicianship Approach, including ideas from Brinson and
                                             Apfelstadt
                                           • facilitate engaged learning
                                           • videotape for self-assessment
         Due: Video Review and Reflection (In-Class Teaching)

T-25   Music Education in the Choral Classroom; Learning Environments and Educational Priorities
         Focus: Planning; Strategies and Procedures; Instructional Representations
         In-Class Presentation: Rehearsal/Learning Sequence (cont.)
                                           Prepare and present twenty-minute rehearsal sequence (typed).
                                           Extension of previously introduced piece and inclusion of new selection:
                                           • explicitly incorporate National Achievement Standard(s) within com-
                                             prehensive Musicianship Approach, including ideas from Brinson and
                                             Apfelstadt
                                           • facilitate engaged learning
                                           • videotape for self-assessment
         Due: Video Review and Reflection (In-Class Teaching)

Th-27   Music Education in the Choral Classroom; Learning Environments and Educational Priorities
         Focus: Planning; Strategies and Procedures; Instructional Representations
         In-Class Presentation: Rehearsal/Learning Sequence (cont.)
                                           Prepare and present twenty-minute rehearsal sequence (typed).
                                           Extension of previously introduced piece and inclusion of new selection:
                                           • explicitly incorporate National Achievement Standard(s) within com-
                                             prehensive Musicianship Approach, including ideas from Brinson and
                                             Apfelstadt
                                           • facilitate engaged learning
                                           • videotape for self-assessment
         Due: Video Review and Reflection (In-Class Teaching), Course Notebook and Portfolio
         Assigned Readings: Brinson, Ch. 12
                                           Lee, "Selecting, Staging, and Singing a Show," and Bogar, "From the
                                           Drama Director's Chair" in *MEJ,* Sept. 1983, pp. 41–48. (Course Notebook)

May
T-2   Jazz/Show Choirs, Musical Productions
         Discuss: Assigned Readings Above
         Due: Video Review and Reflection (In-Class Teaching)
         Assigned Readings: Brinson, Ch. 13
                                           "Setting the Record Straight: Give and Take on the National Standards for
                                           Arts Education, Part I." ACDA *Choral Journal,* Nov. 1995, pp. 17–24.
                                           (Course Notebook)

Th-4   Advocacy; Professionalism; and Organizational/Administrative "Nuts and Bolts"
         Discuss: Assigned Readings Above
         Due: Final Project

T-9   8–9:50 a.m. *Final Project Presentations*

MUE 445: Choral Methods
Nolan W. Long
University of North Dakota
Fall 2002–2003

Credit:	3 semester hours
Time:	Tuesday, Thursday: 9–10:30
Instructor:	Mr. Nolan W. Long
Office:	Campus Box 7125, Hughes Fine Arts Center
Phone:	701-777-2814
E-mail:	nolan.long@und.nodak.edu

Required Texts

Brinson, B. (1996). *Choral music, methods, and materials: Developing successful choral programs (Grades 5–12)*. New York: Schirmer Books.

Ehmann, W., & Haaseman, F. (1981). *Voice building for choirs*. Chapel Hill, NC: Hinshaw Music.

Ehret, W. (1959). *The choral conductor's handbook*. Milwaukee: Edward B. Marks Company.

Jorgensen, N. S., & Pfeiler, C. (1995). *Things they never taught you in choral methods*. Milwaukee: Hal Leonard.

Suggested Activities

- Join ACDA (American Choral Directors Association). Includes subscription to *The Choral Journal*
- Attend state, regional, and national ACDA conventions
- Attend state, regional, and national MENC conventions
- Attend as many choral rehearsals/concerts of junior/senior high schools or colleges as possible
- Attend a madrigal dinner
- Attend a choral music reading clinic

Course Description

This course is designed to prepare prospective teachers for the choral music classroom, elementary through high school. It will address both musical and non-musical aspects of being a choral teacher, including such things as the development and evaluation of a choral curriculum, behavior management in rehearsal, planning/organizing/directing rehearsals, choosing/programming music, seating, the changing voice, directing the musical theater and the madrigal dinner, and managing the overall program. Students will finalize their philosophy of music education to provide a solid foundation for their future as music educators.

The lab component of the course will include field experience in a variety of settings and schools; students will evaluate those experiences, both positively and negatively, for their own growth and understanding as a choral music educator.

MUE 445 is a final "capstone" course in the music education sequence. The course goals and objectives highlight the philosophy of the division of education to prepare informed, thoughtful, and sensitive teachers. The course will increase the knowledge of choral/vocal professional educators in their specialty; time in observation, discussion, and reflection will occur as students learn to assimilate and use their choral/vocal knowledge. Critical thinking and decision-making processes will be stressed. Students will use the current research in music education available in books, periodicals, and on the Internet. The professional and ethical responsibilities of a teacher, school/community relations, and values will be addressed.

COURSE GOALS
- To provide students with an understanding of various philosophies of music education specific to choral music
- To provide students with the musical knowledge and skills necessary to successfully lead a choral program at the elementary, intermediate, and secondary levels
- To provide students with the administrative and class management skills necessary to successfully lead a choral program at the elementary, intermediate, or secondary levels

COURSE OBJECTIVES
Students will
- Formulate their philosophy of choral music education
- Learn how to recruit and retain singers to/for their programs
- Learn how to audition choral singers
- Understand the placement of voices and seating arrangements
- Learn and identify how, when, and where to select music
- Learn how to create music and administrative files
- Explore general programming tips and put together sample programs of their own
- Learn how to do musical analysis and score preparation
- Learn how to plan a rehearsal using a simple flowchart and detailed lesson plans
- Develop strategies for behavior management in the choral rehearsal
- Discuss and practice the various techniques/musicianship skills necessary for a choral program
- Understand other specialized choral/vocal training including directing pop/show choir ensembles and musical productions and madrigal dinners
- Learn what it takes to manage a choral program, including discussions on such topics as choral parent organizations, student leadership, budget, scheduling, performance attire, equipment, etc.
- Meet, talk to, and get to know the music teachers, administrators, staff persons, and other teachers in the school
- Observe the musical/nonmusical characteristics of learners at the elementary, middle, and secondary school levels
- Observe the teaching methods practiced by certified choral music teachers
- Identify specific ways that classroom management is handled in classes observed
- Identify specific ways the musical goals of the rehearsal were/were not accomplished
- Observe how the classroom environment and physical arrangement of the room helps/hinders the learning process
- Look for evidence and ways to apply what is learned in MUE 320

COURSE REQUIREMENTS
- Complete assigned readings prior to the next class session
- Participate in class discussions
- Be prepared to sing/conduct/demonstrate and/or play piano in class
- Successfully complete all mini-projects assigned
- Fill out observation sheets for each observation
- Keep all written materials and handouts in a notebook. The notebook should be neat and organized so that it can be used not only for reflection on what has been learned and observed, but also as an important reference for the future

GRADING PROCEDURES
Daily grades will be taken for class participation. This is not a lecture course; therefore, all individuals are expected to contribute to the classroom discussion.

- There will be daily assignments and four tests
- Grades will be based upon the following:
  - MUE 445—Choral Methods
    - 50%   Tests (4)
    - 40%   Daily mini-projects and assignments
    - 10%   In-class participation and attendance
  - MUE 445—lab
    - 20%   Observation Sheets
    - 20%   Notebooks
    - 60%   Class attendance/participation

Grading Scale

A: 100–94   B: 93–85   C: 84–78   D: 77–70   F: 69–0

While it is possible to pass the course with a 70%, the instructor feels that a prospective teacher should earn no lower than a B in the course. Meeting the requirements of this course are important and help to show tangible evidence of the student's abilities as a future choral music educator.

COURSE POLICIES

- Attendance is mandatory and is necessary for successful completion of this course. Excuses include (1) college-sponsored activities (e.g., music touring) when the office of the Vice President for Academic Affairs excuses the student, (2) the student is seriously ill and misses more than this class for illness, and (3) documented emergencies. In all cases, the instructor must be notified *prior* to the class (in the case of an unexpected emergency, please contact the instructor as soon as possible). An unreported absence is considered unexcused, regardless of the reason, and will affect the student's grade. Three unexcused absences are considered grounds for failure of the course. After the second unexcused absence, notice will be sent to the student, the student's academic advisor, the Music Department Chairperson, and the Vice President for Academic Affairs.

- Make-up material will only be given if the absence is excused. In this case, all material must be presented *prior* to the next class period.

- Assignments are due and tests are to be taken on the day indicated. No written assignments, observations, or other assignments will be accepted late. Typed observation sheets are due at the next class meeting.

REFERENCE/SUPPLEMENTAL READING

Articles and books as assigned.

Ades, H. (1983). *Choral arranging.* Delaware Water Gap, PA: Shawnee Press, Inc.

Boyd, J. (1970). *Rehearsal guide for the choral director.* Champaign, IL: Mark Foster Music Co.

Collins, D. L. (1999). *Teaching choral music.* Upper Saddle River, NJ: Prentice Hall.

Collins, D. L. (1981). *The cambiata concept: A comprehensive philosophy and methodology of teaching music to adolescents.* Conway, AR: Cambiata Press.

Cooper, I. (1970). *Teaching junior high school music: General Music and Vocal Program.* Boston: Allyn and Bacon.

Crowther, D. S. (1981). *Teaching choral concepts: Simple lesson plans and teaching aids for in-rehearsal choir instruction.* Bountiful, Utah: Horizon Publishers.

Decker, H. A., & Herford, J. (1973). *Choral conducting: A symposium.* Englewood Cliffs, NJ: Prentice Hall.

Garretson, R. (1993). *Choral music: History, style, and performance practice.* Englewood Cliffs, NJ: Prentice Hall.

Green, E. A. (1987). *The modern conductor.* Englewood Cliffs, NJ: Prentice Hall.

Hawkins, M. B. (1976). *An annotated inventory of distinctive choral literature for performance at the high school level.* Lawton, OK: American Choral Directors Association.

Hoffer, C. (1985). *Teaching music in the secondary schools.* Belmont, CA: Wadsworth Publishing
 Company.

Lamb, G. H. (1979). *Choral techniques.* Dubuque, IA: Wm. C. Brown.

Robinson, R., & Winold, A. (1992). *The choral experience: Literature, materials, and methods.* Prospect
 Heights, IL: Waveland Press, Inc.

Ulrich, H. (1973). *A survey of choral music.* New York: Harcourt Brace Jovanovich, Inc.

Helpful Web site: Changing Voices: http://sites.entscape.net/cambiatapress

SCHEDULE– MUSIC 445

Day 1, Tues., Aug. 27 Intro., Distribute Syllabus, **Philosophy of Choral Music Education**
 Assignment due Thurs., 8/31: Brinson: Ch.1
 Assignment due Thurs., 9/1: mini-project p. 14, #1 & 3
  Jorgenson pp. 76–104

Day 2, Thurs., Aug. 29 Continue **Philosophy of Choral Music Education**
 Assignment for next class: finalize/rewrite philosophy
  Brinson: Ch. 2, 3 (pp. 29–43) and #3
  Jorgensen: Ch. 1, 2, 6

Day 3, Tues., Sept. 3 **Recruitment of Singers, Auditions**
 Assignment for next class: Jorgensen: Ch. 4, 5
  Brinson: mini-project p. 53 #1, 2, 3

Day 4, Thurs., Sept. 5 Ensembles Retreat—no class

Day 5, Tues., Sept. 10 Continue
 Assignment for next class: Brinson: Mini-project p. 27 #1 or 2

Day 6, Thurs., Sept. 12 Continue
 Assignment for next class: Brinson: Ch. 4, Mini-project p. 27 #3
  Ehret: Ch. 7, 12
  Blend Handout

Day 7, Tues., Sept. 17 **Blending/Tone Quality**
 Assignment for next class: Ehmann: pp. 3–22

Day 8, Thurs., Sept. 19 Continue
 Assignment for next class: Ehmann: pp. 24–59

Day 9, Tues., Sept. 24 Continue

Day 10, Thurs., Sept. 26 Test #1
 Assignment for next class: Brinson: Ch. #3, pp. 43–53

Day 11, Tues., Oct., 1 **Seating Arrangements**
 Assignment for next class: Create seating chart: assignment of voices

Day 12, Thurs., Oct. 3 Continue
 Assignment for next class: Robinson: Ch. 11 (library reserve)
  Ehmann: pp. 68–75

Day 13, Tues., Oct. 8 **Choral History/Performance Practice: Renaissance**
 Assignment for next class: Robinson:Ch. 12 (library reserve)
  Ehmann: pp. 76–78

Day 14,Thurs., Oct. 10 **Choral History/Performance Practice: Baroque**
 Assignment for next class: Robinson: Ch. 13 (library reserve)
  Ehmann: pp. 78–81

Day 15, Tues., Oct. 15   **Choral History/Performance Practice: Classical**
                          Assignment for next class: Robinson: Ch. 14, 15 (library reserve)
                                        Ehmann: pp. 82–91

Day 16, Thurs., Oct. 17   **Choral History/Performance Practice: Romantic & 20th Century**
                          Assignment for next class: Brinson: Ch. 9
                                        Hoffer: Ch 15, 16 (library reserve)

Day 17, Tues., Oct. 22   **Behavior Management in Rehearsal**

Day 18, Thurs., Oct. 24   Test #2
                          Assignment for next class: Jorgenson: Ch. 3
                                        Brinson: Ch. 5, Mini-project p. 89, #2, 3
                                        Handout

Day 19, Tues., Oct. 29   **What is Quality Choral Music?**
                          Assignment for next class: Brinson: Ch. 6
                                        Ehret: Ch 14, 16

Day 20, Thurs., Oct. 31   **Choosing/Programming Choral Music**
                          Assignment for next class: Brinson: Ch. 11
                                        Brinson: mini-project p. 104, #3 & 4

Day 21, Tues., Nov. 5   **The Changing Voice**
                          Assignment for next class: Handout
                                        Brinson mini-project p. 104, #2: for changing voices
                                        Ehret: Ch. 8, 9, 10, 11

Day 22, Thurs., Nov. 7   **Choral Diction**

Day 23, Tues., Nov. 12   **Choral Diction**

Day 24, Thurs., Nov. 14   Test #3
                          Assignment for next class: Brinson: Ch. 7

Day 25, Tues., Nov. 19   **Score Preparation**
                          Assignment for next class: Brinson: mini-project p. 126, #1, 2 & 4, Ch. 8
                                        Ehret: Ch. 3, 4, 5, 6

Day 26, Thurs., Nov. 22   **Planning the Rehearsal**
                          Assignment for next class: Brinson: mini-project p. 152, #1
                                        Ehret: Ch. 1, 2
                                        Handout

THANKSGIVING VACATION

Day 27, Tues., Dec. 3   **Madrigal Dinners**
                          Assignment for next class: Brinson: Ch. 12
                          Ehret: Ch. 13
                          Handout

Day 28, Thurs., Dec. 5   **Musical Theatre Production**
                          Assignment for next class: Brinson Ch. 9, 13
                                        Jorgenson: Ch. 7, 8, 9, 10

Day 29, Tues., Dec. 10   **Choral Administration**

FINAL EXAM: test #4

INSTRUMENTAL METHODS

MUSIC 57-360,860: BRASS METHODS
DR. LEWIS H. STROUSE
CARNEGIE MELLON UNIVERSITY
FALL 2000

Instructor: Lewis H. Strouse D.A.
Office: CFA 162, x1432, 2372
E-mail: Strouse+@Andrew.cmu.edu

REQUIRED TEXTS
Colwell & Goolsby (1992). *The Teaching of Instrumental Music.*
Pearson (1993). *Standard of Excellence Comprehensive Band Method,* Book 1—Conductor's Score.
Strouse. Course packet for *Brass Methods.*
Additional materials may be provided in class or placed on library reserve.

COURSE FOCUS
Introduction to brass instrument technique and pedagogy

MATERIALS
2" notebook (suggest slant-ring)
Notebook index sheets/dividers for sectioning of course notebook content
VHS tape

DESCRIPTION
This course is designed to develop an understanding of brass playing techniques and related pedagogy, with special attention to beginning-level instruction.

DETAILED STATEMENT OF INTENT
The main purpose of the course is to bring students to a satisfactory level of competence in regard to
- an understanding of brass instrument pedagogy designed for individual and ensemble instruction through
- the development of an elementary brass playing technique on trumpet, horn, trombone, and baritone, and the preparation of assigned readings leading to
- the presentation of demonstration lessons for a heterogeneous ensemble class

EVALUATION
The final evaluation estimate will comprise the grade average obtained from the midterm and final comprehensive exams (40%); brass score for beginning band (10%); four playing tests (30%); a grade average of four technique reports and the course notebook (10%); and one demonstration lesson (10%). See the "Course Evaluation Outline" for specific descriptions of evaluation areas.
Exams will be rescheduled only in cases of personal or family emergencies. Grades are not curved.

Grading scheme for this course:

A = 90–100   B = 80–89   C = 70–79   D = 60–69   F = 0–59

Letter grades earned for the brass score, technique reports, and demonstration lesson will be translated as follows:

A+ = 100	B+ = 89	C+ = 79	D+ = 69	F = 0–59
A = 95	B = 85	C = 75	D = 65	
A- = 91	B- = 81	C- = 71	D- = 61	

The final grade for this course reflects a level of professional discipline as well as an understanding of course information and skill. Attendance variations will be reflected in grading (see below).

STATEMENT OF PROFESSIONAL STANDARDS

Class Attendance. Class activities and discussion are intended to clarify and reinforce elements of course content. Regular and prompt class attendance is of paramount importance. Two absences will be permitted. Each absence beyond the limit of two will lower the next playing-test grade by ten points. *Students anticipating some problem with regular class attendance should speak with Dr. Strouse.*

Instruction. Class instruction will derive from a mixture of lecture, discussion of assigned readings, and discussion of problems related to individual practice and in-class performance. Students will be expected to demonstrate solo and ensemble playing skills at each class session.

Instrument Exchange. Prior to each instrument exchange class, it is the responsibility of the student to clean his or her instrument. Following each instrument exchange, class members will introduce their "old" instruments to the new assignees and demonstrate proper assembly, holding and finger positions, proper embouchure formation, and the first tones.

Class Preparation. Motto: "Panic at the beginning and relax at the end!" (i.e., complete new assignments as soon as possible so that your mind will have ample time to assimilate the learning of new information and skills).

Practicing. With regard to brass instrument performance, a practice routine of 10–15 minutes per day is the typical requirement for elementary beginners. The primary components of playing skill that you are developing include physical skills of embouchure muscle strength, finger dexterity, and breath control. Acquiring these skills requires regular, systematic practice. Further information regarding practice will be presented in class; however, it is important not to exceed these brief practice periods prescribed for the early stages of instrument playing. Excessive or careless playing can damage the embouchure and require several days of rest before regular practice can be resumed. Students should practice their exercises with a metronome and insist on on-time attacks via air control.

Overall Class Preparation. Prepare study-guide questions for the Colwell and Goolsby chapters, course packet material, and assigned reserve readings as due dates are indicated in the course schedule. Preparation of the readings is essential to reinforce lecture information and understand practical applications discussed in class. The satisfactory completion of focused practice, assigned readings, and a hearty enthusiasm for class participation will play an important part in your successful completion of the course. If you find yourself struggling in a particular area, see Dr. Strouse as soon as possible.

Late work. Assigned reading and written work are discussed as part of class instruction. Failure to meet a due date and contribute informed discussion handicaps learning for you and your classmates.

Micro-Teaching. Beginning with the Instrument #2 section of the course, students will be randomly chosen to lead the class in playing exercises and diagnosing problems with playing technique.

COURSE SCHEDULE
(**) Indicates Pedagogical Protocol
8/29   Course Introduction.

Instrument #1.
8/31   Topics: Screening Beginners; Instrument Assignments; Instrument Loan Form and Card; Embouchure Formation and Use of Tonguing Syllable to Focus Air Flow; Mouthpiece Tone; Composing Unit Objectives (A12).

9/5 *Standard of Excellence,* pp. 58–66.
Topics: Mouthpiece Placement; Instrument Assembly and Holding Position, Posture, First Tone, Tongue Tip Placement; Basic Instrument Care (C12-13).

9/7 *Standard of Excellence,* pp. 74–83.
Topics: Beginner Warm-ups; Technique Report (A4); Topic-Specific Delivery Strategies—Motivation** (A6); Playing In Tune**; Main Tuning Slide.

9/12 *Standard of Excellence,* pp. 84–95.
Topics: Introducing A New Element** (A3); Trade-offs; Solfège**; Kohut, "Teaching Class Lessons" (On Reserve)—complete the study guide (B1) for this article; Introducing Duet Playing.**

9/14 *Standard of Excellence,* pp. 96–107.
Due: Technique Report #1.
Topics: Listening across the Ensemble**; Kodály Rhythm Chant**; Basic Brass Acoustics (C16); Harmonic Series (A25-26); Reviewing an Exercise before Playing.**
C&G, Chapter 15, "Principles for Brass."

9/19 *Standard of Excellence,* pp. 108–17.
Topics: Tuning the Instrument and Ensemble** (A8-9); Harmonic Lip Slurs; Trombone Legato.
C&G, Chapter 8, "An Overview of Brass Instruments."

9/21 *Standard of Excellence,* pp. 118–27.
Topics: Transposition Exercises for Brass (C15); Scoring for Beginning Brass (A18).

9/26 **Quiz: Chromatic Scale and Fingerings.**
Instrument Exchange.

Instrument #2 (Micro Teaching begins)
9/28 *Standard of Excellence,* pp. 58–83.
Topics: Vibrato—C&G, pp. 135–37; Student Practice Chart (A5).

10/3 *Standard of Excellence,* pp.84–95.
Topic: Horn.
C&G, Chapter 16, "The Horn"; Stringing French Horn Rotary Valves (C14).

10/5 *Standard of Excellence,* pp. 96–107.
Topic: Trombone—C&G, Chapter 18, "The Trombone."

10/10 *Standard of Excellence,* pp. 108–17.
Topic: Advanced Tonguing Technique (B2-8); Studio Lesson Plan** (A13); Half-beat Level Counting** (A7).
Due: Technique Report #2.

10/12 *Standard of Excellence,* pp. 118–27.
Topic: Trumpet and Cornet—C&G, Chapter 17, "The Trumpet and Cornet."

10/17 Quiz: Chromatic Scale and Fingerings.
Instrument Exchange.

10/19 Midterm Exam.

Instrument #3 (Micro Teaching continues)
10/24 *Standard of Excellence,* pp. 58–83.
Topics: Demonstration Lesson Description (A14-17); Ensemble Class Format** (A11). Mutes.

10/26 *Standard of Excellence,* pp. 84–95.
Topics: Recommended Equipment (A23-24); Mouthpieces (C&G, pp. 336-43).

10/31 *Standard of Excellence,* pp. 96–107.

10/31 Topics: Baritone/Euphonium. C&G, Chapter 19, "The Baritone and Euphonium".
(cont.) **Due: Technique Report #3.**

11/2 *Standard of Excellence*, pp. 108–17.
Topic: Band Method Evaluation (A19-22); Chamber Ensemble Project; Harmonic Lip Slur.

11/7 *Standard of Excellence*, pp. 118–27.
Topic: Tuba. C&G, Chapter 20, "The Tuba."
Due: Brass Scoring Project.

11/9 *Standard of Excellence*, pp. 129–47.
Topic: Reading Brass Scoring Projects.

11/14 **Quiz: Chromatic Scale and Fingerings.**
Instrument Exchange.

Instrument #4 (Demonstration Lessons begin)

11/16 *Standard of Excellence*, pp. 58–83.
Topic: Demonstration Lesson.

11/21 No Class (PMEA District #1, Professional Development Workshop)

11/23 No Class (Thanksgiving Break)

11/28 *Standard of Excellence*, pp. 84–95.
Topic: Demonstration Lesson.

11/30 *Standard of Excellence*, pp. 96–107.
Topic: Demonstration Lesson.
Due: Technique Report #4.

12/5 *Standard of Excellence*, pp. 108–17.
Topic: "Trombone Slide Technique" worksheet (C10); Demonstration Lesson.

12/7 *Standard of Excellence*, pp. 118–27.
Topic: Demonstration Lesson.
Due: Course Notebook.

12/12 **Quiz: Chromatic Scale and Fingerings.**
Instrument Turn-in.

TBA Comprehensive Final Examination.

COURSE EVALUATION OUTLINE

Performance. Horn, Trumpet, Trombone, Baritone.
Playing will be graded on the basis of holding position, hand position, embouchure formation, accurate pitch and rhythm, fingering accuracy, steady and appropriate tempo, intonation, tone, articulation, and musicality. Three points will be deducted for each error. The quiz must be performed within a time limit, determined, in part, by the number of students in the class. An error will be scored each time a student "starts over."

Evaluation Components

(1) In-class Playing (20%). Performing prepared exercises from class method demonstrating (a) detached tonguing, (b) legato tonguing, (c) harmonic lip slur, and (d) trombone legato, as assigned.

(2) Chromatic Scale Quiz (40%). Performing a memorized mid-range chromatic scale, range of perfect fifth (student's choice), half-note per pitch, slur-2 @ M.M. quarter = 72, ascending and descending.

(3) Fingering Quiz (40%). A written test in which you will be asked to identify the common fingerings of ten random pitches within the following ranges and within a time limit of one minute: Horn (G3-G5), Trumpet (F#3-G5), Trombone (E2-F4), Baritone/euphonium (E2-F4). Consult the fingering chart in your method book for the common fingerings.

Midterm Exam. A written exam covering all course material assigned prior to the midterm exam date. Study guides are provided for the the Colwell & Goolsby chapters in the course packet.

Projects.

Brass Methods Course Notebook. Your Brass Methods Course Notebook is to be organized into labeled sections by using a set of notebook dividers. In professional practice, your notebook will serve as a key reference for your continuing education in brass instruments. To complete the Course Notebook project, divide your notebook into the following sections:

    (1) Syllabus and Course Schedule

    (2) Course Packet subdivided as per the Course Packet Index categories

    (3) Technique Reports and Student Practice Charts

    (4) Demonstration Lesson Plan

    (5) A minimum of three published journal articles, personalized, on brass technique and related pedagogy (To personalize an article, underline or highlight certain portions of particular import.)

    (6) Reference Section: includes class handouts distributed during the semester as well as a personal collection of information you may view as useful in teaching brass

    (7) You may include additional sections.

Four Technique Reports. Self-assessment of playing technique on each brass instrument with a diagnosis for each problem and a prescribed remedy.

Brass Score for Beginning Band. See "Brass Scoring Project" in CP.

Demonstration Lesson. See "Demonstration Lesson Description" in CP.

Final Exam. A comprehensive examination covering all course material.

SELECTED BIBLIOGRAPHY

Many thanks to CMU Professors Abelson, Erickson, McCulloh, and Pasquarelli for their assistance in the compilation of this bibliography.

General

Farkas, P. (1962). *The art of brass playing.* Bloomington, IN: Brass Publications. (hard)

Whitener, S. (1997). A complete guide to brass instruments and pedagogy. New York: Schirmer Books. (paper)

Horn

Farkas, P. (1956). *The art of French horn playing.* Evanston, IL: Summy-Birchard. (hard)

Schuller, G. (1971). *Horn technique.* London: Oxford University Press.

Yancich, M. (1971). *A practical guide to horn playing.* Rochester, NY: Wind Music.

Cornet, Trumpet

Bach, V. (1969). *The art of trumpet playing.* Elkhart, IN: Vincent Bach Corporation.

Davidson, L. (1970). *Trumpet techniques.* Rochester, NY: Wind Music.

Johnson, K. (1981). *The art of trumpet playing.* Ames, IA: Iowa State University Press. (paper).

Smithers, D. (1973). *The music and history of the baroque trumpet before 1721.* London: J.M. Dent.

Trombone

Fink, R. H. (1977). *The trombonist's handbook: A complete guide to teaching and playing the trombone.* Athens, OH: Accura. (hard)

Kleinhammer, E. (1963). *The art of trombone playing.* Evanston, IL: Summy-Birchard.

Wick, D. (1975). *Trombone technique.* London: Oxford University Press.

Tuba

Bevan, C. (1978). *The tuba family.* New York: Scribner's.

Griffiths, J. R. (1980). *The low brass guide.* Hackensack, NJ: Jerona Music.

Sorenson, R. A. (1972). *Tuba pedagogy: A study of selected method books, 1840–1911* (Doctoral dissertation, University of Colorado). UM 73-1832.

Stewart, M. D. (Ed.). (1987). *Arnold Jacobs The legacy of a master.* Northfield, IL: *The Instrumentalist.*

MED 241: Brass Methods
Dr. Lynn Cooper
Asbury College
Spring 2001

Instructor: Dr. Lynn Cooper
                  McCreless 123 (Office hours posted)
Credits: 1 credit
Time: Mon. at 8 a.m.

Required Textbooks

Introducing The Instruments. Preliminary Book Text and Picture Full Score, James Froseth, pub. by GIA. Publications.
Teaching Brass. Wayne Bailey et al., pub. by McGraw-Hill.

Objectives

By the end of the semester, the student will be able to play two of the five basic brass instruments with a characteristic tone and appropriate technique. The student will be able to teach others to play with correct embouchure, hand position, posture, breath support, and characteristic tone. The student will know the ranges, basic fingerings, transpositions, teaching/playing techniques for all five of the basic brass instruments.

Instructional Methods

The class will be conducted in a demonstration-laboratory fashion. Students will also be given teaching assignments.

Teaching Test

You will have a Teaching Test for each of the two instruments you play in class. You will be given a 15-minute period in which to teach a non-player how to form the embouchure, assemble the instrument, use the correct posture, arm, hand, and instrument position, and produce the first tone on the instrument. A written timed lesson plan must be submitted at the beginning of the teaching test.

Teaching Guides

Teaching Guides for all five basic brass instruments will be developed. These guides are to be in outline form and cover embouchure, instrument assembly, positions (instrument, body, hand), breath support, special performance problems, desirable playing characteristics, and instrument care. Use material from Froseth, Bailey, class discussions, and your own readings. Do not simply copy Froseth but use the material as a guideline for your own work. Collaboration on this project is suggested.

Technology

The recently approved Kentucky New Teacher Standard related to technology is met in this course by the use of a word-processing program (such as Microsoft *Word*) for most assignments.

Attendance

Only one unexcused absence is permitted—each additional unexcused absence will lower your grade 20 points. Three tardies equal one unexcused absence. Tests or quizzes missed because of an unexcused absence may not be made up.

GRADING

The grade in Brass Methods is determined by the following:

Class Attendance and Participation	50 pts.	
Playing Tests (2 @ 20 pts)	40 pts.	**Grade Scale:**
Written Tests (2 @ 20 pts)	40 pts.	91–100% = A
Quizzes (playing and written—4 @ 5)	20 pts.	81– 90% = B
Teaching Tests (2 @25 pts)	50 pts.	71– 80% = C
Teaching Guides (5 @ 10 pts)	50 pts.	61– 70% = D
Final Written Exam	<u>50 pts.</u>	0– 60% = F
	300 pts.	

COURSE OUTLINE

Students will play two instruments during the semester. All students will play cornet/trumpet and trombone unless their major instrument is one of those instruments. There will be regular short playing and fingering quizzes.

Date	Class Activity	Assignment (day assigned)
Jan. 15	Introduction and Assign Instrument #1 (Cornet/Trumpet or Trombone) Embouchure/Positions/Assembly	*TB*, Ch. 1–3 & 6 or 8 Froseth readings* for Instr. #1
Jan. 22	Review and Discuss Readings Begin Exercises	*TB*, Ch. 4 & 5. Memorize fingering chart in Froseth for Instr. #1.
Jan. 29	Fingering Quiz: Instr. #1 Continue Exercises	Exercises
Feb. 5	Continue Exercises and Discuss Readings	Exercises
Feb. 12	Playing Quiz: Instr. #1 Continue Exercises and scales.	Exercises and Scales
Feb. 19	Written Test: Instr. #1 Continue Exercises & Scales	Exercises and scales T.G. #1 is due
Feb. 26	Playing Test: Instr. #1 Teaching Test #1 Assign Instrument #2	*TB*, Ch. 6 or 8 Froseth readings* for Instr. #2
Mar. 5	Instr. #2: Trombone or Cornet/Trumpet Embouchure/Positions/Assembly	Memorize fingering chart in Froseth* for Instr. #2
Mar. 12	Discuss Readings Review and Exercises National Standards in Beginning Band	Exercises Froseth, remain. readings* *TB*, remaining chapters
March 19–25—Spring Break		
Mar. 26	Fingering Quiz: Instr. #2 Continue Exercises and Scales	Exercises and Scales
Apr. 2	Playing Quiz: Instr. #2 Continue Exercises and Scales	Exercises and Scales

| Apr. 9 | Discuss Readings | Exercises and Scales |
| | Continue Exercises and Scales | T.G. #2 is due |

| April 16 | Easter Holiday | |

| Apr. 23 | Written Test: Instr. #2 | Exercises and Scales |
| | Exercises and Scales | |

April 30	Playing Test: Instr. #2	Prepare for Exam
	Teaching Test #2	T.G. #3, 4, 5 are due
	Clean and Return two instruments by Monday, May 7.	

Final Exam. May 8 (Tuesday) from 10:30 a.m. to 12:30 p.m. or TBA (because of String Methods). This will be a written exam covering all five of the basic brass instruments (including fingerings for the two instruments actually played).

*Froseth Readings. (all read pp. 2–3)
Cornet/Trumpet: 12, 26–28, 44–46, 72–73, 110–11, 141–42, 157, 166–69, 205, 226.
Horn: 13, 26–28, 47–49, 74–75, 112–13, 143, 152, 158–59, 170–71, 186–87, 206, 227.
Trombone: 15, 26–28, 53–55, 78–79, 117–19, 145, 164–65, 177–79, 208, 229.
Euphonium: 16, 26–28, 53–55, 78–79, 120–21, 146, 154, 161, 180–83, 209, 230–31.
Tuba: 17, 26–28, 57–59, 80–81, 122–23, 147, 155, 162–63, 184–85, 189, 210, 232–33.

MED 365: Elementary and Middle School Instrumental Music Methods

Dr. Lynn Cooper
Asbury College
Fall 2000

Instructor: Dr. Lynn Cooper
McCreless 123 (Office hours posted)
Credits: 2 credits
Time: Wed. & Fri. at 9 a.m.

Required Textbooks

(1) *A Sound Approach to Teaching Instrumentalists,* Stanley L. Schleuter, pub. by Schirmer Books.
(2) *Teacher's Guide to the Individualized Instructor,* James Froseth, pub. by GIA.
(3) *Preliminary Book, Teachers Book,* James Froseth, pub. by GIA.
(4) *The School Music Program: A New Vision,* MENC.
There is a $3.00 copy fee for this course. Please pay Mrs. Moore by Sept. 6.

Objectives

- The student will be able to discuss and/or demonstrate appropriate teaching techniques, strategies, and materials for elementary and middle school instrumental music programs
- The student will demonstrate an understanding and knowledge of music education history, significant philosophical positions, and contemporary music learning theory
- The student will develop skills in the additional non-musical activities needed to initiate and maintain a successful elementary and middle school instrumental music program

Instructional Methods

The class will be conducted in a lecture-demonstration-laboratory fashion. Students will be given opportunities to demonstrate appropriate teaching techniques and strategies during the various sections of the course.

Attendance and Participation

Participation in class discussion and demonstrations is a vital part of this class. Each student will teach various assignments to the class. Assignments are due at the beginning of class on the dates indicated. Late assignments are lowered one full grade for each day late. Regular attendance is assumed. Each unexcused absence past the second will result in the final grade's being lowered by a one-third grade. Three tardies will equal one unexcused absence. Tests, class teaching assignments, etc. missed during an unexcused absence may not be made up.

Technology

The recently approved Kentucky New Teacher Standard related to technology is met in a number of ways in this course. Most assignments require the use of a word-processing program (such as Microsoft *Word*). In addition, a major assignment (a recruiting presentation) uses *PowerPoint*.

Special Projects

Project 1. This project is due on or before Oct. 18.
Schedule a visit and interview with an elementary instrumental music teacher now in the field. This visit is to include an observation of at least one beginning instrumental class. Document the type of program, materials for teaching, schedules, equipment, facilities and the objectives that the program uses. Include a description of the instructional techniques, student's responses, etc. from the class observation.

Project 2. This project is due on or before Nov. 3.

Design and produce a recruiting presentation to be used with fifth-grade students and their parents. The presentation must include at least six screens in *PowerPoint*. Be prepared to give your presentation in class on the due date (10 minutes each).

Project 3. This project is due on or before Nov. 15.

Prepare (as a collaborative class project) a Physical Characteristics Checklist for each of the following instruments: flute, oboe, bassoon, clarinet, saxophone, horn, cornet/trumpet, trombone and euphonium, tuba, percussion, violin, viola, cello, and string bass. This should be a thorough but concise checklist of desirable and/or undesirable physical characteristics. Many resources are available in our library and from our college studio faculty.

Project 4. This project is due on or before Nov. 29.

Compare two of the newer band or orchestra beginning methods. Discuss content, layout, charts, pictures, features, starting notes, how special problems are handled, the teacher's book (is it in a series?), etc. Try to choose different materials than your colleagues so that you can share your findings with each other.

Project 5. This project is due on or before Dec. 6.

Turn in a notebook of typed class notes, assignments, and materials collected in class or at conferences, etc. The notebook is to be categorized and indexed. Include a blank comments page for my use at the beginning of the notebook. Include a written evaluation of the use of technology in this course. Neatness and thoroughness are very important.

GRADING

The final grade is determined by the following:

Project 1	25 pts.		
Project 2	25 pts.		
Project 3	25 pts.	**Grading Scale**	
Project 4	25 pts.	91% –100% = A	
Project 5	50 pts.	81%– 90% = B	
Class Assignments (5 @ 10)	50 pts.	71%– 80% = C	
Class Teaching (4–7 @ 10)	40+ pts.	61%– 70% = D	
Final Exam	50 pts.	0%– 60% = F	
Total possible points	290+		

Note. All assignments and projects are due at the beginning of class on the due date. Grades will be lowered one full grade for each day late.

COURSE OUTLINE

Some readings are on reserve in the Library. Others may be assigned.

Date	Class Discussion	Assignment (listed on the date assigned)
Aug. 23	Introduction/Syllabus	Schleuter: Pref., Ch. 1. H & J: Ch. 1 & 2
Aug. 25	Past and Current Practices I	Read articles assigned
Aug. 30	Past and Current Practices II	
Sept. 1	Past and Current Practices III	Assign. #1: p. 16, #9 (1–3 pages, typed) Schleuter: Ch. 2 (plus)
Sept. 6	The Process of Learning Music Philosophy of Music Ed. handouts	Assign. #1 is due Assign. #2: p. 39 (7, 8, or 9—one-page typed) Schleuter: Ch. 3; T.G.: pp. 2–14, 36, 49–50
Sept. 8	Teaching a Sense of Tonality I	Begin Project 1
Sept. 13	Teaching a Sense of Tonality II	Assign. 2 is due. Teaching Assignments
Sept. 15	Class Teaching Assignments	Schleuter: Ch. 4. T.G.: pp. 15–35, 37–48

Sept. 20	Teaching Rhythmic Feeling I	
Sept. 22	Teaching Rhythmic Feeling II	Teaching Assignments
Sept. 27	Class Teaching Assignments	Schleuter: Ch. 5
Sept. 29	Teaching Performance Skills	Teaching Assignments
Oct.4	Flash Card Teaching Assignments	Schleuter: Ch. 6. H & J: Ch. 8
Oct. 6	Some Aspects of the Teaching Process	Assign. #3: p. 175 (2 & 5, 1–2 typed pages) Schleuter: Ch. 7
Oct. 11	Assessment of Music Achievement and Music Aptitude	Cooper: Ch. 1
Oct. 13	The Role of the Beginning Program Types of Instructional Groupings	Assign. #3 is due
Oct. 18	Which Instruments Are Taught? Goals and Objectives	Project 1 is due Cooper: Ch. 2 Assign. #4: Cooper, Ch. 1, p. 15, #1 *or* 2
Oct. 20	Fall Break—no class	
Oct. 25	Recruiting the Beginning Class: Communication and Planning, Gathering Data, Recruiting Activities, Additional Resources	*Jump Right In* reading, Introduction (pp. 1–2) Begin Project 2
Oct. 27	Aptitude Tests. Retaining Students	Assign. #4 is due
Nov. 1	Review *Jump Right In* concepts	Cooper: Ch. 3
Nov. 3	Present *PowerPoint* Recruiting Project	Project 2 is due; Begin Project 3
Nov. 8	The Curriculum: Materials and Materials Evaluation. The First Lessons	Assign. #5: pp. 16 & 17; Choose 2 from #3, 4, 5
Nov. 10	Lesson Plans Student Evaluation and Communication Teacher Self-Evaluation	Begin Project 4
Nov. 15	The School Music Dealer—Kerry Davis of Don Wilson Music, Inc.	Assign. #5 is due Project 3 is due
Nov. 17	The School Music Dealer—Kerry Davis (or School Visit)	*New Vision*: pp. v, 1–20
Nov. 22	Non-verbal Communication (video) Teaching Assignments	*New Vision*: pp. 21–42
Nov. 22–27	Thanksgiving Holiday (no classes)	
Nov. 29	The National Standards for Music Ed.	Project 4 is due
Dec. 1	Class Teaching Assignments (Instr. Care/ Instr. Positions/Breathing/Posture/etc.)	
Dec. 6	The Habits of Effective Music Teachers	Project 5 is due
Dec. 8	Review for Final Exam	

Final Exam. ***Wednesday (December 13) from 10:30 a.m. to 12:30 p.m.

SUPPLEMENTARY READING
Grunow, R., & Gordon, E. (1989). *Jump right in: The instrumental series teacher's guide.* Chicago: GIA Publications.

MED 4540: Instrumental Music
Methods and Materials for the Elementary School
Dr. Stephen F. Zdzinski
Wayne State University
Fall 1998

Hours:	3 Credit Hours
	11:45 to 12:40 Mondays, Wednesdays, and Thursdays, Room 305
Instructor:	Dr. Stephen F. Zdzinski (pronounced GIN-ski)
Office:	310 Music
Office Hours:	9:30 a.m. to 11:00 a.m. Mondays and Wednesdays, other times by appointment
Phone:	(313) 577-2674 (office)
E-mail:	s.zdzinski@wayne.edu

Purpose

This course is designed to provide the student with those competencies needed for effective teaching of instrumental music at the elementary level. The course is designed to provide experiences in synthesizing previously learned competencies and skills, as well as to specifically address issues important to instrumental music instruction. Opportunities will be provided to review string, wind, and percussion instruments through performance, course readings, and classroom discussion.

Required Texts and Materials

Fraedrich, E. (1997). *The Art of Elementary Band Directing* [F]
Schleuter, S. (1997). *A Sound Approach to Teaching Instrumentalists* [S]
Walker, D. E. (1989). *Teaching Music: Managing the Successful Music Program* [W]
Soprano Recorder

Texts On Reserve

Bollinger, *Band Director's Complete Handbook.*
Cook, *Teaching Percussion*
Froseth, *The NABIM recruiting manual*
Greer, *Design for Music Learning*
Hunt, *Guide to Teaching Brass*
Klotman, *Teaching Strings*
Kohut, *Instrumental Music Pedagogy*
Lacy, *Organizing and Developing the High School Orchestra*
MENC, *The School Music Program: Description and Standards*
MENC, *Course of Study for Wind and Percussion Instruments*
MENC, *Course of Study for String Instruments*
MENC, *Complete String Guide*
MENC, *National Standards for Music Education*
MENC, *Guidelines for Performance of School Music Groups*
Rolland, *String Syllabus*
Westphal, *Guide to Teaching Woodwinds*

Course Objectives

As a result of this course, the student will be able to
  • write a personal educational philosophy that includes instrumental music and its justification
  • identify significant historical developments in instrumental music education

- demonstrate skills in class lesson instruction
- demonstrate skills in teaching musical concepts
- sequence instruction to teach instrumental music content
- provide appropriate content for instrumental instruction at various levels
- demonstrate a knowledge of materials and music literature appropriate for various types of music instruction
- compare and contrast various instrumental music instructional modes (i.e., lessons, small groups, large groups)
- evaluate instructional materials in instrumental music
- implement appropriate instrumental music recruiting procedures
- design appropriate instrumental music schedules for various types of instructional delivery
- demonstrate knowledge of public relations and personal communication strategies useful in an instrumental music setting
- apply knowledge of measurement and evaluation strategies useful for instrumental music education
- demonstrate skill and knowledge of motivation and classroom management techniques with large and small instrumental groups and individuals
- demonstrate knowledge of basic instrumental technique for each band and string instrument
- demonstrate basic performance demonstration skills on string, wind, and percussion instruments

CLASSROOM PARTICIPATION/ATTENDANCE

Classroom participation is expected during each and every class session. Attendance is mandatory. Each unexcused absence is worth half a grade point. (In other words, every two absences lowers your final grade a letter). Excellent classroom participation will raise your semester grade.

EVALUATION

Your course grade will be determined using the following criteria:

Instrument Proficiencies	5%
Fingering Quizzes (2)	5%
Written Exams (2)	25%
Teaching Demonstrations (3)	15%
Intern Experience & Report	10%
Notebook and Portfolio	10%
Assignments/Class Participation	30%

MED 4540 INSTRUMENT PERFORMANCE PROFICIENCIES

The following instrument proficiencies must be completed during MED 4540, not including your major instrument. *All* proficiencies must be completed prior to student teaching.

	Instrument	Task (Play)
A.	Flute	(low C–E)
B.	Single Reeds, Clarinet	(low E–F)
	or Saxophone	(low B♭–F)
C.	Double Reeds, Oboe	(low C–E)
	or Bassoon	
D.	High Brass, Trumpet	(A–E)
	or Horn	(A–E)
E.	Low Brass, Trombone	(F–C)
	or Tuba	(B♭–D)
F.	Upper Strings, Violin	(low G–G)
G.	Lower Strings, Cello	(low C–C)
H.	Percussion	

Note. All playing is to be chromatic within the ranges in parentheses. A grade 2 solo is to be performed. Any major scale ascending/descending, one octave minimum, through three sharps or flats may be requested.

In addition to playing the instruments, you must demonstrate knowledge of the following:
- Proper assembly of each instrument
- Correct playing position
- Correct embouchure and how to teach embouchure
- How to tune each instrument and play with good intonation
- Care of the instrument
- You must demonstrate an acceptable sound on each instrument

WRITTEN EXAMS
Written exams will be held at the midterm and final exam periods. All tests will include both objective items (i.e., true/false and multiple choice) and essay questions.

TEACHING DEMONSTRATIONS
Each student will have the opportunity to teach simulated beginning music lessons in class. Appropriate lesson plans will be submitted prior to each demonstration, at least one class period in advance. Lessons will be evaluated both on lesson plan content and lesson execution.

Teaching A: Rote Song
Teaching B: Sound Approach Class Lesson (recorders)
Teaching C: Mixed Instrument Class Lesson (National Standards)

INTERN EXPERIENCE
Choose an elementary school music teacher. Arrange to spend a minimum of one class period per week with that teacher. (See the outline titled "Intern Experiences" for specific instructions). Keep a log of each school visit, and turn in a summary of your experiences no later than the date of the final examination. (See "Intern Experience Report" form.)

COMPREHENSIVE NOTEBOOK/PORTFOLIO
Your portfolio will contain any information that you believe documents your achievement and progress in this course, and will be used later in your student-teaching portfolio. The emphasis should be placed on your achievement and personal thoughts. Appropriate materials could include (but are not limited to) the following:
(a) personal journal that reflects on your progress in the course
(b) comments on assignments and a reflection on the results obtained from these assignments
(c) audio or visual tapes of work related to the course
Your notebook is to be typed and is to contain class notes and handouts, tests, assignments, and individual research. The evaluation of the notebook will include organization and usability of material.

ASSIGNMENTS
Assignments will be given related to course material studied in class, in order to apply material studied in practical situations. Evaluation of class participation will include knowledge of reading assignments.

Philosophy Statement. Write a personal philosophy of music education, suitable for inclusion in a job application. Be prepared to discuss your written statement in class.

Sample Lesson Plans. Provide lesson plans for the first ten lessons of a like instrument beginning class, using guidelines given by your instructor in class. Include behavioral objectives in the psychomotor, cognitive, and affective domains.

Method Book Evaluation. Select three different elementary instrumental method book series of your choice and write a review of each book, using criteria given by your instructor in class and the MENC National Standards for Music Education.

Music Literature Catalog. Each student will prepare a microcomputer database of a minimum of 25 selections appropriate for large instrumental ensemble performance in the first three years of a band or string program. You will search and select pieces from a variety of sources (W.S.U. files, music stores, promotional materials, conferences) for your catalog. For each entry, you will indicate title, publisher, pub. #, composer, arranger, type, style, range, rhythmic patterns, tempo, harmony, melodic tonal patterns, tonality, form, accompaniment, difficulty, and comments. Each catalog will be prepared on a microcomputer database of your choice.

Grading Progress Report. Create a student progress report suitable for use with beginning instrumental music students. Explain your criteria for student evaluation.

Classroom Management Plan. Create a written document stating your philosophy of classroom management and a discipline plan.

TENTATIVE SCHEDULE OF TOPICS, READINGS, DUE DATES, AND EXAMINATIONS

Date	Topic	Reading	Due
9/9	Introduction to Class; History of Instrumental Music in Schools	S, Ch. 1 W, Ch. 13	
9/10	Philosophy and Justification for Instrumental Music	MENC, *Guidelines for Performance of School Music Groups* *The Complete String Guide,* pp. 3–8 *Description and Standards,* pp. 3–5 W, Ch. 14	
9/14	National Standards for Music	MENC *National Standards*	
9/16	The Michigan Teacher Examination and State Standards		
9/17	Process of Learning Music	S, Ch. 2	Philosophy
9/21	The Teaching Process	S, Ch. 6	Intern Site
9/23	Lesson Planning	Rolland, *String Syllabus* Bollinger, pp. 323–86 MENC *Courses of Study*	Proficiency Test (Prof 1)
9/24	**Demo A**		
9/28	**Wind Fingering Quiz** Brass Refresher		
9/30	Woodwind Refresher		
10/1	Percussion Refresher		
10/5	String Fingering/Bowing Quiz String Refresher		Prof 2
10/7	Class Lessons, Traditional Approaches	F, Ch. 5 Kohut, Ch. 2 & 7	
10/8	Teaching Tonal Content I	S, Ch. 3	

10/12	Teaching Tonal Content II		Prof 3
10/14	Teaching Rhythm Content I	S, Ch. 4	
10/15	Teaching Rhythm Content II		
10/19	Teaching Performance Skills	S, Ch. 5	Lesson Plans
10/21	Teaching Interpretation and Style	Kohut, Ch. 3–5	
10/22	**Demo B**		
10/26	**Midterm Exam**		
10/28	**Demo B**		Prof 4
10/29	Method Books I	F, Ch. 3	
11/2	Method Books II		
11/4	Beginning Literature—Band	F, Ch. 9, 13; NYSSMA Manual	
11/5	Beginning Literature—Strings	Lacy, pp. 79–99	
11/9	Elementary Scheduling	F, Ch. 4, 8; W, Ch. 7 *Description and Standards,* pp. 31–32 *The Complete String Guide,* pp. 9–10	Prof 5
11/11	Elementary Concert Planning	F, Ch. 10	
11/12	Elementary Ensembles	F, Ch. 11, 13	Method Book Reviews
11/16	Instrumental Music Grading I	S, Ch. 7; W, Ch. 9; F, Ch. 7	Prof 6
11/18	Instrumental Music Grading II		
11/19	Recruiting	F, Ch. 1–2; *NABIM Recruiting Manual*	
11/23	**Proficiency Day**		Prof 7
11/24	Old St. Mary's Concert		
11/30	Instrument Repair	F, Ch. 6	Grading
12/1	Classroom Management I	W, Ch. 2–3; Greer, Ch. 4	
12/3	Classroom Management II		
12/7	Teaching Special Learners		
12/8	Motivation	F, Ch. 12	Literature
12/10	Demo C		
12/14	Demo C		
12/16	Demo C/Review		Discipline Plan
12/18	**Final Exam** (10:40 a.m.)		Portfolio/Notebook

MED 455: Instrumental Music
Methods and Materials for the Secondary School
Dr. Stephen F. Zdzinski
Wayne State University
Winter 1999

Meeting: 11:45 to 12:40 Mondays, Wednesdays, and Thursdays, Room 305
Instructor: Dr. Stephen F. Zdzinski
Office: 310 Music
Phone: Office (313) 577-2674
E-mail: s.zdzinski@wayne.edu

Purpose

This course is designed to provide the student with those competencies needed for effective teaching of instrumental music to secondary school students. The course is designed to provide experiences in synthesizing previously learned competencies and skills, as well as to specifically address issues important to instrumental music instruction.

Texts
Required
> Walker, D. E., *Teaching Music: Managing the Successful Music Program*
> Lisk, E., *The Creative Director: Alternative Rehearsal Techniques*
> Labuta. J., *Teaching Musicianship in the High School Band*

Recommended
> Dvorak, Grechesky, & Ciepluch, *Best Music for High School Band*
> Dvorak, Taggart, & Schmalz, *Best Music for Young Band*
> Garafalo, *Blueprint for Band, Rehearsal Handbook for Band and Orchestra Students*
> Hendrickson, *Handy Manual Fingering Charts*
> Whaley, *Basics in Rhythm*

Reserve Books
> Bollinger, *Band Director's Complete Handbook* (**B**)
> Cook, *Percussion Pedagogy*
> Dillon & Kriechbaum, *How to Design and Teach a Successful School String and Orchestra Program* (**D&K**)
> Doerksen, *Guide to Evaluating Teachers of Music Performance Groups* (**D**)
> Hoffer, *Guidelines for Performances of School Music Groups*
> Hunt, *Guide to Teaching Brass*
> MENC, *Music Booster Manual* (**MBM**)
> New York State School Music Association, *NYSSMA manual of graded solo and ensemble music suitable for contests and festivals, volume XXI* (**NYSSMA**)
> Smith & Stoutamire, *Band Music Notes* (**S&S**)
> Westphal, *Guide to Teaching Woodwinds*

Course Objectives
- write a personal educational philosophy that includes instrumental music and its justification
- identify significant historical developments in instrumental music education
- implement appropriate instrumental music recruiting procedures
- apply knowledge of budgeting procedures common to school music situations
- apply inventory, organizational, and management procedures used in instrumental music settings

- design appropriate instrumental music schedules for various types of instructional delivery
- demonstrate knowledge of public relations and personal communication strategies useful in instrumental music settings
- demonstrate knowledge of parent organizations used to support school music programs and their structure
- explain how computers can be used in instrumental music teaching situations
- demonstrate skills in class lesson instruction
- demonstrate skills in teaching musical concepts
- sequence instruction to teach instrumental music content
- provide appropriate content for instrumental instruction at various levels
- demonstrate skills in teaching correct intonation
- evaluate instructional materials in instrumental music
- demonstrate a knowledge of materials and music literature appropriate for various types of music instruction
- compare and contrast various instrumental music instructional modes (i.e., lessons, small groups, large groups)
- demonstrate a knowledge of instrumentation and seating arrangements for various small and large instrumental ensembles
- apply knowledge of measurement and evaluation strategies useful for instrumental music education
- articulate appropriate performance expectations of instrumental music ensembles of various types and levels
- demonstrate skill and knowledge of motivation and classroom management techniques with large and small instrumental groups and individuals

EVALUATION

Your course grade will be determined using the following criteria:

Written Exams (2)	25%
Ann Arbor Conference Report	5%
Internship Experience and Report	10%
Classroom Participation/Attendance	5%
Notebook	5%
Teaching Demonstrations (2)	10%
Assignments	40%

Written Exams. Midterm and final exams will be held covering course content. Each test will include both objective items (i.e., true/false and multiple choice) and short essay questions.

Classroom Participation/Attendance. Classroom participation is expected during each and every class session. Attendance is mandatory. Each unexcused absence is worth half a grade point. (In other words, every two absences lowers your final grade a letter). Excellent classroom participation will raise your semester grade.

Ann Arbor Conference Report. You must attend the Midwestern Conference on School Vocal and Instrumental Music in Ann Arbor, and write a written summary of the concerts and clinic sessions attended. You must have attended at least eight sessions, including at least one clinic session in vocal music.

Intern Experience and Report. Choose a secondary school and music teacher. Arrange to spend a minimum of one class period per week with that teacher (see the outline titled "Intern Experiences" for specific instructions). Keep a log of each school visit, and turn in a summary of your experiences no later than the date of the final examination (see "Intern Experience Report" form).

Comprehensive Notebook/Portfolio. You will develop a comprehensive notebook/portfolio for your present and future teaching needs, using class handouts, assignments, and other material you may gather. You are to include each of the twelve student-teaching competencies in your portfolio. The portfolio must be typed and indexed.

Teaching Demonstrations

(1) *Standards Lesson.* This mini-lesson will incorporate the National Standards for Music Education in a mixed instrument lesson setting. Obtaining all materials (including books, etc.) is your responsibility. Some books are available for your use, but we may not have full sets. You have the option of a full band class, or a mixed string class.

Your lesson plan must be provided to the instructor at the beginning of your lesson. The format of the lesson should follow the lesson formats discussed in class, with modifications as needed due to time limitations (15 minutes per lesson). You must include objectives and at least four of the standards (including the required standards of playing, singing, and reading notation) in your lesson.

The evaluation form includes questions from Dr. Martin Bergee's "Student Teachers' Rehearsal Effectiveness Rating Scale," which is used during student-teaching visits.

(2) *Band or Orchestral Rehearsal.* Students will conduct a band or orchestral rehearsal at one of the following sites: (a) public school band or orchestra, grades 7–12, or (b) a portion of a rehearsal of the WSU concert band. You will provide a written rehearsal plan to your instructor in advance, using outlines provided in class. At the conclusion of the rehearsal segment, you will be asked to provide any fingerings that are in the music for any instrument.

The evaluation form will be Dr. Martin Bergee's "Student Teachers' Rehearsal Effectiveness Rating Scale," which is used during student-teaching visits. If you are conducting a public school group, you must either make arrangements with Dr. Zdzinski to attend your rehearsal or make arrangements to have the rehearsal, including fingering questions, videotaped.

Assignments. Assignments will be given related to course material studied in class. Assignments will not be accepted for any reason after their due date. Written assignments will be given in order to apply material studied in practical situations. All written assignments *must* be typed, including all class notes, which will be included in your portfolio.

Topic 1: Grading (5%)

(1) Grading Policy. Your music department chairperson has asked that you prepare a written statement outlining instrumental music grading policies in grades 5–12. Your task is to state your philosophy towards grading, identify specific grading practices that you believe should be utilized, and justify your position with appropriate documentation.

Topic 2: Administration (5%)

(2a) Budget for School Instrumental Program. Prepare a mock budget request for a typical public school instrumental music program, providing documented justification for each of your requests suitable for administrative and public consumption. You may wish to use the music administration software found in the Music Listening Lab.

AND

(2b) Press Release. Create a typical press release suitable for newspaper use, as detailed by Walker.

Topic 3: Advanced Instrumental Techniques (5%)

(3) Transposition Check. On your instrument, be able to demonstrate the ability to sight-read three tunes from a second-year method book for any instrument in proper transposition, as if you were playing along with the student. I will be checking for treble clef C, bass clef C, B-flat, E-flat, and F transpositions.

Topic 4: Concert Organizations (5%)

(4) Contest Position Paper. Write a position paper stating your position on large-ensemble contest and solo and ensemble festival participation for elementary, middle school, and senior high instrumentalists. Justify your position with appropriate documentation.

Topic 5: Rehearsal/Instructional Techniques (5%)

(See teaching demonstrations, above.)

(5) Pedagogical Score Analysis and Plan. Using a Junior or High School composition of your choice, complete a pedagogical task analysis as outlined in the *Blueprint for Band* pages given in class (pp. 33–37). Extract objectives from your analysis. Using those objectives, prepare (at least) four detailed 20-minute lesson plan segments (as part of a 50-minute rehearsal with other pieces being played as well) to achieve these objectives. Try to include as many of the MENC National Standards as you can in your plans. Include in each plan the following:
- behavioral objectives
- materials needed (if not obvious)
- instructional sequence of student activities
- methods to evaluate achievement of objectives
- possibilities for remediation when needed

Topic 6: Teaching Materials and Literature (5%)

(6) Concert Organization Core Repertoire Listing. Provide a four-year listing of repertoire for grades 9–12 which all band or orchestra students should encounter during their years of instrumental ensemble participation. Include in your listing for each year one example of a concert overture, a Sousa march, another march selection, two contest pieces, a solo with band, a transcription, a novelty piece, a suite, and a patriotic selection. Your listing should include all style periods (contemporary, romantic, classical, and medieval/Renaissance) and should be grades 3–5 in difficulty (on a six-point grading scale). For each entry, you will indicate title, publisher, pub. #, composer/arranger, type, tempo, harmony/tonality, difficulty, National Standards addressed, and comments.

Topic 7 & 8: Marching Band and Jazz Band Techniques (5%)

(7) Computer Charting Assignment. You are to design a pregame show, selecting music and charting one tune for a 64-member band and 12-member guard, with instrumentation of your own choosing. Use the *Pyware 3D* charting program found in Dr. Zdzinski's office and in the Music Listening Lab. Details will be given in class.

OR

(8) Jazz Pedagogy Project. Create a jazz pedagogical assignment suited to your future plans and needs. This may take the form of a jazz improvisation syllabus, jazz band chart list, short historical paper, a jazz performance project, or another project to be mutually agreed upon.

Topic 9: Special Topics (5%)

(9) Bibliography Assignment. Locate and summarize at least fifteen articles in one or two of the following subject areas (listed below) related to instrumental music education. Each class member will select a different topic area. Suggested sources include (but are not limited to) *Music Educators Journal, Update: Applications of Research to Music Education, Instrumentalist, American String Teacher, Contributions to Music Education, Journal of Band Research, Dialogue in Instrumental Music, Council for Research in Music Education Bulletin,* and other periodicals and books found in the Library and in Dr. Zdzinski's office. Copies of your project will be distributed to all members of the class, and you will present a short summary of your project findings to the class. The subject areas include:

Band or Orchestra Literature (Analyses)   Brass Instrument Techniques
Classroom Management   Competition

Conducting	Instrumental Music Education History
Jazz	Marching Band
Modeling	Motivation
Multiculturalism	Musical Theatre
Music Preference	Music Learning Theory
Parental Involvement	Philosophy
Predictors of Achievement	Rehearsal Techniques
Sight Reading	Small Ensembles
String Instrument Techniques	Student Retention and Dropout
Suzuki	Technology
Teacher Effectiveness	Woodwind Instrument Techniques

Alternative and Extra Credit Projects (up to 10%)

(1) *Contest Adjudication.* Serve as precontest adjudicators for area instrumental music ensembles preparing for MSBOA contests. You will use the MSBOA forms, and provide both constructive criticism and concrete suggestions for improvement.

(2) *Special Event Plan.* Create a detailed schedule and plan for one of the following. Include budget, rehearsal, organization details, and staff and chaperons needed.

      (a) A week-long marching-band camp

      (b) A 3–4 day band or orchestra trip

      (c) An all-state adjudication festival

      (d) A rehearsal schedule for a school musical

      (e) A fund-raising campaign

(3) *Instrumental Music Handbook.* Create a detailed policy handbook outlining your discipline, attendance, scheduling details, grading, and other policies, suitable for student and parental consumption. Also include samples of letters home to parents for encouragement, discipline problem, concert reminders, fund-raising, and trip information.

(4) *Sample Concert Program.* Create a sample concert program with program notes for each selection. Keep in mind programming considerations, timings, etc., as well as the inclusion of a variety of musical styles. Student names and designations should be listed (chairs, honors, etc), as well as acknowledgements of important administrative personnel and staff.

TENTATIVE SCHEDULE OF TOPICS

Date	Area	Topic	Assignment Due
1/11		Syllabus	
1/13	I	Grading I: Testing Basics	
1/14		Vocal Music Education Search, no class	
1/18		Grading II: Performance Measurement	
1/20		Grading III: Grading Systems	
1/21		Secondary Classroom Management	
1/25	II	Administration: Budget	Ann Arbor
1/27		Administration: Facilities	
1/28		Administration: Music Library and Copyright	Grading
2/1		Administration: Scheduling	
2/3		Administration: Public Relations and Booster Organizations	
2/4	III	Advanced Instrumental Techniques	Budget

2/6		Advanced Instrumental Techniques and Instrument Repair	
2/10		Concert Organizations: Programming and Concert Planning	
2/11		Concert Organizations: Contests and Festivals	Press Release
2/15, 17, 18		**Teaching I**	
2/22		**Teaching I/Review**	
2/24		**Exam #1 (10%)**	
2/25	IV	Rehearsal/Instructional Techniques I	
3/1		Rehearsal/Instructional Techniques II	Contest Paper
3/3		Rehearsal/Instructional Techniques III	
3/4		Rehearsal/Instructional Techniques IV	
3/8	V	Teaching Materials and Literature I	
3/10		Teaching Materials and Literature II	
3/11		Teaching Materials and Literature III	Ped. Analysis and Plan
3/15–19		Spring Break (Dr. Z in Japan)	
3/22	VI	Marching Band: Marching Fundamentals	
3/24		Marching Band: Instruction	
3/25		Marching Band: Charting	
3/29		Marching Band: Organization, Band Camp	Core Rep
3/31		Jazz Band: Jazz Fundamentals	
4/1	VII	Jazz Band: Improvisation	
4/5		Jazz Band: Organization	
4/7		Jazz Band: Instructional Techniques	
4/8		**Transposition Check Day**	
4/12	IX	Special Topics: Strolling Strings	Bibliography
4/14		Special Topics: Musical Theatre	
4/15		Special Topics: Trips and Commissions	
4/19		Teaching/Student Presentations II	
4/21		Teaching/Student Presentations II	
4/22		Teaching/Student Presentations II	Jazz/MB
4/26		Review	
4/29		**(10:40 a.m. to 1:10 p.m.) FINAL EXAM (15%)**	Other stuff

COURSE READINGS

Topic 1: Grading and Secondary Classroom Management
- Measurement and Evaluation II (D, all)
- Student Characteristics (B, pp. 46–64)
- Walker, Chs. 2–4, 9

Topic 2: Administration
(a) Budgeting
- Walker, Ch. 5
- *Description and Standards,* pp. 29–32

(b) Facilities
- Walker, Ch. 6

    (c) Music Library and Inventory
- Walker, Ch. 8
- *Description and Standards*, pp. 33–41
- MENC (1988). *The Complete string guide: Standards, programs, purchase, and maintenance.* Reston, VA: MENC. pp. 20–51

    (d) Scheduling
- Walker, Ch. 7
- *Description and Standards*, pp. 31–32
- *The Complete String Guide*, pp. 9–10

    (e) Public Relations
- Walker, Ch. 11
- MENC, *TIPS: Public Relations*

    (f) Booster Organizations
- Walker, Ch. 12
- *Music Booster Manual*

Topic 3: Advanced Instrumental Techniques
- Percussion Pedagogy (Cook)
- String Pedagogy (D&K)
- Advanced Wind Instrument Pedagogy (Hunt, Westphal, Hendrickson)
- Instrument Repair (Videos and Filmstrips)

Topic 4: Concert Organizations
- Programming and Concert Planning (B, Ch. 4, pp. 247–53, Hoffer)
- Performance Considerations (B, pp. 79–93)
- Contests and Festivals (B, Ch. 15; Walker, Ch. 10)

Topic 5: Rehearsal/Instructional Techniques
- Large Concert Ensembles (B, pp. 64–78, 121–161; D&K, pp. 187–230)
- Small Ensembles (B, pp. 220–46)
- Individual Instruction (B, pp. 79–120, 160–219)
- Comprehensive Musicianship (*Blueprint for Band, Rehearsal Handbook*)
- Labuta, Lisk, Whaley

Topic 6: Teaching Materials and Literature
- Large Concert Ensembles (S&S, NYSSMA, J&K, pp. 229–51, K)
- Small Ensemble (NYSSMA)
- Etudes and Study Material (NYSSMA)
- Solo Material (NYSSMA)
- Garofalo, *Guides to Band Masterworks I & II*

Topic 7: Marching Band Techniques
- Organization (Articles)
- Charting (*Pyware* Charting)
- Teaching Techniques (Wells)

Topic 8: Jazz Band Techniques
- Organization (*MENC Course of Study: Jazz*)
- Improvisation (Articles)
- Teaching Techniques (Articles)

Topic 9: Special Projects
- Musical Theatre Productions (Articles)
- Band Camp
- Trips (B, pp. 274–78)
- Commissions (Articles)

MED 363: High School Instrumental Music Methods
Dr. Lynn Cooper
Asbury College
Spring 2001

Office: MC 123 (hours posted)
Hours: Two credits—Mon. and Wed. at 9:00 a.m.

Required Textbooks

- *Teaching Band and Orchestra,* Lynn G. Cooper (unpublished).
- *Effective Performance of Band Music,* W. Francis McBeth, pub. by Southern Music Co.
- *The Choral Conductor's Handbook,* Walter Ehret, pub. by ProArt.
- *Rehearsal Handbook for Band and Orchestra Students,* Robert Garofalo, pub. by Meredith Music Pub.
- *The Marching Band Program,* Bentley Shellahamer et al., pub. by Barnhouse Co.
- $10.00 copy fee due by January 22

Objectives

- The student will develop his or her own philosophy of music education
- The student will be able to discuss and/or demonstrate appropriate teaching techniques, strategies, and materials for high school instrumental music programs
- The student will develop skills in the additional non-musical activities needed to initiate and maintain a successful instrumental music program

Instructional Methods

The class will be conducted in a lecture-demonstration-laboratory fashion. Students will be given opportunities to demonstrate appropriate teaching techniques and strategies during the various sections of the course.

Attendance and Participation

Participation in class discussion and demonstrations is a vital part of this class. Each student will teach the class various assignments. Assignments are due at the beginning of class on the dates indicated. Late assignments are lowered one full grade for each day late.

Regular attendance is assumed. Each unexcused absence past the second will result in the final grade being lowered by one-third grade. Three tardies will equal one unexcused absence. Tests, class teaching assignments, etc. missed during an unexcused absence may not be made up.

Technology

The recently approved Kentucky New Teacher Standard related to technology is met in a number of ways in this course. Most assignments require the use of a word-processing program (such as Microsoft *Word*). In addition, various assignments will require proficiency in using a database (such as *Excel* or *AppleWorks*), a grading program (like *MicroGrade*), and the ability to do Internet searches (related to copyright law and future employment issues). Students will also be using *BandChat*.

Special Projects

Project 1. This project is due on or before April 25.
Submit a printed copy of your computer database file of music for the concert band and/or orchestra. Information should include correct (and complete) title, composer, arranger (if any), publisher, date published, grade, character (ex., oboe solo with band, or march, or overture, etc.), any special needs or characteristics (ex., requires 25 oboes!), a brief description of the piece, etc. A minimum of 75 entries is

expected with an additional set of 10 entries for method book series, techniques, or warm-up books. On 15 of the 75 concert pieces, please listen to a recording while following the score and include those observations in your data file.

Note: Start this project early in the semester.

Project 2. This project is due on or before February 19.
Attend the KMEA In-Service in Louisville on Feb. 3–5. Go to at least five of the clinics offered in instrumental music (note suggestions on the program on my bulletin board) and turn in a typed copy of your thorough notes.

Project 3. This project is due on or before April 30.
Please state your personal Philosophy of Music Education. This scholarly paper (1–2 pages only) should be a concise and thoughtful reflection of your own beliefs about music education in the schools. It is the type of document many prospective employers will request. Develop a real "lighthouse" statement for yourself.

Project 4. This project is due on or before May 2.
Turn in a notebook of typed class notes, assignments, materials collected in class or at conferences, etc. The notebook should be categorized and indexed. Include a blank comments page for my use at the beginning of the notebook. Include a written evaluation of the use of technology in this course. Neatness and thoroughness are very important.

GRADING

The final grade is determined by the following:

Project 1	25 pts.		
Project 2	100 pts.	**Grading Scale**	
Project 3	50 pts.	91% –100% = A	
Project 4	75 pts.	81% – 90% = B	
Class Assignments (13 @ 10)	130 pts.	71% – 80% = C	
Class Teaching (2 @ 10)	20 pts.	61% – 70% = D	
Final Exam	50 pts.	0% – 60% = F	
Total possible points	**450**		

Note: All assignments and projects are due at the beginning of class on the due date. Grades will be lowered (see previous section) for all late work.

COURSE OUTLINE

Note: Some readings are on reserve in the Library.

Date	Class Discussion	Assignment (listed on the date assigned)
(1) Jan. 15	Introduction/Syllabus	Cooper, Ch. 4
(2) Jan. 17	Building a Curriculum: Program Balance and What to Teach	Assign. 1 (p. 26, #1)
(3) Jan. 22	Curriculum Planning: Course Descriptions/ Sequential Instruction/Scheduling	Assign. 1 is due Assign. 2 (p. 26, #3) Cooper, Ch. 5
(4) Jan. 24	Selecting Literature: "Good" Music/ A Core Repertoire	Assign. 2 is due Project 1 and Project 2
(5) Jan. 29	Organizing the Music Library	Assign. 3 (copyright info) Cooper, Ch. 6

(6) Jan. 31	Running Effective Rehearsals: Quality Rehearsals/A Success Plan	Assign. 3 is due Assign. 4 (reh. plan)
(7) Feb. 5	Effective Rehearsals: Environment/ Teaching Ensemble Sight-Reading	Assign. 4 is due Assign. 5 (p. 20, #2) Garofalo, pp. 1–40
(8) Feb. 7	KMEA (no class—attend conference)	
(9) Feb. 12	KMEA Review Comprehensive Musicianship	Teaching Assignment Assign. 5 is due
(10) Feb. 14	Teaching Assignment (instr. skill)	McBeth, I & II
(11) Feb. 19	Teaching Techniques: Tone, Pitch, Balance, and Articulation. McBeth video.	McBeth, III & IV Project 2 is due
(12) Feb. 21	Teaching Techniques: Technique and Rhythm Reading	McBeth, V
(13) Feb. 26	Percussion Techniques ("Tricks of the Trade")	McBeth, VI & VII Casey, pp. 231–38, 385–401
(14) Feb. 28	Effective Podium Technique Interpreting Twentieth-Century Band Music	Teaching Assignment
(15) Mar. 5	Class Teaching Assignments	Cooper, Ch. 7
(16) Mar. 7	Programming and Performing: The Performance Year/Logistics/Audience Development/Programs and Ushers	Assign. 6 (program) Cooper, Ch. 8
(17) Mar. 12	Core Issues: Motivation and Discipline	Assign. 6 is due Ehret, pp. 5–29
(18) Mar. 14	Core Issues: Major Events and Competition	Assign. 7 (p. 24, #2, 3, 4) Ehret, pp. 29–55

March 19–25 is Spring Break

(19) Mar. 26	Choral Methods	Assign. 7 is due Assign. 8 (*BandChat*-3 wk.) Cooper, Ch. 9 *MBP*, Ch. 10
(20) Mar. 28	Organizing and Administering: Organization/ Facilities and Equipment	*MBP*, Ch. 12 Begin Project 4 (notebook)
(21) Apr. 2	Administering: School-Owned Things/ Student Help/Parent Help/Boosters	Cooper, Ch. 10
(22) Apr. 4	Planning for the Classroom: Organization/ Technology/The Other Areas	Assign. 9 (*MicroGrade*) Cooper, Ch. 11 *MBP*, Ch. 11
(23) Apr. 9	Handling Business Issues: A Public Relations Program/Business Skills and Fund-Raising/The School Music Dealer	Assign. 9 is due Assign. 10 (news) Cooper, Ch. 12

(24) Apr. 11	Knowing the Profession Today: National Standards/Program Goals/Research/Music Learning Theories/Advocacy/Educational Reform	Assign. 10 is due Cooper, Ch. 14 Assign. 11 (budget)
Apr. 16	Easter Holiday (no classes)	
(25) Apr. 18	Then, Now, and Why: Historic and Current Influences	Assigned readings Assign. 8 is due
(26) Apr. 23	Then, Now, and Why: A Personal Philosophy	Assign. 11 is due Begin Project 3 Cooper, Ch. 13
(27) Apr. 25	Personal Issues: The Job Search/Ethics/Relational Skills	Assign. 12 (MENC/Job) Project 1 is due
(28) Apr. 30	Personal Issues: Professional Development/A Complete Education/Habits	Assign. 12 is due Assign. 13 (resume) Project 3 is due
(29) May 2	Interview Exercises /Review for Exam	Project 4 is due Assign. 13 is due

Final Exam: Wednesday (May 9) from 10:30 a.m.

The Final Exam will be a Mock Job Interview. Each student will have a 20–30 minute interview with the professor and at least two other persons who will form the "interview committee" and grade the interview. Each student will have previously selected a specific type of job for which to interview. The student will use the material studied in this course as the source of his or her preparation for the interview.

MUSED 355: Instrumental Music Methods
Dr. William I. Bauer
Ball State University
Fall 1999

Section 1:   M, W (10:00)
Section 2:   M, W (11:00)
Office: MU 308
Office Hours: As posted or by appointment
Telephone: 285-5493
E-mail: wbauer@bsu.edu
WWW: http://bsuvc.bsu.edu/home/wbauer/

CATALOG DESCRIPTION

Examines issues related to the teaching of instrumental music. Special emphasis on program goals and curriculum development, instructional planning, and materials and techniques designed for teaching musical concepts in performance class or lesson settings.
Prerequisite: MUSED 200.

TEXTS

Coursepack for MUSED 355. Available at T.I.S. College Bookstore, 1717 University Avenue.

SUPPLIES

One VHS videotape

OTHER RESOURCES

- On-line resources have been established for use in this course. To access these, use a World Wide Web browser such as *Netscape Navigator* or *Internet Explorer* and open the following URL: http://www.bsu.edu/classes/bauer/mused355/
- Selected readings will be placed on reserve at Bracken Library and/or in the Music Technology Resource Lab in room 301

GOALS AND OBJECTIVES

At the conclusion of this course, undergraduate instrumental music education majors will

- describe recruiting procedures useful for the school band and orchestra
- discuss the content and sequencing of curricula in instrumental music
- exhibit growth in classroom teaching skills by completing brief teaching episodes and micro-teaching experiences
- list materials used for instrumental music instruction
- write lesson plans for instrumental music instruction
- demonstrate techniques for teaching/rehearsing elementary and secondary instrumental music classes and ensembles
- describe ways to implement the National Standards for Music Education in instrumental music education through the principles of comprehensive musicianship
- describe techniques for assessment in instrumental music
- exhibit organizational skills through assembly of a resource notebook

Note: If you need course adaptations or accommodations because of a disability, if you have emergency medical information to share with me, or if you need special arrangements in case the building must be evacuated, please make an appointment with me as soon as possible. My office location and hours are listed on the first page of this syllabus.

EXPECTATIONS

Attendance. Prompt attendance is expected as a demonstration of professional commitment. The heart of education at Ball State is the teaching/learning interaction between you, the student, and your instructors. Because of this belief, class attendance is regarded as an essential part of the "contract" between you and the University. You are expected to attend all classes for which you are registered. If you know you must be absent from this class, you should speak, before your absence, with Dr. Bauer, stating the reasons for your absence and agreeing upon a way to make up the work. Absences for illness and other valid reasons will be excused when *advance notice* is provided. If you have a valid reason for an absence on an examination day, and you let me know in advance, you will be permitted to make up the test at a mutually convenient time. Exams must be made up as soon as possible after your return to class, and no later than one week following your return. Because attendance and punctuality are such an important part of being a professional music educator, you will receive full attendance credit for being on time to class and partial attendance credit for being in class but arriving after class has begun. No attendance credit will be given for arrival to class later than ten minutes into the class period. Faculty members are responsible for keeping a record of attendance of all students registered in the class. Significant absences may be reported to the Registrar's Office.

Class Participation. Because active and articulate oral interchange increases verbal skills and promotes a stimulating classroom atmosphere, the instructor will evaluate the quality, quantity, and appropriateness of each student's oral contributions to the class. Although no attempt will be made to translate this evaluation into an objective number of points, the instructor will use his subjective judgment of this behavior in the determination of borderline final grades. The dynamics of this class, and its ultimate value to you, require you to come to class prepared (read assignments), bringing questions and comments to stimulate discussions.

Honor Policy. Students of the university must conduct themselves in accordance with the highest standards of academic honesty and integrity. Academic dishonesty by a student will not be tolerated and will be treated in accordance with the "Student Academic Ethics Policy." Please see the Student Code in the Ball State University Calendar Book.

Copyright Policy. Plagiarism or violation of copyright policies are a form of academic dishonesty and are treated as an ethics violation. See the Student Academic Ethics Policy for more details.

MENC. It is *strongly* suggested that all students enrolled in this course become members of the MENC Chapter. Belonging to and participating in professional organizations are an important part of being a professional music teacher. Student MENC members also receive the *Music Educators Journal, Teaching Music,* and the *Indiana Musicator.* See Dr. Burns and/or Dr. Woody for more information on the BSU MENC chapter.

ASSIGNMENTS

All assignments are due on the date specified. Grades on late assignments will be lowered by 10% for each day they are late. No credit will be given for assignments received later than two weeks following the due date. An exception to this policy is if the student is personally ill (doctor's excuse required) or has a death in his or her immediate family. The student should see the instructor immediately upon returning to class to make arrangements to complete missed assignments at the earliest possible date.

inQsit Reading Quizzes. Students will take an on-line (accessed through course Web page) reading quiz for each daily class reading assignment. Reading quizzes must be completed prior to the start of the class for which the reading is assigned. The inQsit quizzes *may not be printed* from your Web browser. The quizzes are meant to be used on-line exclusively. Printing of quizzes will be considered a breach of the Ball State University "Student Academic Ethics Policy."

Method Book Evaluation and Presentation. Small groups of students will evaluate assigned elementary instrumental method books. Each group will present an overview of the book to the class and provide each class member with a one-page, word-processed description which outlines the features of the method book series.

First Lesson. Each student will teach a "first lesson" on an assigned instrument to one other class member. The lesson should follow the format provided in class. A handout of the first lesson procedures will be provided to each class member, and a copy will be provided to the instructor. Your lesson will be videotaped. You must complete and hand in a self-critique of your teaching no later than one week after you teach. More discussion of this assignment will take place in class.

Micro-teaching. Two micro-teaching units will be presented by the students which focus on the three-step teaching/rehearsal cycle and good teaching presentational factors. Criteria for each of these teachings is listed below and will be discussed in class. Submit your "Lesson Plan" prior to teaching.

    #1:   Good Example = DS w/elevated posture and effective eye contact.
              Poor Example = At least one of the three factors missing.
    #2:   Good Example = Present a total cycle(s) using good presentational factors including facial expressions and the incorporation of effective natural gestures as covered in class. The performance aspect may be live or presumed (pretend the band/orchestra is playing). Poor Example = One or more of the necessary elements is missing.

Warm-up/Rehearse Teaching Episode. Each student will be responsible for teaching a brief episode from an instrumental ensemble rehearsal (other class members will serve as the lab ensemble for this assignment).

    (1) Prepare the lesson, including a complete written lesson plan using the format discussed in class. Hand in a copy of the lesson plan to Dr. Bauer prior to teaching.
    (2) The lesson should demonstrate your understanding of concepts and techniques discussed in class regarding the warm-up and rehearsal of an instrumental ensemble.
    (3) Teach the lesson. The lesson will be videotaped.
    (4) View your videotape. Complete and hand in the self-critique form within one week of teaching your lesson.

On-line Activities. The Internet is becoming an increasingly valuable resource for instrumental music educators. To acquaint you with, and give you practice using, some of these resources, the following assignments should be accomplished:

    (1) All students need to regularly check their e-mail. Important communication regarding this course may take place via e-mail. Make it a part of your daily routine.
    (2) Subscribe to one of the music education listservs discussed in class by the date listed in the course calendar. When you receive confirmation of your subscription to the listserv, forward a copy of it to Dr. Bauer. Follow the discussions on the listserv throughout the semester. After you become familiar with the "culture" of the list, post a question related to the content of this class to the list *at least one time*. Send a "Cc"(copy) of your question to Dr. Bauer and forward a copy of all responses you receive to Dr. Bauer as well.
    (3) Explore some of the Web sites linked from the course homepage. Select any three of these resources and evaluate them according to the criteria provided to you in class. These evaluations should be e-mailed to Dr. Bauer no later than the date on the course calendar.

Notebook. Each student will complete an Instrumental Pedagogy Notebook for use as a resource during student teaching and the early years of his or her teaching career. This notebook will consist of all materials from this class and any other materials the student may deem appropriate. The notebook must be one with *large* rings so that pages can be easily turned. If the notebook has pockets, nothing should be placed in these pockets. In the front of the notebook should be the syllabus for this class followed by a typed table of contents (put your name someplace on the table of contents). Use the table of contents of your *Coursepack* as an example of the type of table of contents to include in your notebook. The notebook should be separated into appropriate content areas with divider pages that have *typed* index tabs. For ease of retrieval, sections should be *alphabetized* in the notebook. Sections should also not contain too many topics. Possible sections for the notebook are: Administration, Assessment, Comprehensive Musicianship, Elementary Instrumental Music, Planning, Recruitment, Rehearsal Procedures. (This is just an example; you do not have to use these exact sections.) The coursepack should be included in the notebook, divided up into appropriate sections with the divider pages.

Professional Development. Continual growth and development as a musician and teacher throughout a career is essential. For this class, students will exhibit a commitment to professional growth and development by completing four professional development hours through at least two different activities. MENC meetings, ASTA meetings, and Career Services workshops are among those events that can be used to fulfill this requirement. Other events will be discussed in class. Students should obtain the permission of the instructor prior to attending any event (in order to receive professional development credit) that has not been discussed in class. Turn in the professional development log form to Dr. Bauer no later than the due date indicated on the course calendar.

Please note:

- A music-teaching experience (for example, teaching a private lesson or directing a church choir) can be used for one of the four required professional development hours. A reflective essay on lesson content and how your teaching is evolving needs to be stapled to the professional development log.
- Fraternity or sorority events and meetings do not count toward this requirement
- A BSU faculty member or speaker must sign the professional development log for you to receive credit for the event.

ASSESSMENT

Students can check their grades via the course Web page at any time.

Assignment	Grading Criteria	Weight
Attendance	Prompt attendance at each class session	.05
inQsit Quizzes	Correct answers completed on time	.05
Method Book Evaluation and Presentation	Well-organized, thoughtful presentation. Neatly word-processed handout with complete information and free of grammar, spelling, and punctuation errors	.05
First Lesson	Lesson plan, presentation, completion of self-assessment, neatly word-processed handout with complete instructional sequence outlined and free of grammar, spelling, and punctuation errors	.10
Micro-teachings	Lesson plan, presentation	.05
Warm-up/Rehearse Teaching Episode	Lesson plan, presentation, completion of self-assessment	.15
On-line Activities	Completion of activities as assigned on time	.025
Notebook	Content, organization, neatness	.10
Professional Development	Completed Professional Development Log handed in on time	.025
Midterm	Percent of correct answers, depth of thought, clarity of expression	.20
Final Exam	Percent of correct answers, depth of thought, clarity of expression	.20

Grading Scale			Letter to Numerical Grade Conversion	
			Letter Grade	*Numerical Equivalent*
93 –100	A		A	100
90 – 92	A-		A	95
87 – 89	B+		A-	90
83 – 86	B		B+	87
80 – 82	B-		B	85
77 – 79	C+		B-	80
73 – 76	C		C+	77
70 – 72	C-		C	75
67 – 69	D+		C-	70
63 – 66	D		D+	67
60 – 62	D-		D	65
			D-	60

COURSE CALENDAR

Key

A =   Article to be given to you
CP =   Course Packet
G =   Garofalo, Robert. (1983). *Blueprint for Band*—on reserve in MU 3011
S =   Schleuter, Stanley. (1997). *A Sound Approach to Teaching Instrumentalists* (2nd edition)—on reserve in MU 301

Date	Topic	Assignment	
Aug. 23	Course Overview/Syllabus		
Aug. 25	A Philosophy for Teaching Instrumental Music	Read:	A, "The Philosophy in Action: The Performance Program" (excerpt) CP, "Are Students Learning Music in Band?"
Aug. 30	Philosophy/History of Instrumental Music	Read:	CP, "Music Is for Life," "Leading the Way" S, Preface, Ch. 1 (see reading guide in coursepack)
Sept. 1	Recruitment	Read:	CP, "Concert Band Instrumentation"
Sept. 6	Labor Day—No Classs		
Sept. 8	Recruitment	Read:	CP, "Going beyond Recruiting"
Sept. 13	Selecting a Method Book		
Sept. 15	The First Lesson/Scheduling and Grouping of Beginning Instrumental Music Instruction	Read:	A, "Teaching Class Lessons" (Kohut) S, p. 142–43
Sept. 20	Method Book Presentations	Due: Read:	Method book handouts and presentations S, Chapter 2
Sept. 22	Teaching Music Reading	Read:	CP, "Teaching Music Reading"
Sept. 27	First Lesson Presentations	Due:	First lesson handouts and presentations
Sept. 29	First Lesson Presentations	Due:	First lesson handouts and presentations

Oct. 4	First Lesson Presentations	Due:	First lesson handouts and presentations
		Read:	CP, "Why Wait to Start Beginning Band Rehearsals?"
Oct. 6	Teaching Class Lessons	Read:	CP, "Bringing General Music Techniques to the Instrumental Class"
Oct. 11	Teaching Class Lessons	Read:	CP, "Teaching through Rain, Sleet, Snow, and a Seventh-Grade Fire Drill"
Oct. 13	Midterm		
Oct. 18	Fall Break—No class		
Oct. 20	Planning for Instrumental Music Instruction; Three-Step Teaching/ Rehearsal Cycle; Presentational Factors in Instrumental Music Teaching—Posture and Eye Contact	Read:	S, Ch. 5 & 6
Oct. 25	Rehearsal Techniques; Presentational Factors in Instrumental Music Teaching—Reading Cues, Using Names, Facial Expressions	Due: Read:	Micro-teaching #1 CP, "How Do You Behave?" "Teaching Music in the Ensemble Rehearsal through Multiple Intelligences"
Oct. 27	Rehearsal Techniques; Presentational Factors in Instrumental Music Teaching—Gestures, Varying Proximity, Vocal Inflection	Due: Read:	Micro-teaching #1 CP, "Instrumental Warm-ups to Improve Skills," "Warm-ups that Work"
Nov. 1	Rehearsal Techniques	Due: Read:	Micro-teaching #2 CP, "Listening: Teach Your Instrumental Students to Listen"
Nov. 3	Rehearsal Techniques	Due:	Micro-teaching #2
Nov. 8	Warm-up/Rehearse Teaching Episode	Due:	Warm-up/Rehearse Teaching Episode
Nov. 10	Warm-up/Rehearse Teaching Episode	Due:	Warm-up/Rehearse Teaching Episode
Nov. 15	Warm-up/Rehearse Teaching Episode	Due:	Warm-up/Rehearse Teaching Episode
Nov. 17	Warm-up/Rehearse Teaching Episode	Due:	Warm-up/Rehearse Teaching Episode
Nov. 22	Developing Comprehensive Musicianship via the National Standards	Read: Due:	G, pp. i–27 Listserv posting
Nov. 24	Thanksgiving Break—No Classs		
Nov. 29	Developing Comprehensive Musicianship via the National Standards	Read:	CP, "To Sing or Not to Sing in Instrumental Class," "Comprehensive Musicianship Research"
Dec. 1	Developing Comprehensive Musicianship via the National Standards	Read: Due:	CP, "Teaching Ensembles to Compose and Improvise" Web Site Evaluations

Dec. 6	Developing Comprehensive Musician-ship via the National Standards	Due:	Notebooks
Dec. 8	Assessment in Instrumental Music Education; Review for Final Exam	Due:	Professional Development Logs
Dec. 13	Administration of Instrumental Music Programs		
Dec. 14	Section 2 Final Exam: 9:45–11:45		
Dec. 15	Section 1 Final Exam: 9:45–11:45		

This syllabus is a guide. It may be varied as needed.

COURSEPACK ARTICLES

Austin, J. R. (1998, Fall–Winter). Comprehensive musicianship research: Implications for addressing the National Standards in music ensemble classes. *UPDATE: Applications of Research to Music Education, 25–32.*

Bauer, W. I. (1998, September). Teaching music in the ensemble rehearsal through multiple intelligences. *Indiana Musicator, 37–39.*

Burnsed, V., & Fiocca, P. (1990). Bringing general music techniques to the instrumental class. *Music Educators Journal, 76*(6), 45–49.

Byo, J. (1990). Teach your instrumental students to listen. *Music Educators Journal, 77*(4), 43–46.

Conway, C. (1997). Why wait to start beginning band rehearsals. *Teaching Music, 5*(1), 36+.

Dodson, T. (1989). Are students learning music in the band? *Music Educators Journal, 76*(3), 25–29.

Ely, M., & Rashkin, A. (1999, March). Warm-ups that work. *The Instrumentalist, 12–16.*

Fallis, T. L. (1999, January). Standards-based instruction in rehearsal. *Music Educators Journal, 85*(4), 18–23, 50.

Hickey, M. (1997, May). Teaching ensembles to compose and improvise. *Music Educators Journal, 83*(6), 17–21.

Hughes, J. R. (1981, January). How do you behave? *Music Educators Journal, 87*(6).

Linklater, F. (1995). Instrumental warmups to improve skills. *Music Educators Journal, 82*(3), 31–34.

Pasqua, F. A. (2000, April). Teaching tuning through cooperative learning. *School Band and Orchestra.*

Prentice, B. (1994, October–December). Recruitment. *Bandworld, 12.*

Robinson, M. (1996). To sing or not to sing in instrumental class. *Music Educators Journal, 83*(1), 17–21, 47.

Rodgers, G. L. (1991). Concert band instrumentation: Realities & remedies. *Music Educators Journal, 77*(9), 34–39.

Sandene, B. A. (1994). Going beyond recruiting: Fighting attrition. *Music Educators Journal, 81*(1), 32–34, 61.

MUSIC EDUCATION 261.03 AND 262.03: STRING METHODS
DR. ROBERT GILLESPIE
OHIO STATE UNIVERSITY

MUSIC ED. 261.03 (STRING METHODS—VIOLIN AND VIOLA)

Meetings: 8:30/9:30 MTWR
8:30 Class Professor—Dr. Robert Gillespiee
9:30 Class Graduate Teaching Associate—Andrea Olijnekk

Dr. Gillespie	**Andrea Olijnek**
Office Hours: 10:30 Tuesday and Thursday or by appointment	Office Hours: By appointment
Phone: 292-2336	Phone: 292-0473
Office: 308B Hughes Hall	Office: 308A Hughes Hall
E-mail: gillespie.5@osu.edu	E-mail: olijnek.1@osu.edu

REQUIRED TEXTS
Allen, M., Gillespie, R., Hayes, P. (1995). *Essential Elements for Strings. Book 1 Teacher Manual.* Milwaukee, WI: Hal Leonard Corporation.
Text available only at the Ohio Union Long's Book Store.
Music Education 261.03 *Course Pack,* available at the Ohio Union Cop-Ez Center.

OBJECTIVES OF THE COURSE
To acquire string instrument skills and pedagogical understanding of
- teaching beginning upper string (violin, viola) instruction
- orchestra program curricula
- unique aspects of string recruitment
- aural-skill string training in the school orchestra
- string instrument repair
- teaching the National Standards for Music Education in the orchestra program
- tuning the orchestra efficiently and accurately using an electronic tuning device

GRADING POLICY
30%	Average of all playing tests
10%	Article reviews (minus five points every review not turned in)
10%	Playing final exam
10%	Written final exam
20%	Notebook
10%	Diagnostic skill competency
10%	Attendance
	(minus two points per day if absent; minus one point per day if late but do come to class)

Note: Article reviews are due on Thursdays, once per week.

GRADING POLICY
98–100	A+	93–97	A	90–92	A-
88–89	B+	83–87	B	80–82	B-
78–79	C+	73–77	C	70–72	C-
68–69	D+	63–67	D	60–62	D-

IMPORTANT CLASS DATES

Sept. 28	Playing Test #1: Pizzicato D String Notes (#19 & # 33)
Oct. 4	Lecture: Model School Orchestra Programs
Oct. 5	Playing Test #2: #41
Oct. 11	Lecture: String Recruitment
Oct. 12	Playing Test #3: Bowing Open Strings #52 & #53
Oct. 18	Lecture: School Orchestra Curriculum
Oct. 19	Playing Test #4: Bowing #66
Oct. 25	Lecture: String Instrument Repair
Oct. 26	Playing Test #5: Bowing #74
Oct. 30	Switch Instruments
Nov. 2	Diagnostic Skills Pretest
Nov. 8	Lecture: Teaching National Standards in the Orchestra
Nov. 9	Playing Test #6: Bowing #88
Nov. 15	Lecture: Aural Training in the String Class
Nov. 16	Playing Test #7: #101
Nov. 22	Diagnostic Skills Posttest
Nov. 30	Written Final Exam and Notebook Due in Class
Dec. 4	7:45 Playing Exam for 8:30 Class—#113, #126 (memory)
Dec. 5	7:45 Playing Exam for 9:30 Class—#113, #126 (memory)

READING ASSIGNMENTS FOR 261.03

Model School Orchestra Programs: Oct. 4

Culver, R. (1981, Summer). Goals of a string program. *American String Teacher,* 21–24.

Tatton, T. (1988, Summer). A model public school string program. *American String Teacher,* 59–62.

String Recruitment: Oct. 11

Allen, M. L. (1992, Summer). Flinging strings in spring. *American String Teacher,* 67–70.

Dillon, J. (1978, Fall). Twenty tips for successful string-class recruiting. *Orchestra News, 16*(2).

Gillespie, R. (1989, January). Strategies for string recruitment. *The Instrumentalist,* 50–54.

Perkins, D. (1989, Autumn). Getting students and parents involved in recruiting. *American String Teacher,* 88–90.

School Orchestra Curriculum: Oct. 18

Allen, M. (1994, Summer). Introducing and integrating basic skills in the beginning. *American String Teacher,* 69–72.

Hanson, D. A. (1999, February–March). Organizing and operating an orchestra program. *TRIAD,* 11–15.

Instrument Repair: Oct. 25

Sibert, P. (2001, November). Stringed instrument maintenance and repair. *American String Teacher,* 80–87.

Teaching National Standards in the Orchestra: Nov. 18

Allen, M. (1995, Summer). The national standards for arts education: Implications for school string programs. *American String Teacher,* 30–33.

Gillespie, R. (1998, Summer). National standards for successful school string and orchestra teachers. *American String Teacher,* 30–33.

Aural Training in the String Class: Nov. 15

Gillespie, R. (1990, Autumn). Jazz up your orchestra life! *American String Teacher,* 52–54.

Erwin, J. (1995, December). Beyond the page. *Teaching Music,* 28–30.

Wagner, M. (1987, Spring). Improvisation and musical problem solving: Music with the young string
player. *American String Teacher,* 43–44.

MUSIC EDUCATION 262.03 (STRING METHODS—CELLO AND DOUBLE BASS)

REQUIRED TEXTS

Allen, M., Gillespie, R., & Hayes, P. (1995). *Essential Elements for Strings. Book 1 Teacher Manual.*
Milwaukee, WI: Hal Leonard Corporation.

Music Education 262.03 *Course Pack,* available only at Copez at the Ohio Union.

Required Music Stand. You must bring your own music stand to class. Music stands are not provided by
the School of Music.

PURPOSE OF THE COURSE

- To acquire fundamental cello and double bass performance skills and pedagogical understanding for teaching beginning lower strings
- To acquire fundamental understanding of the values of orchestra programs, string instrument
availability, evaluation process, guidelines for organizing an orchestra rehearsal, recommended
orchestra music, technique for developing community support of the orchestra program
- To offer a beginning string class peer-teaching opportunity

IMPORTANT CLASS DATES

Jan. 12	Lecture: Values of Orchestra Programs
Jan. 13	Playing Test #1: #22, #24 (pizzicato)
Jan. 19	Lecture: Delivery Principles for String Teaching
Jan. 20	Playing Test #2: #33, #34 (pizzicato)
Jan. 26	Lecture: Instrument Availability
Jan. 27	Playing Test #3: #52 (arco)
Jan. 31–Feb 7	Observation in the Schools
Feb. 2	Lecture: Developing Community Support for School Orchestras
Feb. 3	Playing Test #4: #67
Feb. 7	Values of Orchestra Programs Paper Due
Feb. 7	Switch Instruments
Feb. 9	Lecture: Designing a School Orchestra Rehearsal
Feb. 14	Peer Teaching Begins
Feb. 16	Lecture: Evaluating Orchestra Students
Feb. 17	Playing Test #5: #69
Feb. 23	Lecture: Recommended Orchestra Music and Method Books
March 2	Playing Test #6: #74
March 8	Written Final Exam and Notebooks due in Class
March 14	7:30 Playing Exam for 8:30 Class—#132, #136
March 15	7:30 Playing Exam for 9:30 Class—#132, #136

READING ASSIGNMENTS FOR 262.03

Values of Orchestra Programs: Jan. 12

Atwood, J. (1991, Autumn). The winners—Lottery and otherwise. *American String Teacher,* 60–63.

District adds music teachers after violins overrun inner-city school. (1998, February). *Teaching Music,* 31–32.

Ensley, J. (1991, Autumn). Hispanic student participation. *American String Teacher,* 53–54.

Ensley, J. (1991, Autumn). The estudiantina of East Los Angeles. *American String Teacher,* 62–63.

Hernandez, E., Jr. (1991, Autumn). The violin as a bridge. *American String Teacher,* 55–56.

Mahany, B. (1991, Autumn). They've got pluck. *American String Teacher,* 57–59.

Developing Community Support for School Orchestras: Feb. 2

Benham, J. (1992, November). Forestalling budget problems. *The Instrumentalist,* 12–17.

Culver, B. (1999, February). How to develop community-wide support for string study. *American String Teacher,* 48–54.

Gillespie, R. (1987, Summer). Getting the community behind your orchestra program. *American String Teacher,* 52–54.

Kendall, S. (1997, Spring). Securing our string programs. *American String Teacher,* 47–51.

Designing A School Orchestra Rehearsal: Feb. 9

Dillon-Krass, J. (2000, November). Productive orchestra rehearsals guarantee high-quality performances. *American String Teacher,* 29–30.

Gillespie, R. (1990, February). String orchestra rehearsal techniques. *The Instrumentalist,* 50–54.

Gillespie, R. (1993, October). Recurrent problems in string sections. *The Instrumentalist,* 83–90.

Nelson, C., & Scott, L. (1993, Autumn). Making full orchestra work. *American String Teacher,* 73–74.

Evaluating Orchestra Students: Feb. 16

Frankel, J. (1999, Fall). The computer as an assessment tool in the band room. *Soundtree,* 6(1).

Hamann, D., & Baker, H. Assessing music teaching effectiveness in diverse environments. Copyrighted paper. (Please note I have a letter in my office from the authors giving me permission to place their article/form in the 262.03 course pack for duplication purposes)

Recommended Orchestra Music & Method Books: Feb. 23

Littrell & Racin. (2001) *Teaching music through performance in orchestra.* Chicago: GIA Publications.

GRADING POLICY

25%	Average of all playing tests
10%	Playing final exam
10%	Written final exam
15%	Notebook
10%	Attendance
	(minus two points per day if absent; minus one point per day if late but do come to class)
10%	Peer Teaching
5%	School Observation
10%	Values of Orchestra Programs paper
5%	Article reviews

Note: Article reviews are due on Thursdays, once per week. The Observation Report is due the last day of class.

GRADING POLICY

98–100	A+	93–97	A	90–92	A-
88–89	B+	83–87	B	80–82	B-
78–79	C+	73–77	C	70–72	C-
68–69	D+	63–67	D	60–62	D-

MUSE 346: String Techniques and Methods
Dr. Margaret Schmidt
St. Cloud State University
Spring 1999

Instructor:	Dr. Margaret Schmidt
Office:	PAC 144
Phone:	255-2295
Office Hours:	as posted and by appointment
Class Meetings:	Tuesdays and Thursdays, 8:25–9:15

Required Text

Allen, M., Gillespie, R., & Hayes, P. T. (1994). *Essential Elements for Strings, Book I.* Milwaukee, WI: Hal Leonard.

Recommended

Student membership in American String Teachers Association, including subscription to *AST Journal.* ($15)

Course Objectives

The prospective music teacher will
- perform, with good posture, playing position, tone, and intonation, music appropriate for beginning and intermediate string class
- develop a repertoire of teaching strategies appropriate for string class instruction and rehearsal
- develop assessment skills to diagnose and correct problems common to beginning and intermediate string players
- develop skills to analyze string solo and ensemble literature and select appropriate repertoire for students
- discuss strengths and weaknesses of major text published methods for beginning string class instruction
- demonstrate proper care and minor repair of string instruments
- become familiar with a variety of professional and community resources for string teachers

The National Standards For Music Education

From *National Standards for Arts Education* (Reston, VA: MENC, 1994):
(1) Singing, alone and with others, a varied repertoire of music
(2) Performing on instruments, alone and with others, a varied repertoire of music
(3) Improvising melodies, variations, and accompaniments
(4) Composing and arranging music within specified guidelines
(5) Reading and notating music
(6) Listening to, analyzing, and describing music
(7) Evaluating music and music performances
(8) Understanding relationships between music, the other arts, and disciplines outside the arts
(9) Understanding music in relation to history and culture

Assignments

(1) Be on time and participate fully in all class discussions and activities. Practice regularly between class meetings (20 minutes daily is a suggested minimum). You will lose ten points for each absence, excused or unexcused; however, points lost for excused absences may be made up. For an excused absence, please talk to the instructor or leave a message at 255-2295. (300)

(2) Write summaries of articles from at least two different volumes of *American String Teacher*. Choose topics of interest to you, such as: technical issues like vibrato, bowing, or shifting; recruiting; letters to parents; working with administrators; working with the community; curriculum; string literature; developing a private studio. Your summary should be about one page long, and should include complete bibliographic information. Add one or two paragraphs of your own response to the article. (20 each)

Sample bibliographic citation: Shipps, S.B. (1993). The influence of Lucien Capet on teaching violin. *American String Teacher 53*(1), 65–68.

(3) Review two beginning string method texts, using the assigned format. Turn in two copies of your reviews. (20 each)

(4) Attend at least two sessions for string teachers at the MMEA Midwinter Clinic, February 15–17, in Minneapolis. Write a brief summary of each presentation. (60)

(5) Develop an annotated bibliography of references from the list of "Resources for Teachers." For each reference, give complete bibliographic information, and write a paragraph or two describing what information the book contains. You need to include enough information so that, if you needed ideas for teaching, you could decide which resources would be most helpful in a given situation. You might also want to attach a photocopy of the Table of Contents. (40)

For each resource, copy the complete bibliographic citation, correctly formatted. Then write a paragraph or two describing what is in the book. Your description should be complete enough that, several years from now, you could decide if this is a book that would be useful for you to purchase to use in whatever job you hold. You may wish to include a copy of the Table of Contents of some of these references, to remember exactly what is included. Print a copy of your description to bring to class, and—before class—also e-mail your description to: mschmidt@stcloudstate.edu.

Sample bibliographic annotation:

Matesky, R., & Rush, R. (1963). *Playing and teaching stringed instruments (Parts I and II)*. Englewood Cliffs, NJ: Prentice Hall, Inc.

Together, these two volumes address all aspects of string technique for all four stringed instruments. They are intended to be used in college-level string methods courses, and to provide good references for teachers. Book I covers care of the instruments, tuning, basic bowing and instrument positions, all finger patterns, cello extensions, and half position. Bowing styles (legato, staccato, spiccato, and slurs) are introduced through musical excerpts scored for all instruments. Book II addresses shifting, double stops, other bowings, harmonics, vibrato, and a short chapter on organization of the school string program. Musical excerpts in Book II are primarily etudes and scales. This is an encyclopedia-like approach, a good teachers' reference, but not good pedagogical order for students. The pictures are dated, but the musical examples are useful.

(6) Develop a notebook or file of resource ideas for teaching string instruments. The file should contain class notes and handouts, using dividers to show your choice of organization for easy future additions. Some of the following categories may be useful to you when you begin teaching:

Principles of movement and posture
Establishing the instrument and left hand position
Fingerboard geography
Establishing the bow hold
Bowing styles
Aural skills
Principles of teaching and learning
Teaching techniques
Teaching resources
Care of instruments, supplies, repairs
Building a program, concert ideas, recruiting, public relations (30)

(7) Analyze a Grade 1 or 2 orchestra score, using the assigned format. Bring copies of your analysis for each of the other class members. (40)

(8) Observe an elementary or junior high string class or orchestra rehearsal (one 45-minute or two 30-minute lessons). Write a summary of what you observe. Discuss in as much detail as you can: (a) the physical arrangement of the classroom and routines for entering, unpacking, packing up, and leaving; (b) how the instruments were tuned; (c) specific teaching techniques and games that were used; (d) the teacher's pedagogical goals for that class. (Recommended: observe Spiritoso Strings rehearsal, every Sunday, 5:00–6:30 in PA 113). (50)

(9) Participate in four playing and teaching quizzes. Write comments about your colleagues' performances to demonstrate your understanding of string techniques. (75 each)

GRADING

Approximately one third of the course grade may be earned in each of three areas: class attendance and participation, playing quizzes, and written work. Of the total points:

> 90% are needed to earn an A
> 80% are needed to earn a B
> 70% are needed to earn a C

Point values for assignments may vary from those listed in this syllabus. Grades are based on percentages of points earned for each completed assignment.

A professional attitude towards attendance and assignments is expected. All assignments are due at the beginning of class on the day specified. Late assignments will receive a proportion of the points otherwise earned:

> | Same or next school day | 90% |
> |---|---|
> | Within one week | 70% |
> | More than one week | 50% |
> | After class final | 0% |

Habits such as good spelling, appropriate grammar, organized writing, and neatness are essential for teachers, as is the ability to read and follow instructions. On all assignments, points earned depend on attention to these details.

If you achieve less than 80% success on an assignment, you will be given an opportunity to redo the assignment. Points to be made up must be completed within three school days of the original due date to receive credit. Extra credit assignments may be arranged only in unusual circumstances.

The reading assignments are the references you choose from the "Resources for Teachers" list in order to complete your annotated bibliography assignment.

COURSE SCHEDULE—SPRING 1999

Tues., Jan. 12	Introduction, check out instruments
Thurs., Jan. 14	The basics: bow hold, statue of liberty, mouse house
Tues., Jan. 19	D and G scales, marching fingers, lift bows
Thurs., Jan. 21	Finger patterns; **Article summary 1 due**
Tues., Jan. 26	Bow distribution and bowing marks
Thurs., Jan. 28	**Playing quiz; bring paper and pencil**
Tues., Feb. 2	C scale, slurs and bowing marks, principles of left hand
Thurs., Feb. 4	Beginning class instruction; method books
Tues., Feb. 9	Beginning class instruction; method books
Thurs., Feb. 11	**Method Book evaluations due (Make copies for class)**

Feb. 11-13: MMEA Clinic in Minneapolis

Tues., Feb. 16	Shifting and fingerboard geography; class instruction
Thurs., Feb. 18	Class instruction and rehearsals; shifting
Tues., Feb. 23	Resources for teaching; **Conference summaries due**
Thurs., Feb. 25	**Playing quiz**
Tues. March 2	Shifting, vibrato
Thurs., March 4	Shifting, vibrato; **Annotated bibliography due**
Tues., March 16	Class instruction and rehearsals
Thurs., March 18	String bass
Tues., March 23	Bow distribution; **Article summary 2 due**
Thurs., March 25	Suzuki instruction and repertoire
Tues., March 30	Bowing styles; fingerboard geography
Thurs., April 1	Concerts, recruiting, and program development. **Video review due**
Tues., April 6	Ralph Searles: Instrumental rental, business services
Thurs., April 8	Analyzing string music; planning curriculum
Tues., April 13	Beginning-level songs and games
Thurs., April 15	Planning for class instruction
Tues., April 20	**Teach a song or Rehearsal observation report due**
Thurs., April 22	**Teach a song or Rehearsal observation report due**
Tues., April 27	Planning ensemble rehearsals; curriculum development **Teaching self-evaluation due**
Thurs., April 29	Instrument repair and maintenance
Thurs., May 6	Class final, 8:00–9:50 **Notebooks due; Playing quiz** **Quiz on clefs and fingerboard geography**

RESOURCES FOR TEACHERS

Allard, M. A. (1989). *Razzle dazzle: Marketing the school orchestra*. Elkhart, IN: Glaesel/Selmer.

Bearden, G. (1982). *Emergency string repair manual for school orchestra directors*. St. Louis, MO: Bearden Violin Shop.

Bunting, C. (1982). *Essay on the craft of cello-playing (Vol. I and II)*. Cambridge: Cambridge University Press.

Dalton, D. (1988). *Playing the viola: Conversations with William Primrose*. Oxford: Oxford University Press.

Dillon, J., & Kriechbaum, C., Jr. (1978). *How to design and teach a successful string and orchestra program*. San Diego: Kjos West.

Dillon-Krass, J., & Straub, D.A. (1991). *TIPS: Establishing a string and orchestra program*. Reston, VA: MENC.

Galamian, I. (1962). *Principles of violin playing and teaching*. Englewood Cliffs, NJ: Prentice Hall, Inc.

Gerber, M. (1989). *Color your teaching green: A framework for implementation of a private music studio*. Ann Arbor, MI: Author.

Gillespie, R., with Gilbert, B., & Jones, M. L. (1995). *Getting started with strolling strings*. Reston, VA: MENC.

Godfrey, J. H. (Ed.). (1989). *The best of the soundpost*. Published by National School Orchestra Association, available through MENC.

Green, B. (1971). *The fundamentals of double bass playing*. Cincinnati, OH: Piper Co.

Green, B., with Gallwey, W. T. (1986). *The inner game of music.* New York: Doubleday.

Green, E. A. H. (1949/1990). *Orchestral bowings.* Bloomington, IN: American String Teachers.

Green, E. A. H. (1966/1987). *Teaching stringed instruments in classes.* Bloomington, IN: American String Teachers.

Green, E. A. H. (1987). *The dynamic orchestra: Principles of orchestral performance for instrumentalists, conductors, and audiences.* Englewood Cliffs, NJ: Prentice Hall, Inc.

Jackson, B. G., Berman, J., & Sarch, K. (1987). T*he A.S.T.A. dictionary of bowing terms for string instruments* (3rd ed.). Bloomington, IN: Tichenor Publishing Group. Available from MENC.

Littrell, D. A. (Ed.). (1997). *String syllabus* (Vol. 1). Bloomington, IN: Tichenor Publishing Group. Available from MENC.

Mayer, F. R. (Ed.). (1993). *The string orchestra super list.* Reston, VA: MENC.

Mullins, S. (1985). *Teaching music: The human experience.* Available from Shirley Mullins, 537 Ridgecrest Dr., Yellow Springs, OH 45387.

MENC. (1988). *The complete string guide: Standards, programs, purchase, and maintenance.* Reston, VA: MENC.

MENC. (1991). *Teaching stringed instruments: A course of study.* Reston, VA: MENC.

MENC. (1994). *Strategies for success in the band and orchestra.* Reston, VA: MENC.

Perkins, M. M. (1995). *A comparison of violin playing techniques: Kato Havas, Paul Rolland, and Shinichi Suzuki.* Bloomington, IN: Tichenor Publishing Group. Available from MENC.

Rolland, P., & Mutschler, M. (1974). *The teaching of action in string playing.* Bryn Mawr, PA: Boosey & Hawkes.

Schaefle, E. (Coordinator). (n.d.). *Community resources and school orchestras: Building bridges.* Bloomington, IN: American String Teachers Association.

Slone, K. C. (1985). *They're rarely too young...and never too old "to twinkle!"* Ann Arbor, MI: Shar Products Co.

Starr, W. (1976). *The Suzuki violinist: A guide for teachers and parents.* Knoxville, TN: Kingston Ellis Press.

Suzuki, S. (1969). *Nurtured by love.* New York: Exposition Press.

Young, P. (1978). *Playing the string game: Strategies for teaching cello and strings.* Austin, TX: University of Texas Press.

Young, P. (1986). *The string play: The drama of playing and teaching strings.* Austin, TX: University of Texas Press.

ME 211: Violin/Viola Class
ME 391: Lab Orchestra
Dr. Susan Quindag
Bob Jones University
Fall 2001

Credits: 1 hour
Time: Monday—9:00–9:50 (ME 211)
              Friday—9:00–9:50 (ME 391)
Location: GFAC 119
Instructor: Dr. Susan Quindag
Office: GFAC 232
Phone: (864) 370-1800, ext. 2785
E-mail: squindag@bju.edu

REQUIRED MATERIALS

Allen, M., Gillespie, R., & Hayes, P. T. (1996). *Essential elements for strings, Bk. 1*. Milwaukee, WI: Hal Leonard. [EE]

Klotman, R. (1996). *Teaching strings*, (2nd ed.). New York: Schirmer Books. [K]

O'Reilly, J. (1996). *Strictly classics, Bk. 2*. Los Angeles: Highland/Etling. [SC]

Pro Audio 9.0 [Computer Software]. (2000). Cambridge, MA: Cakewalk. [In Music Lab]

COURSE DESCRIPTION

This course is designed to provide music education majors the opportunity to develop performance skills necessary for classroom string instruction. Students will learn either violin or viola during the semester in a homogeneous classroom (ME 211) and reinforce their performance skills in a laboratory orchestra (ME 391). Further discussion will ensue regarding teaching methods of stringed instruments and special topics in string education.

OBJECTIVES

- Students will perform either violin or viola with the aural acuity and physical skills at the level of a first- or second-year elementary string student
- Students will discuss the preliminary stages of a stringed instrument program
- Students will discuss various teaching methods in strings regarding technique, classroom discipline, motivation, special education, and aesthetics
- Students will teach a performance skill to other students in the class

ATTENDANCE REQUIREMENT

Students are expected to attend all class sessions on time. Students' absences will be reported to the University Discipline Committee. Students will then be given demerits for unexcused absences.

PRACTICE REQUIREMENT

All students will be required to practice five times each week (35 practice sessions from the first day of class to midterm and 35 sessions from midterm to the final) and will be expected to make up practice sessions missed due to illness, cuts, or official canceled classes. The only exception to the required practice sessions is participation in an official music group tour—three practice sessions will be required upon return. During a recital week, practice sessions may be deferred for two weeks.

WEEKLY READING REQUIREMENT

During each violin/viola class, students will have five minutes to answer one essay question that refers to the weekly reading and information presented in class.

GRADE

Activity	Points Earned
Exam #1—Dichotomous	20
Sequencing Project	10
Exam #2—Videotape Assessment	20
Exam #3—Performance	20
Final Exam—Dichotomous, Performance, and Oral	40
Weekly Reading Essay (7)	35
Weekly Practice Sessions	70
Observation	10
Teaching Segment	20
Total Possible Points for the Course	**245**

SCHEDULE

Students should practice all the exercises in both books and may read the sections in Klotman that pertain to the instrument they are studying.

Week-Date	Behavioral Objectives: (Students will demonstrate, perform, identify, or discuss)	EE	K	National Curriculum Standards*
Introduction in Lab Orchestra 8/30	A philosophy of teaching strings Parts of the stringed instrument. Care of the instrument. Hold of the instrument. Sound production. Right hand pizzicato	2–3		1p, 2p, 5a
I 9/3–9/7	**Quiz 1** Steady beat. Open Strings. The bow hold on a pencil and bow. Open-string quarter notes and rest. Legato bowing by rote. Improvisation of bowing patterns.	4–8	3–44	1p, 2p, 6p 2c, 3c, 5c
II 9/10–9/14	**Quiz 2** Legato bowing while reading notes. First position first finger pattern. Improvisation with first finger pattern.	9–17	47–91	5p, 7p, 2c 3c, 4c, 5c
III 9/17–9/21	**Quiz 3** Simple and folk music in G and D major. Eighth notes Two-four meter. Double-stops. Left hand pizzicato. Duets.	18–24	92–110	5p, 6p, 7p, 10p, 4c, 1m
IV 9/24–9/28	**Examination #1 (Dichotomous)** Crisscross fingering. Tied notes. Two-note slur. String-cross slur.	25–30	111–21	5p, 9p, 1m, 2m, 3a
V 10/1–10/5	**Quiz 4** First position second finger pattern. Three-note slur. C-natural. Improvisation of a theme and variation using half, quarter, and eighth notes and rest. Tempo markings. **Sequencing Project of Non-Western Music Due.**	31–36	122–47	4p, 5p, 6p, 8p, 10p, 12p 1c, 1m, 2m, 3a

Week-Date	Behavioral Objectives	EE	K	Standards
VI 10/8–10/12	**Examination #2 (Videotape assessment)** Staccato. Hooked bowing. Dotted quarter note followed by an eighth note.	37–40	151–176	1p, 2p, 3a
VII 10/15–10/19	**Quiz 5** Spiccato. Music in F and B-flat major.	41–46	179–188	5p, 3a
VIII 10/22–10/26	**Quiz 6** Shifting to third position by rote. Music in F and B-flat major. Tempo changes. **Observation Due.**	1–3	189–198	5p, 11p, 12p, 2a
IX 10/29–11/2	**Examination #3 (performance)**	4–5	199–221	
X 11/5–11/9	**Teaching Segment**	6	222–232	
XI 11/12–11/16	**Quiz 7** Teaching cadences and form.	7		5p, 3a, 6a
XII 11/19	Classroom discipline, motivation, and special learners.	8		5a, 6a
XIII 11/26–11/30	Developing aesthetic sensivity through listening	9		5p, 11p, 12p 6c, 7c, 1a, 2a, 3a
XIV 12/3–12/7	Review for final examination **Recital during Lab Orchestra**			

A final examination will be administered during the finals week (December 10–13). This final will include a dichotomous written test, a performance test, and an individual oral test.

MUSIC FOR LAB ORCHESTRA

Composer-Arranger	Title	Publisher
Allen, M., et al.	*Essential Elements, Bk. 1*	Hal Leonard
Caponegro, J.	*Bow-Regard's Parade*	Kendor Music
Frost, R. S.	*Countdown March*	Lake State
Frost, R. S.	*Step Ladder*	Kendor Music
McLeod, J.	*Festival March*	Kjos
Niehaus, L	*Bows and Arrows*	Kendor Music
O'Reilly, J.	*Strictly Classics, Bk. 2*	Highland/Etling
Pinner, J.	*Downtown Suite for Strings*	Alfred

*NATIONAL CURRICULUM STANDARDS

BASED ON THE SOUTH CAROLINA VISUAL AND PERFORMING ARTS FRAMEWORK
(November, 1993)

Aesthetic Perception

    1p. Continue to identify and describe sound and methods of changing sound

    2p. Categorize sounds by method of sound reproduction

    3p. Identify and demonstrate pitch from musical notation

    4p. Discriminate and identify major and pentatonic tonalities

5p. Perform melodic patterns (melodies from notation)

6p. Identify steady beat in musical examples

7p. Recognize relationship of accents to meter

8p. Identify and discriminate between duple and triple meters including syncopated rhythm patterns

9p. Identify chord changes, descants, obbligatos, counter melodies, rounds, and canons

10p. Identify monophonic, homophonic, and polyphonic textures

11p. Identify introduction, interlude, cadence, and coda

12p. Identify simple forms such as binary (AB), ternary (ABA), and rondo (ABACA)

13p. Identify common musical terms related to tempo and dynamics

Creative Expression

1c. Sing expressively a repertoire of familiar songs from varied styles including rounds, partner-songs, and two-part songs with or without accompaniment

2c. Play simple patterns on rhythmic or melodic instruments

3c. Demonstrate elements of space, energy, and time through expressive movement

4c. Read and write basic notation symbols for rhythm and melody with comprehension

5c. Improvise and compose rhythmic and melodic phrases

6c. Aurally identify, by listening, a basic repertoire of standard instrumental and vocal compositions

7c. Aurally identify instruments and vocal types

Musical Heritage

1m. Sing, play, and listen to music of one's own and a variety of ethnic and cultural groups

2m. Sing, play and listen to music from a variety of periods and musical styles and from different geographical areas

Aesthetic Valuing

1a. Continue to recognize historical and cultural characteristics that determine the source of musical style

2a. Continue to demonstrate a developing awareness of musical quality by describing music and by applying musical concepts, ideas, and values

3a. Continue to give examples of music that are part of celebrations, ceremonies, and many other special occasions

4a. Continue to use elements of music to describe and classify music

5a. Continue to explain ways that music is an important part of everyday life as a vocation and as an avocation

6a. Develop and defend criteria to judge the worth/value of music heard, performed, or created

GRADUATE

MUS 862: SEMINAR IN MUSIC CURRICULUM AND METHODOLOGY
DR. COLLEEN CONWAY
MICHIGAN STATE UNIVERSITY
SUMMER 1999

Instructor: Dr. Colleen Conway
Office: 206PB
Telephone: 355-7658
E-mail: conwayc@pilot.msu.edu
Office Hours: Mon.–Thurs. 10:00–11:00 and 12:30–1:30, or by appointment

REQUIRED TEXTS

Flinders, D. J., & Thorton, S. J. (Eds.). (1997). *The curriculum studies reader*. New York: Routledge.

Walker, F. D., & Soltis, J. F. (1997). *Curriculum and aims* (3rd ed.). New York: Teachers College Press.

Course Packet (Available from Neds)

RECOMMENDED TEXTS

(On reserve in the Music Library)

Mark, M. (1996). *Contemporary music education* (3rd ed.). New York: Schirmer Books.

MENC Task Force for National Standards in the Arts. (1994). *The school music program: A new vision*. Reston, VA: MENC.

MENC Committee on Performance Standards. (1996). *Performance standards for music: Strategies and benchmarks for assessing progress towards the national standards*. Reston, VA: MENC.

Publication Manual of the American Psychological Association (4th ed.). (1994). Washington, DC: American Psychological Association.

COURSE DESCRIPTION

Seminar in Music Curriculum and Methodology will include study and discussion of the following:

- **Curriculum.** Definition, history, theory, designs in music, research on curriculum in music.

- **Assessment.** Types of assessment, grading procedures, connection of assessment and curriculum, alternative assessment techniques.

- **Methodology.** Student presentations of various methods and curricular areas including: Orff, Kodály, Dalcroze, Manhattanville Music Curriculum Project, Gordon Music Learning Theory, Suzuki Talent Education, Comprehensive Musicianship, Early Childhood Education, Technology in Education, Multicultural Music Education, Curriculum for Special Populations, etc.

COURSE OBJECTIVES

- To become familiar with the research and scholarship in the field of general curriculum studies
- To understand the close connection between educational history, philosophy, and curriculum
- To become aware of recent reforms in school curriculum which may interact with music education
- To understand research and curriculum with regard to design, implementation, and dissemination of research on curriculum

- To review various methodologies in music education that may provide the conceptual framework for the development of K–12 music curriculum
- To become articulate with regard to issues facing K–12 comprehensive music education curriculum development
- To understand the various assessment options available to music teachers for evaluating student learning in music

COURSE REQUIREMENTS

Attendance/Class Participation. Students are expected to attend all classes. Please notify me in advance if you are to be absent from class. In addition, students are expected to have prepared for the class seminar by reading the assigned material and preparing personal responses and commentaries. (10% of final grade)

Weekly Journal. Each week (or sometimes twice each week) the student must submit an electronic version of a two- to three-page journal entry which includes personal reflections and commentary regarding the upcoming assigned readings. I will respond to each entry so that the journal offers the student and the instructor an opportunity to communicate informally about the course content. In addition, journal response "teams" will be organized so that students may share responses with one another. As a general rule, journal entries will not be accepted late. (20% of final grade)

Book Review. Each student will prepare a book review (3–5 pages written) for presentation at a book share poster session held on July 9, 1999. Books to be reviewed should be chosen from the list provided. Students are encouraged (but not required) to complete this assignment in groups of two or three. The poster session will include a poster describing the book and copies of your review for each student in the class. Choices for the book review should be submitted no later than July 5th. (15% written, 5% poster)

Methodology Review. During the week of July 26, 1999, each student will present to the class the philosophies and ideals of a chosen music education method. Presentations should last approximately five to seven minutes and should include a one-page class handout which highlights the themes presented to the class. A five- to eight-page written overview of the concepts and ideals of the methodology should be turned in on the day of the presentation. A methodology project proposal with references must be submitted by July 19, 1999. (15% written, 5% oral)

Final Project. The final course project, due July 30, 1999, requires the student to design a curriculum for a chosen music course. The curriculum may cover yearly objectives or a specific unit (8-week session, etc.). It may include a specific methodology discussed in class or it may be an eclectic presentation of music education ideals. A one-page project proposal must be approved by the instructor and should be submitted by July 19, 1999. The final document should be between 15–20 pages long and should be written in APA style. It should include the type of curriculum chosen; a description of the course and the time schedule for the curriculum; a music course philosophy; course goals and objectives; a list of developmental skills and/or benchmarks; requirements for facilities, equipment, supplies, budget, and scheduling; a list of resources to be used (books, recordings, etc.); sample teaching strategies and sample assessment procedures. Papers will be evaluated on both content and style. Student will present their projects during class on July 30, 1999. (30% of final grade)

EVALUATION

As a group, we will develop rubrics to determine grades for the journal responses, the written book review, the book review poster, the methodology review, the methodology presentation, and the final project. In addition to these rubrics, the following qualities will be valued in your written work:
- Attention to APA editorial style
- Relevance. Connections between your work and the content and orientation of this course should be clear. Your work should show evidence of your understanding of course readings and discussions.

- Responsiveness to the task or question. Are you fulfilling the requirements of the assignment?
- Conciseness. Clear and organized writing style will be valued. Writing should be concise yet complete. Write as though your audience is not an expert on your topic.

COURSE CALENDAR/ASSIGNMENT SCHEDULE

June 14, 15   Course Introduction/Overview. What are Curricula/Assessment/Methodology? How Do They Relate to Teaching Music in the Schools? Personal Assumptions. Grading Rubric Development.

Curriculum

June 16   Journal #1 is due. Walker and Soltis, Ch. 1–3. Flinders and Thorton, Ch. 2, 3, 6, 7.

June 17, 18

June 21   Journal #2 is due. Walker and Soltis, Ch. 4. Flinders and Thorton, Ch. 17, 18, 28.

June 22–24

June 25   Journal #3 is Due. Walker and Soltis, Ch. 5. Flinders and Thorton, Ch. 1, 10, 14.

June 28, 29   Book review choices due.

June 30   Journal #4 is due. Walker and Soltis, Ch. 6. Flinders and Thorton Ch. 4, 29.

July 1, 2

July 5   Journal #5 is due. Walker and Soltis, Ch. 7. Flinders and Thorton, Ch. 5, 19, 23, 30.

July 6–8

July 9   Book Review Poster Session

Curriculum in Music

July 12   Journal #6 is due. Wing (1992) in course pack. Methodology Project Proposal with References is due.

July 13

July 14   Journal #7 is due. Elliott (1995) in *Course Pack*.

July 15, 16

Assessment

July 19   Journal #8 is due. Abeles, Hoffer, and Klotman (1994) in *Course Pack*, NAEP information at: http://www.menc.org/naep/naep.html. Final Project Proposal is Due.

July 20–23

Methodology

July 26–29   Student presentations.

July 30   Final project presentations; final paper due.

CHOICES FOR THE BOOK REVIEW ASSIGNMENT

This assignment may be done in groups of two to three students.

- Choose any book source from the chapter notes or the annotated bibliography provided in Walker and Soltis on pages 123–30.
- Choose any book source from the notes and reference sections in each article in the Flinders and Thorton book.
- Any work by the following authors: Ted Sizer, Ann Lieberman, Linda Darling-Hammond, Elliott Eisner, Ernest Boyer, John Goodlad, Michael Fullan, Seymour Sarason.

• Choose one of the following:

> Caine, R. N., & Caine, G. (1994). *Making connections: Teaching and the human brain.* Menlo Park, CA: Addison-Wesley Pub.
>
> Marzano, R. J. (1988). *Dimensions of thinking: A framework for curriculum and instruction.* Alexandria, VA: Association for Supervision and Curriculum Development.
>
> Doll, W. E. (1993). *A post-modern perspective on curriculum.* New York: Teachers College Press.
>
> Jacobs, H. H. (1989). *Interdisciplinary curriculum: Design and implementation.* Alexandria, VA: Association for Supervision and Curriculum Development.
>
> Slattery, P. (1995). *Curriculum development in the postmodern era.* New York: Garland.

• Other choices may be proposed by the student and approved by the instructor.

REFERENCES

Conway, C. M. (1998). Book review: Curriculum and aims. *Journal of Music Teacher Education, 8* (1), 25–26.

Wing, L. B. (1992). Curriculum and its study. In R. Colwell (Ed.) *Handbook of Research on Music Teaching and Learning.* New York: Schirmer Books, 196–217.

Elliott, D. J. (1995). *Music matters.* New York: Oxford University Press. (Ch. 10–11, pp. 241–95.)

Abeles, H. F., Hoffer, C. R., & Klotman, R. H. (1994). *Foundations of music education* (2nd ed.). New York: Schirmer Books. (Ch. 10, pp. 303–41.)

MUED 623: BUILDING INSTRUCTIONAL PROGRAMS (CURRICULUM)
DR. ED DULING
BOWLING GREEN STATE UNIVERSITY
SPRING 2000

CATALOG DESCRIPTION
Applications of humanist and behaviorist views, concept learning, sequencing and assessment of musical instruction, and motivation to the development of instructional programs in music education.

INSTRUCTOR'S FOCI
Students should be prepared to think "outside the box" in curricular terms as this instructor attempts to balance the more traditional types of extant curricula in music education with "the teacher as curriculum." That is, the course emphases will be not only upon what has existed traditionally, but also upon qualitative examination of the influences upon and resulting structure of each student's practice as a teacher and, in turn, his or her own music education curricula.

Instructor:	Dr. Ed Duling
Location:	MMAC 2008
Times:	Thursdays, 6–9 p.m.
Office Hours:	before or after class or by appointment
Phone:	2-0281 (Office)
E-mail:	eduling@bgnet.bgsu.edu

TEXTS
Required
"TPT"

Ross, E. W., Cornett, J. W., & McCutcheon, G. (1992). *Teacher personal theorizing: Connecting curriculum practice, theory, and research.* Albany, NY: SUNY Press.

"TSAS"

Waldron, P. W., Collie, T. R., & Davies, C. M. W. (1999). *Telling stories about school: An invitation.* Upper Saddle River, NJ: Merrill.

Optional Texts and Readings—as needed: (Copies on reserve in 2115)

Ohio Department of Education. (1996). *Comprehensive arts education: Ohio's competency-based model.* Columbus, OH: ODE. (may be able to order, or bring from your school.)

Eisner, E. W. (1994). *Cognition and curriculum reconsidered.* New York: Teachers College Press.

Jacobs, H. H. (Ed.). (1989). *Interdisciplinary curriculum: Design and implementation.* Alexandria, VA: ASCD.

Labuta, J. A., & Smith, D. A. (1997) *Music Education: Historical contexts and perspectives.* Upper Saddle River, NJ: Prentice Hall.

Lehman, P. (1994). *Opportunity-to-learn standards for music instruction.* Reston, VA: MENC.

Snyder, S. (1996). *Integrate with integrity: Music across the elementary curriculum.* W. Norwalk, CT: Ideas Press. (may be found in MUED 248 section of reserve.)

GOALS OF THE CLASS
The broad goals of this graduate music education class are threefold: (1) to extend and review knowledge of curricular models, methodologies, and frameworks in education and music education, (2) to provide a structural model for graduate students' reflections upon examination of their own practices as music educators—the "hows" and "whys"—arising from their memories and influences, and (3) to spur the creation of some type of curricular material applicable to the teaching practice of the teacher.

Please inform the instructor if you have any special needs of ANY type.

EVALUATION
Based on 400 points
- Participation: 50 points. Be ready to discuss/write in class based upon readings; must be present to get points. Save ALL ALL ALL materials from both out-of-class and in-class assignments! They will become part of your references for a final project.
- Curricular Generation Project: 75 points
- Final Teacher Practice Paper: 75 points
- Midterm (Take-home and in-class): 55 points
- "Data gathering" items are 145 points as follows:

> Mentoring Survey (20)
> Stimulated Recall (20)
> Philosophy Draft (20)
> Your Curricular Model (20)
> Concept Maps (30)
> Guided Interview (20)
> Setting Description (15)

Grade Ranges
A = 360–400
B = 320–359
C = 280–319
D = 240–279
239 or below (oops!)

TENTATIVE SCHEDULE OF ACTIVITIES
Assignment at end of each session is for following session(s).

Jan. 13　　Intro./Syllabus/Procedures; "The Bell" or "The Death of Myrtle Reiss"/Caring.
In class: Your own story shared.
A: Another story. Read *TPT,* 35–53 (Ch. 3); *TSAS,* iii–xiv. Definitions.

Jan. 22　　Speed and Accuracy.
In class: Read story, write another story, discuss readings, what do you need?
A: Read *TSAS,* 1–8; *TPT,* xi–18. Bring your Philosophy on 2/3.

Jan. 27　　OMEA—No class: work ahead on readings

Feb. 3　　In class: "Why I am in Music Education" and sharing and discussion of end products of MUED 623. **Sharing of philosophies of education.**
A: Read *TSAS,* 8–24; *TPT,* 19–34 (Ch. 2). Handout: Duling's "Reflection in Music Teaching" and "Teachers as Researchers."

Feb. 10　　In class: Discussion of "Reflection in Music Teaching" and "Teachers as Researchers" and readings and Teacher thinking. "-isms" review and implications for curriculum in schools—especially music, readings, concept maps.
A: Concept map of "influences;" Read *TSAS,* 25–46; *TPT,* 179–90 (Ch. 11) and 137–57 (Ch. 9).

Feb. 17　　In class: What is a Curricular Model? Making Curriculum from CAE, Objectives, Standards, and The Ohio Model. Influence maps.
A: Review National Standards and Ohio CAE model. Concept maps: teacher planning and the role of music. Read *TSAS,* 47–62.

Feb. 24	In class: **Mentoring res. and questionnaire.** Discuss reading. Handout "Let More Teachers;" Catch-up day. Assign out-of-class portion of midterm. Discuss models assignment. A: Read "When 'Method' Becomes Authority," role and planning maps.
Mar. 2	In class: Integrated curricula—various types. Discuss reading. Discuss "Let More Teachers." **Describe teaching setting.** A: Read *TSAS,* 63–89; *TPT,* 114 (Ch. 7).
Mar. 9	**No Class—Spring Break! (MENC)**
Mar. 16	In class: Discuss readings, Turn in drafts of CG project, Catch-up day. Start Guided Interview. A: Finish interview. Read *TPT,* 191–205 (Ch. 12).
Mar. 23	In class: Drafts returned. **In-class portion of midterm.** Schedule stimulated recall. **Turn in OOC Midterm.**
Mar. 30	In class: **Turn in interview. CG projects due.** Discuss reading. **Curricular Models Due.** A: Read Maxine Greene; *TSAS,* 91–114.
Apr. 6	No class: **Stimulated Recall as Scheduled: 1/2 hr. each (S)**
Apr. 13	In class: Maxine Greene discussion. Advocacy for Music Curricula—a Model. Discuss reading. A: Read *TSAS,* 115–47.
Apr. 20	**Practice Papers Due.** In class: catch up as needed, deferred topics. **Student Presentations of Practice Papers**
Apr. 27	**Student Presentations**
May 4	**Exam Day. Final Draft of Practice Papers Due (My Practice as a Teacher)**

SOME POLICIES

It is the instructor's feeling that a class of this nature is a collaboration among the participants, including the instructor. The instructor will facilitate thinking about curricula in general and in music particularly. Because there will be times when he must be absent to conduct other professional business, or for illness, he understands that this may be the case for you also. *Therefore, one absence is allowed.* Beyond that, allowances for absence must be made on a case-by-case basis, always with some prior notice to the instructor whenever humanly possible (voice-mail, note, e-mail). In any event, work due must be left prior to class unless some *very* specific prior agreement is reached with the instructor.

Unless specifically directed to the contrary, all work is to be word-processed, double-spaced, and in APA style. Save a hard copy and save the work to disk, of course. Any curricular materials created may be partially or mainly in chart or outline form. Details on contents of this and the Teacher Practice Paper will be given.

There will be times that you will need to meet with the instructor outside of class to facilitate your classwork. Outside meetings will probably occur mostly, though, before or after class and on class days.

SUPPLEMENTAL BIBLIOGRAPHY

Abeles, H. F., Hoffer, C. R., & Klotman, R. H. (1994). *Foundations of music education* (2nd ed.). New York: Schirmer. ISBN 0-02-870011-2.

Alig, K. J. (1992). Factors in the development of leading general music educators. Unpublished dissertation, University Microfilms #9237234.

Bridges, M. S. What our graduates wish we had told them. *The Quarterly Journal of Music Teaching and Learning, 4*(1), 68–72.

Brinkman, D. J. (1995). Teaching about thinking: Thinking about teaching. *Journal of Music Teacher Education, 5*(1), 8–14.

Colwell, R. (1993). *Handbook of research on music teaching and learning.* New York: Schirmer.

Duling, E. (1990). *Curriculum mapping.* Unpublished paper for graduate curriculum class, Ohio State University.

Duling, E. (1991). Reflection in music teaching: Revealing our theories of practice. *TRIAD, 58*(5).

Duling, E. (1999/00). TRIAD etc.

Duling, E. (1992). *The development of pedagogical-content knowledge: Two case studies of exemplary general music teachers.* Unpublished dissertation, University Microfilms #9227261.

Eisner, E. W. (1985). *The educational imagination* (2nd ed.). New York: Macmillan.

Jackson, P. W. (1968). *Life in classrooms.* New York: Holt. (pp. 115–43.)

May, W. T. (n.d.) Teaching for understanding in the Arts, etc. *Quarterly Journal of Music Teaching and Learning, 1*(1&2), 5–16.

McCutcheon, G. (1988, September). Theory and practice: Considerations for the 1990s and beyond. *NASSP Bulletin,* 33–34, 36–42.

Consortium of National Arts Education Associations. (1994). *National standards for arts education.* Reston, VA: MENC.

Oakes, J., & Lipton, M. Examining Curriculum in "best" schools. *Education Week.*

Schleuter, L. (1991). Student teachers' preactive and postactive curricular thinking. *Journal of Research in Music Education, 39*(1), 46–63.

Wells, R. (1997). Designing curricula based on the standards. *Music Educators Journal, 84*(1), 34–39.

Wing, L. (Ed.). (1999, Spring.) *The Mountain Lake Reader.*

Yatvin, J. (1990). Let more teachers "re-invent the wheel." *Education Week, 10*(3).

MUE 503: Philosophical Foundations of Music Education
J. Bryan Burton
West Chester University

Meetings:	Monday Evenings, 5–8 p.m.
Instructor:	J Bryan Burton, Professor of Music Education
Office:	Swope 36
Telephone:	610-436-2222
E-mail:	jburton3@wcupa.edu

Catalog Statement

This course shall include the study of historical and philosophical foundations of music education, the application of principles of education to music, and major emphasis on the development of a philosophy of the discipline.

Textbooks
Required Texts

Foundations of Music Education. Harold Abeles, Charles Hoffer, & Robert Klotman. Schirmer Books. *Music Matters.* David J. Elliott. Oxford University Press.

Supplemental Materials

Readings will be assigned from texts on bibliography list (books on reserve in Music Library) and copies of materials from current journals and various resources will be distributed as necessary to provide current information in the field.

Class Description

MUE 503 will consist of lectures on historical, philosophical, and curricular issues of music education, presentations by class members, and outside readings—both specifically assigned articles and student-selected materials related to the topics under discussion. Class discussion will be of paramount importance in developing an understanding of historical, philosophical, and curricular issues.

Course Objectives

The following course objectives for instrumental music education students have been designed to meet the Statement of Overarching Goals for Teacher Education at West Chester University as adopted Spring 1995 by the WCU Teacher Education Council. By meeting these objectives, students will have gained: (1) knowledge of the learner, (2) knowledge of content, (3) knowledge of pedagogy, (4) personal knowledge, and (5) professional knowledge.

As a result of participation in MUE 503, students will

- demonstrate, through discussion and written assignments, knowledge and understanding of the history of music education in the United States including various individuals, curricular innovations, historical events
- demonstrate, through discussion and written assignments, knowledge and understanding of the major philosophical issues in music education, including types of philosophical approaches, individual writers and philosophers in the field, and historical and contemporary texts in music education philosophy
- formulate a personal philosophy of music education
- formulate a music education curriculum based upon philosophical principles encountered in MUE 503

ASSIGNMENTS AND GRADING

- **Readings.** Readings will be assigned from class textbooks and handouts on a weekly basis. Students are to make an outline of each assigned reading to be placed in a course notebook. These will be checked weekly to determine timeliness of assignment completion.

- **Written Exams.** There will be at least one written quiz covering definitions of terms used in philosophical discussions, identification of writers, music educators, etc., historical information.

- **Research Papers/Presentations.** Two research papers will be completed as part of MUE 503. (a) One will focus on an individual music educator or music philosopher. This paper will be approximately three double-spaced pages in length and will include a bibliography. A ten-minute presentation covering major points of this paper will be given in class. (b) A 2,500 word (plus bibliography) paper will focus on a topic of philosophical, historical, or curricular interest. This may be an examination of a major section of a book from the reading list or a general examination of the topic. A 10-minute class presentation covering major points of this paper will be given in class.

- **Class Discussions/Participation.** Each student is required to take an active, positive part in class discussions on each topic, reading, and paper.

- **Class Notebook.** Each student will compile a comprehensive notebook containing handouts, reading outlines, class notes, assignments, and any other materials the student feels may be relevant to the discussion of historical, philosophical, and curriculum issues in music education.

- **Grading.** A final course grade will be determined through use of the following weighted scale:

Reading Outlines	15%
Average of Written Exams	25%
Papers/Presentations	40%
Comprehensive Notebook	10%
Class Participation/Discussion	10%

Late Assignments. Assignments not completed on time will be subject to lowering of the assignment grade by 10% for each day late.

Grading scale. A = 90–100%, B = 80–89%, C = 70–79%, D = 60–69%, F = 0–59%

- **Student Conduct.** Inappropriate student conduct will provide grounds for removal from the class and/or lowering of the final grade for the course. WCU policies and procedures are clearly stated in the University handbook and *Ram's Eye View*. A student whose conduct is determined by the instructor to be disruptive of the learning process will be requested to leave the classroom. If the student refuses to leave upon request, University Public Safety personnel may be called to remove the student. A conference with appropriate WCU officials will determine if and when the student may return to class.

- **Academic Dishonesty.** WCU policies regarding academic dishonesty (see current WCU Catalog and *Ram's Eye View* for details) will be strictly enforced in this class. At a minimum, a failing grade will be assigned to any project, assignment, or presentation in which academic dishonesty is evident, with further academic/judicial action as determined by the MUE faculty. Copyright issues, paraphrasing, and plagiarism have been taught in courses by the English Department and Music Education Department.

- **Social Equity and Students with Disabilities.** WCU conforms to all state and federal policies regarding social equity issues including race, ethnic origin, gender, physical/mental disabilities, and these policies will be strictly enforced in this class. Students with disabilities must make special needs known to the Music Education Department and Office of Services for Students with Disabilities (x3217). Sufficient notice is needed in order to make the accommodations possible.

- **Beepers, Phones, etc.** All beepers, pagers, and cell phones will be turned off during class. Exception is made for students who serve as members of emergency units (fire, rescue, ambulance) who are "on call."

- **Attendance.** This is a professional preparatory course with appropriate expectations for attendance (including promptness). Students are expected to be in the classroom with required texts, materials, equipment, and instruments when attendance is checked and instruction begins. Absences are considered unexcused unless prior arrangements have been made or reasonable cause can be verified to the satisfaction of the instructor. Excessive absenteeism or tardiness may result in a student's being requested to withdraw from the class. Five percent will be deducted from the final course grade for each unexcused absence. The instructor may be contacted at the telephone and e-mail addresses above in case of emergency.

- **Inclement Weather and Emergency Closures/Delays.** In the event of inclement weather or emergency University closure or delay, area media will carry an appropriate announcement. For media using number codes for school closing/delay information, 853 is the code for West Chester University.

BIBLIOGRAPHY AND READING LIST

Abeles, H., Hoffer, B., & Klotman, R. (1994). *Foundations of music education* (2nd ed.). New York: Schirmer Books.

Boardman, E. (Ed.). (1989). *Dimensions of musical thinking*. Reston, VA: MENC.

Bowman, W. D. (1998). *Philosophical perspectives on music*. New York: Oxford University Press.

Burton, J. B. & Dunbar-Hall, P. (2002). Music education in a post-Colonialist world. Unpublished manuscript.

Campbell, P. S. (2001). The survival of cultural traditions in a changing world. *International Journal of Music Education, 37,* 59–64.

Consortium of National Arts Education Associations. (1994). *National standards for arts education.* Reston, VA: MENC.

Elliott, D. (1995). *Music matters*. New York: Oxford University Press.

Gardner, H. (1983). *Frames of mind: The theory of multiple intelligences*. New York: Basic Books.

Jorgensen, E. (1997). *In search of music education*. Urbana, IL: University of Illinois Press.

Madsen, C. (2000). *Vision 2020: The Housewright Symposium on the future of music education.* Reston, VA: MENC.

Reimer, B. (1989). *A philosophy of music education* (2nd ed.). Englewood Cliffs, NJ: Prentice Hall.

Reimer, B., & Wright, J. (Eds.). (1992). *On the nature of musical experience*. Evanston, IL: Center for the Study of Education and the Music Experience. Northwestern University Press.

Rideout, R. (Ed.). (1997). *The sociology of music education*. Norman, OK: University of Oklahoma Press.

Small, C. (1996). *Music, society, education* (3rd ed.) Middletown, CT: Wesleyan University Press.

Small, C. (1998). *Musicking: The meanings of performing and listening*. Middletown, CT: Wesleyan University Press.

Older Texts of Historical Value (Most have been excerpted in current anthologies)

Birge, E. B. (1928) *History of public school music in the United States*. Reprinted by MENC (Reston, VA: 1988.).

Cooke, D. (1959) *The language of music*. London: Oxford University Press.

Copland, A. (1957) *What to listen for in music*. New York: McGraw-Hill.

Dewey, J. (1934). *Art as experience*. New York: Minton, Balch & Co.

Langer, S. (1942). *Philosophy in a new key*. Cambridge, MA: Harvard University Press.

Meyer, L. (1956). *Emotion and meaning in music*. Chicago, IL: University of Chicago Press.

MUE 503 PROJECT/PRESENTATION TOPICS

Group Project Subject Choices

Groups of 3–4 students prepare paper and presentation on one chapter/topic below. Some time will be given during class for group preparation. In-class presentation of 20 minutes on Oct. 30; paper to be turned in.

Abeles, et al.:	Chapter 5:	"Sociological Foundations of Music Education"
Rideout:	Part II:	"Music Education and Sociology"
Abeles, et al.:	Chapter 6:	"Social Psychological Foundations of Music Education"

Abeles, et al.:	Chapter 8:	"Applications of Psychology to Teaching"
Abeles, et al.:	Chapter 10:	"Assessing Music Behaviors"
Elliott:	Chapter 7:	"Musicing in Context"
Elliott:	Chapter 9:	"Musical Creativity in Context"

Final Project Subjects/Issues

Individual student-prepared paper and presentation on one of the following topics, persons, texts, etc.—focus on philosophical applications. In-class 20-minute presentations on December 4 and 11.

(I) Any book selected from class reading list/bibliography. Other books may be selected with the approval of the course instructor.

(II) Music educator, philosopher, etc. from the following list. Other educators/philosophers may be selected with the approval of the course instructor:

Bennett Reimer	Susanne Langer	John Dewey
Christopher Small	Thomas Regelski	Terry Gates
Edwin Gordon	Harry Broudy	Leonard Meyer
Elliott Eisner	Howard Gardner	Charles Leonard
James Mursell	Charles Fowler	Richard Colwell
Paul Lehman	Carl Orff	Zoltan Kodály

WEEK-BY-WEEK ASSIGNMENTS AND READINGS

Books and sources other than class textbooks will be on reserve in the Music Library

Week 1	No class—Labor Day Holiday.
Week 2	Introduction: Reimer, "Why Humans Value Music" (*Vision 2020*); Elliott, "On the Nature and Significance of Music" (Elliott Web site).
Week 3	Historical Contexts: Abeles et al. text, pp. 3–36; Marks, "From Tanglewood to the Present" (*Vision 2020*).
Week 4	Philosophical Foundations: Abeles et al. text, pp. 41–60; Elliott, pp. 3–17 & 18–45; Elliott, "A Praxial Philosophy" (Elliott Web site).
Week 5	Aesthetics and Music Listening: Abeles et al. text, pp. 65–95; Elliott, pp. 78–106; Group assignment—selection of group members and topic.
Week 6	Aesthetics and Music Listening: Elliott, pp 109–35, 137–58
Week 7	Aesthetics and Music Listening: Elliott, pp. 184–212; Take-home test to be distributed via Internet/e-mail.
Week 8	Take-home test to be returned: may turn in hard copy or via Internet/e-mail; Groups meet and research group project topic and presentation format.
Week 9	Presentation of group projects.
Week 10	Psychology: Abeles et al. text, pp. 189–228.
Week 11	Curriculum Issues: Abeles et al. text, pp. 271–98; Elliott, pp 241–67.
Week 12	Curriculum Issues: Elliott, pp. 269–94; Lehman, "How Can Skills/ Knowledge Called for in the National Standards Best Be Taught?" (*Vision 2020*).
Week 13	Practical Applications of Philosophical Foundations in Teaching: Elliott, pp. 296–310.
Week 14	Final Individual Project Presentations.
Week 15	Final Individual Project Presentations.

MUED 790: Problems in Music Education
Dr. Stephen F. Zdzinski
University of South Carolina
Spring 2001

Meetings: 6 pm to 8:45 p.m., Tuesdays
Office: 320 Music, (803) 777-0791
E-mail: szdzinski@mozart.sc.edu

Course Objectives
As a result of this course, the student will be able to
- Identify and discuss the major features of the "Music Education as Aesthetic Education" Philosophy
- Identify and discuss the major features of the "Praxial" Philosophy of Music Education
- Compare and contrast major philosophical schools of music education philosophy
- Identify and discuss major issues and events in music education history
- Identify and discuss major individuals and organizations in music education history
- Discuss the major conceptualizations of multiculturalism in music education and their implications for music education
- Discuss the implications of mainstreaming and inclusion on music education
- Discuss the impact and implementation of the MENC National Standards for Music Education
- Discuss the impact and implementation of block scheduling for music education
- Discuss the impact of technology on music education

Required Texts
Reimer, B. (1989). *A Philosophy of Music Education*
Elliott, D. (1995). *Music Matters: A New Philosophy of Music Education*
Mark & Gary. (1992/1998). *A History of American Music Education*
MENC. (1996). *Aiming for Excellence: The Impact of the Standards Movement on Music Education*
Rudolph, Richmond, Mash, & Williams. (1997). *Technology Strategies for Music Education*

Texts on Reserve
Fowler, C. (1996). *Strong Arts, Strong Schools*
Hodges, D. A. (1996). *Handbook of Music Psychology*
Jorgensen, E. (1997). *In Search of Music Education*
Miles R. B., & Blocher, L. R. (1996). *Block Scheduling: Implications for Music Education*
MENC. (1994). *The School Music Program: A New Vision*
MENC. (1994). *Teaching Examples: Ideas for Music Educators*
MENC. (1996). *Performance Standards for Music: Strategies and Benchmarks for Assessing Progress toward the National Standards, Grades PreK–12*
MENC. (1994). *Opportunity-to-Learn Standards for Music Instruction: Grades PreK–12*
MENC. (1999). *Opportunity to Learn Standards for Music Technology*
Rudolph, T. E. (1996). *Teaching Music with Technology*
Volk, T. (1997). *Music, Education, and Multiculturalism*
Music Educators Journal articles

Evaluation
Quizzes & Short Assignments (presentations)	20%
Technology & National Standards Presentation	10%
Class Participation	20%
Seminar Paper	20%
Exams (3)	30%

TENTATIVE TOPIC OUTLINE BY WEEK

	Topic	Assignment Due
1/16	Intro to Class	
1/23	Music Education Philosophy	
1/30	Music Education Philosophy	Quiz
2/6	Music Education Philosophy	Participation
2/13	Music Education Philosophy	Participation
2/20	Music Education History	Take-home Exam (trends)
2/27	Music Education History	Quiz
3/6	Music Education History	Participation
3/13	Music Education History	Participation
3/20	National Standards	Take-Home Exam (History)
3/27	Technology	Participation
4/3	Block Scheduling	Participation
4/10	Mainstreaming/Inclusion	Participation
4/17	Multiculturalism	Participation
4/24	Student Presentations	Technology/Standards
5/1	Student Presentations	Seminar Paper
5/8	Student Presentations	Take-Home Exam (trends)

TOPICS AND READINGS

A. Music Education Philosophy

Topic 1: Music Education as Aesthetic Education
A Philosophy of Music Education, Bennett Reimer (1989)

Topic 2: Praxial Philosophy of Music Education
Music Matters: A New Philosophy of Music Education (1992/1999)

Topic 3: Eclectic Philosophies in Music Education
In Search of Music Education, Estelle Jorgensen (1997)

B. Music Education History

Topic 4: Early Music Education History
Mark & Gary, Ch. 1–5

Topic 5: The Beginnings of Music Education in America
Mark & Gary, Ch. 6–8

Topic 6: The Growth of Music Education
Mark & Gary, Ch. 9–13

Topic 7: Current Developments in Music Education
Mark & Gary, Ch. 14–17

C. Current Trends in Music Education

Topic 8: The MENC National Standards for Music Education
Aiming for Excellence: The Impact of the Standards Movement on Music Education (1996)
The School Music Program: A New Vision (1994)
Teaching Examples: Ideas for Music Educators (1994)
Performance Standards for Music: Strategies and Benchmarks for Assessing Progress toward the National Standards, Grades PreK–12 (1996)
Opportunity-to-Learn Standards for Music Instruction: Grades PreK–12 (1994)

Topic 9: Music Technology and Music Education
Teaching Music with Technology, Tom Rudolph (1996)
Technology Strategies for Music Education, Rudolph, Richmond, Mash, & Williams (1997)
Opportunity to Learn Standards for Music Technology (1999)

Topic 10: Block Scheduling
    Block Scheduling: Implications for Music Education, Miles & Blocher (1996)
    Scheduling Time for Music, MENC (1995)
Topic 11: Mainstreaming/Inclusion in Music Education
    Bernstorf, E. D., & Welsbacher, B. T. (1996). Helping students in the inclusive class
        room. *Music Educators Journal, 82*(5), 21–26.
    Cassidy, J. W. (1990). Managing the mainstreamed classroom. *Music Educators
        Journal, 76*(8), 40–43.
    Darrow, A. (1990). Beyond mainstreaming: dealing with diversity. *Music Educators
        Journal, 76*(8), 36–39.
    Shuler, S. C. (1991). Music, at-risk students, and the missing piece. *Music Educators
        Journal, 78*(3), 21–29.
    Stambaugh, L. (1996). Special learners with special abilities. *Music Educators Journal,
        83*(3), 19–23.
    Thompson, K. P. (1990). Working toward solutions in mainstreaming. *Music Educators
        Journal, 76*(8), 30–35.
    Walczyk, E. B. (1993). Music instruction and the hearing impaired. *Music Educators
        Journal, 80*(1), 42–44.
    Zdzinski, S. F. (2001). Instrumental music for special learners. *Music Educators
        Journal, 87*(4), 27–29, 63.
Topic 12: Multicultural and International Music Education
    Music, Education, and Multiculturalism, Volk (1997)

TECHNOLOGY AND NATIONAL STANDARDS PRESENTATION

Each member of the class will examine the role of technology as it relates to the National Standards. Each content standard will be assigned to a member of the class, and a 20-minute oral presentation will be given to other members of the class on how technology can be used to teach to that standard. In addition, members of the class may also be asked to make a presentation on the opportunity-to-learn standards for music technology or to examine articles from the eJournal *Technological Directions in Music Learning* for class presentation.

SEMINAR PAPER GUIDELINES

In order to individualize the study of MUED 790: Problems in Music Education, a seminar paper relevant to your area of interest will be written. The preparation of the paper will involve considerable library research. Examine the literature to determine what we do or do not know about your topic. Abstract the sources; then derive implications for practicing musicians. The objective of writing this paper is to make you an expert in one, albeit narrow, area of music teaching or learning.
The following outline should be employed:

(A) **Introduction.** General overview of the topic area, statement of approach to the topic, and general indication of practical importance to musicians/music educators.
(B) **Relevant Research.** The main body of the paper, this section should demonstrate awareness and utilization of major references to the topic area, and should be organized into appropriate subtopics.
(C) **Discussion.** Should demonstrate your ability to synthesize material presented in section B; should extract major findings and summarize related research results.
(D) **Implications & Conclusions.** Should demonstrate the relevance of Section C to the musician; should give example of how principles might be applied.

Style. APA style is required. The paper should be typed, double-spaced. Credibility of presentation will be taken into consideration when grading. Hence, attention should be given to the overall organization of the paper, sentence and paragraph structure, spelling, and documentation (citations in text). Use as your model articles as found in the journal *Update: Applications of Research in Music Education.*

MUED 621: Psychology of Music
Ed Duling
Bowling Green State University
Fall 2000

Instructor:	Ed Duling, Ph.D.
Office:	CMA Office 2161
Telephone:	372-0281
E-mail:	eduling@bgnet.bgsu.edu
Meetings:	Tuesdays, 6–9 p.m.
	In one of two locations as announced: Room 2115 (Curriculum Lab) or Room 2002.

Required Materials

Hargreaves, D. J. (1986). *The developmental psychology of music.* Cambridge: Cambridge University Press.
Norman, G., & Streiner, D. (1997). *PDQ statistics* (2nd ed.). St. Louis, MO: Mosby.

Course Objectives

Given readings, class activities, and personal study, you will

- Review behavioral-associationist, cognitive-organizational, humanist, and neuro-psychological schools of thought
- Formulate a psychology of music question, review research on the topic, prepare an oral presentation on *PowerPoint,* and prepare a written presentation as a culminating project
- Construct a working knowledge of statistical practice applicable to quantitative psychology of music research

National Standards for Music Education

This course is related to people's perceptions of, choices about, and attitudes toward music performance, listening, history, criticism, and philosophy. The work of the class throughout the semester has the potential to address most, if not all, of the National Standards, depending partially upon project choices made by the students in the course.

Grading Procedure

Theory-to-Practice Papers (5 x 15@)	75 points
Stats Assignments	25 points
Final Study Report Paper	75 points
Presentation of Paper	15 points
Gather/Analyze Project (Paper) Data	15 points
Completed Notebook	20 points
"Midterm" Study Evaluation	50 points
Take-Home Stats "Final"	50 points
Research Reviews (5 x 15@)	75 points
Total:	**400 points**

Grading Scale

> 400–360 = A
> 359–320 = B
> 319–280 = C
> 280– (I will talk to you before you get this low!)

Policies and Procedures

Attendance. You may miss one class without penalty. Please leave explanation on voice mail. Your grade may be lowered by one letter if you miss more than one class. Three lates constitute one absence. Absences beyond two classes: the WP drop deadline is October 27.

Assignments. Late assignments receive no credit. Assignments are to be turned in prior to classes that you must miss. Please inform one of the instructors of any planned absence. Some assignments may be rewritten at the instructor's discretion.

TENTATIVE COURSE OUTLINE: FALL 2000

(C = class activity; A = assignment)

First One-Third: The Developmental Psychology of Music

8/29 Getting Started
  C1: PPT: Forgotten Topics of Educational Psychology
  C2: Syllabus. Class cards. Discuss theory-to-practice format.
  C3: Connect: "Facing the Risks of the 'Mozart Effect'" (Reimer, 1999, *MEJ*).
  A1: Read: Hargreaves, pp. 1–30. Write "Theory-to-Practice" Paper on Ch. 1.

9/5 Ch. 1. The Developmental Psychology of Music
  C1: Read theory-to-practice papers aloud. Class discussion.
  C2: Connect: "Music Lessons Enhance Spatial-Reasoning" from *Monitor.*
  C3: Connect: Neuropsychological.
  A1: Read: Hargreaves, pp. 31–59, and "Fertile Minds" and/or other articles from *Time.*
  A2: Theory-to-Practice Paper on Ch. 2, "Fertile Minds," and interesting information found on
    Internet pertaining to neuropsychology and baby brain research.

9/12 Ch. 2. Children's Thinking and Musical Development
  C1: Read Theory-to-Practice Papers.
  C2: *PowerPoint* presentation on *Frames of Mind.*
  C3: Connect: "Applying Multiple Intelligence Theory in the Music Classroom," Mallonee.
  C4: Connect: Cognitive-organizational.
  A1: Read Hargreaves, pp. 60–82, and Gardner article from Ithaca conference. Theory-to-Practice
    Paper on Ch. 3, Gardner's article, and interesting information found on Internet pertain-
    ing to multiple intelligence theory or cognitive approaches.

9/19 Ch. 3. Musical Development in the Preschooler
  C1: Read Theory-to-Practice Papers.
  C2: Direct Instruction, CAI.
  C3: Connect: "The High-Scope Preschool Curriculum Comparison Study through Age 23,"
    Schweinhart and Weikart.
  C4: Connect: Behavioral Associationist (stimulus-response).
  A1: Read Hargreaves, pp. 83–104. Theory-to-Practice Paper on Ch. 4 and interesting information
    found on Internet pertaining to behavioral approaches.
  A2: Myers-Briggs. http://www.keirsey.com/cgi-bin/keirsey/newkts.cgi. Print out and bring
    results next week.

9/26 Ch 4. Musical Development in the Schoolchild
  C1: Read Theory-to-Practice Papers.
  C2: Myers-Briggs, clinical assessments.
  C3: Connect: Humanist school.
  A1: Read Hargreaves, pp. 105–142. Theory-to-Practice paper on Ch. 5 and interesting informa-
    tion found on Internet pertaining to personality, Myers-Briggs, clinical psychology.

10/3 Ch. 5. Development of Responses to Music
  C1: Read Theory-to-Practice Papers.
  C2: Connect: *Nature* article from August 26, 1999, issue.
  C3: Connect: Gromko & Poorman, 1998, "Patterned Art Music."
  A1: Read "A" portion of Pratt's programmed stats; *PDQ*, pp. viii–14, 30, 171–75. Duling Flow

| 10/3 | Chart and "B" portion of Pratt if time. |
| (cont.) | A2: Write a Research Review (#1) on an article related to your small-scale study. |

10/10 Central Tendency and Dispersion

C1: Descriptive statistics: Data (nominal, ordinal, interval, ratio); central tendency (mean, median, mode, range); dispersion (standard deviation, variance); basic types of research as covered in *PDQ* and as conceived by instructors; hypotheses.

C2: Present Research Reviews (#1).

C3: Hand calculate and use computer on descriptive statistics from sample data.

C4: Find examples in *JRME,* etc.

A1: Read "B" portion of programmed stats, *PDQ,* pp. 17–36, 81–83; Madsen Chart.

A2: Write a Research Review (#2) on an article related to your small-scale study.

A3: Gather data for chi-square.

10/17 FALL BREAK: No Class

Second One-Third: Doing Psychology of Music

10/24 Chi-Square: Goodness of Fit and Contingency

C1: Apply descriptive statistics to SYSTAT and other systems.

C2: Present Research Reviews (#2).

C3: Chi-square: Goodness of fit.

C4: Apply chi-square to SYSTAT with sample data.

A1: Gather "*t*" data; read *PDQ,* pp. 37–42.

A2: Write a Research Review (#3) on an article related to your small-scale study.

10/31 *t*-test (Mann Whitney U)

C1: Parametric and non-parametric.

C2: Present Research Reviews (#3).

C3: *t*-test.

C4: Apply *t*-test to SYSTAT with sample data.

A1: Gather ANOVA data; read *PDQ,* pp. 43–54.

A2: Write a Research Review (#4) on an article related to your small-scale study.

A3: Practice *t*-test problem; take-home.

11/7 ANOVA (Kruskal-Wallis H)

C1: Post-hoc tests.

C2: Present Research Review (#4) and go over t-test answer.

C3: Analysis of variance (ANOVA).

C4: Apply ANOVA to SYSTAT with sample data.

A1: Gather "correlational" data; read all pages of *PDQ* on "Pearson correlation," correlation as listed in Index (p. 186).

A2: Prepare Research Review (#5).

A3: Practice ANOVA problem; take-home.

11/14 Correlation

C1: Correlation, Pearson.

C2: Present Research Review (#5) in class and go over ANOVA answer.

C3: Apply Pearson product moment correlation to SYSTAT with sample data.

A1: Practice stats exam and correlation problem; take-home.

A2: Prepare "storyboard" for *PowerPoint* presentation.

11/21 PowerPoint

C: *PowerPoint* from storyboards.

A: Take-home stats exam. Due next week.

11/28   **Psychology of Music Final Project Presentations**
         Take-home stats test due. Other topics as time permits.

12/5   **Psychology of Music Final Project Presentations**
         Go over problematic portions of stats test if necessary. Other topics as time permits.

12/12   **Psychology of Music Final Project Presentations**
         Other topics as time permits.

12/19   **Final Seminar: Probably at 8 Mackenzie Ct. (Duling's)**
         Written papers due.

CITATIONS FOR READINGS

Hargreaves, D. J. (1986). *The developmental psychology of music.* Cambridge: Cambridge University Press.

Gardner, H. (1983). *Frames of mind : the theory of multiple intelligences.* New York : Basic Books.

Mallonee, R. L. (1998). Applying multiple intelligence theory in the music classroom. *Choral Journal, 38*(8), 37–41.

Schweinhart, L. J. & Weikart, D. P. (1997). The high/scope preschool curriculum comparison study through age 23. *Early Childhood Research Quarterly, 12,* 117–143.

Steele, K. M., Dalla Belle, S., Peretz, I., Dunlop, T, Dawe, L. A., Humphrey, G. K. et. al. (1999, August 26). Prelude or requiem for the 'Mozart effect'? [Scientific correspondence]. *Nature, 400,* 826–27.

Gromko, J., & Poorman, A. (1998). Does perceptual-motor performance enhance perception of patterned art music? *Musicae Scientae, 2*(2), 157–70.

THEORY-TO-PRACTICE PAPER FORMAT

Your responses should be written on computer, double-spaced, 10–12 pt. font. After reading and reflecting upon the textbook assignment,

- articulate the meaning that you took from the chapter (synthesize the material into a coherent statement about what the material means)
- choose one of the theories discussed and talk about its ideal manifestation in practice (describe the hypothetical or actual application of the theory in the field)
- connect this material to your own experiences in education or your observations of educators by noting examples (or counter-examples, partial examples) of the theory-in-practice;
- redefine what it means to be a music educator based on these ideas

Maximum: four paragraphs and two pages.

Hint: Look for meanings, manifestations, and connections to practice as you read each chapter.

RESEARCH REVIEW FORMAT

Your responses should be written on computer, double-spaced, 10–12 pt. font. After reading the research article,

- state the problem
- describe the literature review
- state the purpose of the study or state the research question
- describe the method or strategy used
- state the results and conclusions

See Gromko e-mail printout for rubric for grading of the final paper.

ORAL PRESENTATION FORMAT

Follows the outline of the Research Review format. Must be presented using *PowerPoint.*

WRITTEN PRESENTATION FORMAT

Use examples from *JRME, Psychology of Music, Contributions to Music Education, BCRiME* as models. Must conform to APA, 4th edition.

MUS 607: Psychology of Music
Dr. Margaret Schmidt
St. Cloud State University
Spring 2000

Instructor: Dr. Margaret Schmidt
Office: PAC 144
Phone: 255-2295 (office)
320-255-2902 (FAX)
e-mail: mschmidt@stcloudstate.edu
Office hours: MW 11–12, 1–2;
TR 10–11, 12–1, 1:45–3:30;
T 3:30–4:30, and by appointment
Class meetings: Tuesdays, 4:30–6:30, PAC 140

Course Objectives

- To examine the historical antecedents and identify the basic assumptions underlying contemporary Western music psychology and learning theories
- To become familiar with various approaches to research in music psychology and identify their basic assumptions
- To become familiar with various theories of musical intelligence and their implications for music teaching/learning and performance
- To explore recent research in brain biology and its implications for music teaching/learning and performance
- To examine a variety of perspectives on assessment of music learning
- To apply the theories and approaches to practical situations in the music classroom

Materials

- There is no required text. Readings will be selected from a variety of resources, available from the SCSU Library.
- The Write Place at SCSU offers bibliographic formats and all kinds of writing help: http://leo.stcloud state.edu
- Music education materials are available through MENC: www.menc.org
- You may wish to access the complete MENC *Strategies for Teaching* series free at: www.Notation Station.net

Reading Assignments

For each reading, write a summary or response, as assigned. On each assignment, also include a complete, correctly formatted bibliographic citation for each reading. You may use any commonly accepted format, but be consistent within one week's assignments. Typing is not required, but your work must be legible. You may also jot down questions that you wish to discuss in class.

Evaluation

Thoughtful weekly assignments completed on time will earn a course grade of B. (One assignment during the semester may be late with no penalty.) To earn an A, you may propose and complete an additional project. Suggestions include designing an assessment package, researching and reporting on a topic of interest to you, or doing action research applying one or more theories of learning in one of your classes. It is expected that this project be original work, completed for this course.

COURSE TOPICS AND TENTATIVE SCHEDULE OF ASSIGNMENTS DUE

Jan. 18   Introduction. What is psychology? What can it tell us about music learning?

Jan. 25   How did we get where we are today? Music learning theories

Campbell, P. S., & Scott-Kassner, C. (1995). From theory to practice in teaching music to children. In *Music in childhood* (pp. 15–46). New York: Schirmer Books.

Rogers, S. J. (1990). Theories of child development and musical ability. In F. R. Wilson & F. L. Roehmann (Eds.), *Music and child development: Proceedings of the 1987 conference* (pp. 1–10). St. Louis: MMB Music, Inc.

Zentz, D. (1992). Music learning: Greater than the sum of its parts. *Music Educators Journal 78*(8), 33–36.

Feb. 1   How did we get where we are today? Learning theories

Gardner, H. (1999). Perspectives of mind and brain. In *The disciplined mind: What all students should understand* (pp. 60–83). New York: Simon & Schuster.

Strachota, B. (1996). How should I teach? In *On their side: Helping children take charge of their learning* (pp. 1–14). Greenfield, MA: Northeast Foundation for Children.

Maslow, A. (1968). Music education and peak experience. *Music Educators Journal 54*(6), 73–75, 163–71.

Feb. 8   How did we get where we are today? Researching music learning

Seashore, C. E. (1938). The musical mind. The musical medium. The science of music. In *Psychology of music* (pp. 1–32). New York: Dover Publications, Inc.

Mursell, J. (1936). Principles of music education. In G. M. Whipple (Ed.), *The thirty-fifth yearbook of the National Society for the Study of Education, Part II* (pp. 3–16). Bloomington, IL: Public School Publishing Company.

Feb. 15   Directions for research in Music Psychology
Read an article or chapter on a topic of your choice.
Write and present to the class a summary of the study you selected.

Feb. 22   Brain development

Diamond, M., & Hopson, J. (1998). Trees that grow so fair. An enchanted thing. In *Magic trees of the mind* (pp. 10–64). New York: Penguin Group.

Wolfe, P., & Brandt, R. (1998). What do we know from brain research? *Educational Leadership 56*(3), 8–13.

Feb. 29   How the brain learns

Sylwester, R. (1995). How our brain organizes itself on the cellular and systems levels. In *A celebration of neurons* (pp. 25–54). Alexandria, VA: Association for Supervision and Curriculum Development.

Bruer, J. T. (1998). Brain science, brain fiction. *Educational Leadership 56*(3), 14–18.

March 7   Multiple intelligences

Armstrong, T. (1994). The foundations of the theory of multiple intelligences. In *Multiple intelligences in the classroom* (pp. 1–15). Alexandria, VA: Association for Supervision and Curriculum Development.

Scherer, M. (1999). The understanding pathway. *Educational Leadership 57*(3), 12–16.

Gardner, H. (1998). Is musical intelligence special? *The Choral Journal 38*(8), 23–34.

Gardner, H. (1995). Reflections on multiple intelligences: Myths and messages. *Phi Delta Kappan, 77*(3), 200–9.

March 21	Directions for research in Music Psychology
	Read an article or chapter on a topic of your choice.
	Write and present to the class a summary of the study you selected.

March 28   Theories of musical development
Hargreaves, D. (1996). The development of artistic and musical competence. In I. Deliège & J. Sloboda (Eds.), *Musical beginnings: Origins and development of musical competence* (pp. 145–70). New York: Oxford University Press, Inc.
Fogarty, R. (1999). Architects of the intellect. *Educational Leadership 57*(3), 76–78.

April 4   Theories of musical development
Sloboda, J., & Davidson, J. (1996). The young performing musician. In I. Deliège & J. Sloboda (Eds.), *Musical beginnings: Origins and development of musical competence* (pp. 171–90). New York: Oxford University Press, Inc.
Campbell, P. S. (1999). The many-splendored worlds of our children's music. *Update 18*(1), 7–13.

April 11   Defining and assessing musical ability and achievement
Gordon, E. E. (1990). The nature and description of developmental and stabilized music aptitudes: Implications for music learning. In F. R. Wilson & F. L. Roehmann (Eds.), *Music and child development: Proceedings of the 1987 conference* (pp. 325–35). St. Louis: MMB Music, Inc.
Gordon, E. E. (1999). All about audiation and music aptitudes. *Music Educators Journal 86*(2), 41–44.
Rowley, P. T. (1988). Identifying genetic factors affecting musical ability. *Psychomusicology 7*(2),195–200.
Webster, P. R. (1988). New perspectives on music aptitude and achievement. *Psychomusicology 7*(2), 177–94.

April 18   Assessment of learning, Minnesota Profile of Learning
Kohn, A. (1992). Is competition inevitable? The "human nature" myth. In A. Kohn, *No contest: The case against competition* (rev. ed., pp. 11–44). Boston: Houghton Mifflin Company.
Eisner, E. W. (1999) The uses and limits of performance assessment. *Phi Delta Kappan 80*(9), 658–60.

April 25   Directions for research in Music Psychology
Read an article or chapter on a topic of your choice.
Write and present to the class a summary of the study you selected.

May 2   Motivation for learning
Kohn, A. (1993). Hooked on learning: The roots of motivation in the classroom. In A. Kohn, *Punished by rewards: The trouble with gold stars, incentive plans, A's, praise, and other bribes* (pp. 198–227). Boston: Houghton Mifflin Company.

May 9   Research, politics, and policies; course summary
Reimer, B. (1999). Facing the risks of the Mozart effect. *Phi Delta Kappan 81*(4), 278–83.
Weinberger, N.M. (1998). The music in our minds. *Educational Leadership 56*(3), 36–40.
Radocy, R. (1998). SAT scores and the arts: What's next? Music doesn't make you smarter ... but it doesn't hurt. *Kodály Envoy 24*(2), 44–46.

Some Suggested Additional Resources

Aiello, R. (1994). Music and language: Parallels and contrasts. In R. Aiello & J. Sloboda (Eds.), *Musical perceptions* (pp. 40–61). New York: Oxford University Press.

Bamberger, J. (1994). Coming to hear in a new way. In R. Aiello & J. A. Sloboda (Eds.), *Musical perceptions* (pp. 131–51). New York: Oxford University Press.

Blacking, J. (1990). Music in children's cognitive and affective development: Problems posed by ethnomusicological research. In F. R. Wilson & F. L. Roehmann (Eds.), *Music and child development: Proceedings of the 1987 conference* (pp. 68–78). St. Louis: MMB Music, Inc.

Boyle, J. D. (1992). Evaluation of music ability. In R. Colwell (Ed.), *Handbook of research on music teaching and learning* (pp. 247–65). New York: Schirmer Books.

Bruer, J. T. (1999). In search of ... brain-based education. *Phi Delta Kappan 80*(9), 649–57.

Deutsch, D. (1988). The perception of musical configurations. In F. L. Roehmann & F. R. Wilson (Eds.), *The biology of music making: Proceedings of the 1984 Denver conference* (pp. 112–30). St. Louis: MMB Music, Inc.

Graham, C. R. (1987). Music and the learning of language in early childhood. In J. C. Peery, I. W. Peery, & T. Draper, *Music and child development* (pp. 77–183). New York: Springer-Verlag.

Hodges, D. A. (1996). Human musicality. In D. A. Hodges (Ed.), *Handbook of music psychology* (pp. 29–68). San Antonio, TX: IMR Press.

Holahan, J. M. (1987). Toward a theory of music syntax: Some observations of music babble in young children. In J. C. Peery, I. W. Peery, & T. Draper, *Music and child development* (pp. 96–106). New York: Springer-Verlag.

Jourdain, R. (1997). ...to understanding.... In *Music, the brain, and ecstasy* (pp. 269–99). New York: William Morrow and Company, Inc.

Judd, T. (1988). A neuropsychologist looks at musical behavior. In F. L. Roehmann & F. R. Wilson (Eds.), *The biology of music making: Proceedings of the 1984 Denver conference* (pp. 57–76). St. Louis: MMB Music, Inc.

Ostwald, P. F. (1990). Music in the organization of childhood experience and emotion. In F. R. Wilson & F. L. Roehmann (Eds.), *Music and child development: Proceedings of the 1987 conference* (pp. 11–27). St. Louis: MMB Music, Inc.

Pruett, K. D. (1990). Young Narcissus at the music stand: Developmental perspectives from embarrassment to exhibitionism. In F. R. Wilson & F. L. Roehmann (Eds.), *Music and child development: Proceedings of the 1987 conference* (pp. 309–22). St. Louis: MMB Music, Inc.

Serafine, M. L. (1988). The idea of music as cognition. In M. L. Serafine, *Music as cognition* (pp. 29–67). New York: Columbia University Press.

Serafine, M. L. (1988). The problem: Whence music comes. In M. L. Serafine, *Music as cognition* (pp. 1–27). New York: Columbia University Press.

Shuter-Dyson, R., & Gabriel, C. (1981). Cognitive psychology and music. In R. Shuter-Dyson & C. Gabriel (Eds.), *The psychology of musical ability* (2nd ed., pp. 238–57). London: Methuen.

Shuter-Dyson, R., & Gabriel, C. (1981). Introduction to first edition. In R. Shuter-Dyson & C. Gabriel (Eds.), *The psychology of musical ability* (2nd ed., pp. vii–xii). London: Methuen.

Sloboda, J. A. (1990). Music as a language. In F. R. Wilson & F. L. Roehmann (Eds.), *Music and child development: Proceedings of the 1987 conference* (pp. 28–43). St. Louis: MMB Music, Inc.

Sloboda, J. A. (1994). Music performance: Expression and the development of excellence. In R. Aiello & J. A. Sloboda (Eds.), *Musical perceptions* (pp. 152–69). New York: Oxford University Press.

MUED 793M: Topics in Music Education
Measurement and Assessment in Music Education
Stephen F. Zdzinski, Ph.D.
University of South Carolina
Fall 2001

Meetings:	7:00 to 9:45 p.m., Wednesdays
Instructor:	Stephen F. Zdzinski, Ph.D.
Office:	320 Music
Office Phone:	(803) 777-0791
E-mail:	szdzinski@mozart.sc.edu

Purpose

This course is intended to provide music teachers information to improve the effectiveness of their own testing and evaluation procedures.

Texts

Boyle, J. David & Radocy, Rudolf E. *Measurement and Evaluation of Musical Experiences.*
Sax, G. *Principles of Educational and Psychological Measurement and Evaluation.*
Doerksen, G. *Guide to Evaluating Teachers of Music Performance Groups.*
Farrell, S. *Tools for Powerful Student Evaluation.*
Zdzinski, S. F. *Course Handouts.*

Reserve Materials

Bloom B., et al., *Taxonomy of Education Objectives—Handbook I: Cognitive Domain,* pp. 1–8.
Colwell, R. (1970). *The Evaluation of Music Teaching and Learning.*
Colwell, R. (Ed.). (1992). *Handbook of Research in Music Teaching and Learning.*
Music Supervisors Journal Articles.

Course Outline and Readings

Topic 1	Measurement and the Process of Education Sax, Ch. 1–2, pp. 1–53 Boyle & Radocy, Ch. 1–2, pp. 1–48
Topic 2	Principles of Classroom Test Construction Sax, Ch. 3–5, pp. 57–144 Boyle & Radocy, Ch. 4–5, pp. 85–125 Benjamin Bloom et al., *Taxonomy of Education Objectives-Handbook I: Cognitive Domain,* pp. 1–8 (Reserve) Richard Colwell (1970), *The Evaluation of Music Teaching and Learning,* Appendix A, pp. 169–72; Appendix B, pp. 173–77 (Reserve)
Topic 3	Statistical Concepts Related to Measurement Sax, pp. 181–221 Boyle & Radocy, pp. 51–60, 71–81
Topic 4	Criteria for Evaluating Tests and Measurements Sax, Ch. 9–10, pp. 257–314 Boyle & Radocy, pp. 60–72

Topic 5	The Analysis of Examination Items Sax, Ch. 8, pp. 225–56 Boyle & Radocy, Ch. 5, pp. 125–36
Topic 6	The Measurement of Attitudes, Interests, and Values Sax, Ch. 15–16, pp. 467–530 Boyle & Radocy, Ch. 9–11, pp. 195–216 Robert Cutietta, "The Measurement of Attitudes and Preferences in Music Education." In R. Colwell (Ed.) (1992). *Handbook of Research in Music Teaching and Learning,* Ch. 19, pp. 295–309. (Reserve)
Topic 7	The Measurement of Musical Behavior Sax, Ch. 15–16, pp. 467–530 Boyle & Radocy, Ch. 9–11, pp. 171–92
Topic 8	Music Aptitude and Achievement Testing Sax, Ch. 11–14, pp. 315–466 Boyle & Radocy, Ch. 6–7, pp. 139–69 James Mursell, "What about Music Tests?" *Music Supervisor's Journal,* XXIV (Oct.–Nov. 1937), pp. 16–18. (Reserve) Carl Seashore, "Two Types of Attitudes toward the Evaluation of Musical Talent," *MSJ,* XXIV (Dec. 1937), pp. 25–26. (Reserve) Jacob Kwalwasser, "From the Realm of Guess into the Realm of Reasonable Certainty," *MSJ,* XXIV (Feb. 1938), pp. 16–17. (Reserve) James Mursell, "The Issues of the Test Discussion," *MSJ,* XXIV (May 1938), pp. 22ff. (Reserve) J. David Boyle, "Evaluation of Music Ability." In Colwell, *Handbook of Research,* Ch. 16, pp. 247–65. (Reserve) Peter Webster, "Research on Creative Thinking in Music: The Assessment Literature." In R. Colwell *Handbook of Research,* Ch. 16, pp. 266–80. (Reserve)
Topic 9	Alternative Assessment, Portfolio Assessment, and Technology-based Assessment in Music Susan R. Farrell, *Tools for Powerful Student Evaluation* ASBDA Curriculum Guide J. Shively, "Demonstrating Technological Competency as a Component of Initial Licensure in Music," *Technological Directions in Music Learning Ejournal,* 2001. J. Bush, "Informing Others: Using Student Teacher Electronic Correspondence in Undergraduate Music Education Coursework," *Technological Directions in Music Learning Ejournal,* 2001. D. Sebald, "Developing Automated Student Assessment Instruments for the World Wide Web," *Technological Directions in Music Learning Ejournal,* 2000. R. A. Duke, J. J. Buckner, M. E. Cavitt, and E. Colprit, "Applications of SCRIBE: Systematic Observation and Analysis of Teacher Student Interactions in Music," *Technological Directions in Music Learning Ejournal,* 1997. J. A. Taylor and J. J. Deal, "Distance Learning in Music: A Survey of Practice and Plan," *Technological Directions in Music Learning Ejournal,* 1996. D. Gregory, "Reliability of the Continuous Response Digital Interface," *Technological Directions in Music Learning Ejournal,* 1996. W. K. Koehler, "The Effect of Electromyographic Feedback on Achievement in Bowing Technique," *Technological Directions in Music Learning Ejournal,* 1995. D. Bowers, "The Testing/Assessment Phase of Music CAI—Making the Process More Reliable and Efficient," *Technological Directions in Music Learning Ejournal,* 1994.

Topic 10   Assessment and the National Standards for Music Education
MENC, *Performance Standards for Music, Grades PreK–12: Strategies for Assessing Progress toward the National Standards.*
Shuler, "The Effect of the National Standards on Assessment (and Vice Versa)"*
Boyle, "The National Standards: Some Implications for Assessment"*
Colwell, "Why We Shouldn't Change the Standards"*
      *In MENC, *Aiming for Excellence: The Impact of the Standards Movement on Music Education*

Topic 11   Evaluating Students and Programs
Boyle & Radocy, Ch. 12–14, pp. 263–318
Sax, Ch. 17–18, pp. 533–85
Donald Taebel, "The Evaluation of Music Teachers and Teaching." In Colwell, *Handbook of Research,* Ch. 20, pp. 310–30. (Music Library)
David P. Doerksen, *Guide to Evaluating Teachers of Musical Performance Groups.*
Paul Lehman, "Curriculum and Program Evaluation." In Colwell, *Handbook of Research,* Ch. 18, pp. 281–94. (Music Library)

COURSE OBJECTIVES
The objectives of this course are to enable the student to
- Define, explain, and demonstrate the ability to use the basic terms and concepts of the field of educational and psychological measurement
- Construct instructional objectives and identify their distinguishing features
- Apply the taxonomies of educational objectives to music learning
- Demonstrate the ability to construct technically adequate data-gathering instruments
- Carry out procedures for determining descriptive statistics for data-gathering instruments
- Carry out procedures for determining the reliability and validity of data-gathering instruments
- Identify factors possibly influencing the results obtained from data-gathering instruments
- Cite and describe the strengths and weaknesses of commonly used data-gathering instruments
- Describe the relative strengths and weaknesses of commonly used data-gathering techniques
- Demonstrate the ability to organize and code information from data-gathering instruments
- Correctly interpret data provided by data-gathering instruments
- Compare and contrast theories of musical ability
- Identify, describe, and compare standardized musical aptitude and achievement tests
- Identify a cross-section of measurement and evaluation books and authors
- Compare and contrast traditional and alternative assessment strategies and practices
- Identify, describe, and compare strategies and practices used in technology-based assessment in music
- Identify, describe, and compare strategies and practices used to assess the National Standards for Music Education

EVALUATION
Quizzes and assignments	40%
Portfolio	10%
Measurement Project (cognitive, affective, or psychomotor)	20%
Midterm Exam	10%
Final Exam (comprehensive)	20%

PORTFOLIO

Each student in this course will complete a portfolio consisting of any material that documents your learning in this course. This evidence should include tests, projects, assignments, class notes, and other traditional forms of assessment, as well as alternative and authentic forms of assessment (reflective journals, self-evaluations, peer critiques, tape recordings of class discussions, and the like). Any format is appropriate, as long as it demonstrates your learning in the course.

MEASUREMENT PROJECT (COGNITIVE)

- Select a unit of instructional material, and write a set of test specifications to evaluate the area.
- Generate at least 30 items based on your specifications of the area. The items may be either multiple choice, true-false, or matching, depending on the content area being measured.
- Submit a draft copy of the test for review and comment by the class. Revise the instrument based upon class comments.
- Administer your revised instrument to a group of at least 15 students. (The use of an intact classroom group would be preferable.)
- Score the tests; compute the mean, median, mode, range, variance, and standard deviation of the raw scores for the group.
- Do a complete item analysis for your measure; for each item, report the item difficulty and item discrimination.
- Choose the appropriate formula for estimating reliability and then determine the reliability for your measurement instrument.
- Write a report based on this exercise. Organize your report into the following sections: Introduction, Table of Specifications, Description of the Student Sample, Description of the Test Construction Procedures, Descriptive Statistical Summary, Item Analysis, Discussion, Recommended Revisions of the Measure, Conclusions, Appendices to include sample test and raw data.
- Hand in two stapled, typewritten copies of your report. One copy will be graded, commented upon and returned to you. The instructor will retain the second copy.

MEASUREMENT PROJECT (ATTITUDE OR PSYCHOMOTOR)

- Select an attitude or a psychomotor behavior, and write a set of test specifications to evaluate the area.
- Generate at least 40 items based on your specifications of the area.
- Submit a draft copy of the test for review and comment by the class. Revise the instrument based upon class comments.
- Administer your revised instrument to a group of at least 15 students.
- Score the measures; in the case of a rating scale for psychomotor behavior, three judges should be used for the adjudication.
- Compute the mean, median, mode, and standard deviation of the raw scores (for the total measure) for the group.
- Do a complete item analysis for your measure; for each item, report the mean, standard deviation, and item discrimination.
- Choose the appropriate formula for estimating reliability and then determine the reliability for your measurement instrument.
- Write a report based on this exercise. Organize your report into the following sections: Introduction, Table of Specifications, Description of the Student Sample, Description of the Test Construction Procedures, Descriptive Statistical Summary, Item Analysis, Discussion, Recommended Revisions of the Measure, Conclusions, Appendices to include sample test and raw data.
- Hand in two stapled, typewritten copies of your report. One copy will be graded, commented upon and returned to you. The instructor will retain the second copy.

Mus 991: Seminar on Qualitative Research in Music Education
Dr. Colleen Conway
Michigan State University
Fall 2000

Instructor: Dr. Colleen Conway
Office: 206MPB
Telephone: 355-7658
Office Hours: Wed., 2–6, or by appointment

Required Texts

Bogdan, R. C., & Biklen, S. K. (1998). *Qualitative research for education.* (3rd ed.). Boston: Allyn and Bacon.

Patton, M. Q. (1990). *Qualitative evaluation and research methods* (2nd ed.). Newbury Park, CA: Sage Publications.

Course Pack (Available at Neds)

Course Description

This course will provide an overview of qualitative research methods in music education. The term "qualitative" has multiple meanings. For our purposes it will refer to various research methods that depart from quantitative (statistical, experimental, probabilistic, etc.) approaches.

Course Objectives

It is hoped that through this course students will: (1) further develop their understanding of what makes research "qualitative"; (2) develop the ability to discuss strengths and weaknesses of various theoretical frameworks and research methods; and (3) acquire a working knowledge of issues associated with qualitative research.

Course Requirements

Class Participation. Attendance is required, and class participation is requested. There will be occasional class activities based on course readings. Please notify me if you have a reason to be absent from class.

Weekly Journal. E-mail the class on the Monday evening before the Wednesday class regarding personal reflections on the week's reading. In some cases, you will read different readings and report to others who have not read the material. There will be six journal entries marked with a "J" on the syllabus. (20% of course grade/pass or not pass)

Sample Qualitative Study Oral Presentation. Give an oral presentation reviewing two qualitative research studies in music education, music therapy, or education. A one-page handout for the class should be prepared for each study. (Due Oct. 4) (10% of course/graded/rubric developed in class)

Observation Assignment. Observe an event or phenomenon with a partner. Describe your strategies and the experience in a one- to two-page paper. (Due Oct. 11) (5% of course grade/pass or not pass)

Interview Assignment. Conduct an interview with someone and write a one- to two-page paper describing your strategies and the experience. (Due Oct. 18) (5% of course grade/pass or not pass)

Short "Qualitativeness" Paper. A no more than five-page paper which conveys your understanding of "qualitativeness." You may: (1) choose a specific book from the supplemental reading list to focus your essay and weave in content from course readings; or (2) create an alternative format that is not an expository essay (e.g., invent a dialogue between two researchers, compose a musical piece which somehow reflects your understanding of qualitative, incorporate visual art or dance). You may do this assignment collaboratively with a partner or small group. (Due Oct. 25) (15% of course grade/graded or not—student choice)

Qualitative "Mini" Study, Part I. Introduction and statement of research problem, research questions, brief theoretical framework, short review of related literature, methods, and procedure section which focuses on "data collection." (Due Nov. 1) (Will receive an "In-progress" grade)

Qualitative "Mini" Study, Final Report. Expansion of Part I and addition of analysis procedures, results, discussion, and suggestions for practice and research. (Due Dec. 11) (30% of course grade/graded)

Annotated Bibliography. Create an annotated bibliography to use in the future, including books/studies which you came across in the semester. (Due Dec. 11) (10% of course grade/ pass or not pass)

Poster Presentation. Display your qualitative study in a class poster session. (Due Dec. 6) (5% of course grade/pass/not pass)

EVALUATION

- Pass/not pass assignments are "grade neutral" in the sense that as long as you complete the assignment, your course grade will not be affected. If you do an exceptionally fine job, your grade could be made higher.
- Rating scales will be passed out which include criteria for grading the oral presentation and the "mini study."
- In addition, the following qualities will be valued in your written work:
    - (1) Attention to APA editorial style.
    - (2) Relevance. Connections between your work and the content and orientation of this course should be clear. Your work should show evidence of your understanding of course readings and discussions.
    - (3) Responsiveness to the task or question. Are you fulfilling the requirements of the assignment? Or are you answering your stated research questions?
    - (4) Conciseness. Clear and organized writing style will be valued. Writing should be concise yet complete. Write as though your audience is not an expert on your topic.

COURSE CALENDAR/ASSIGNMENT SCHEDULE

*Readings in *Course Pack*

Aug. 30	Course Introduction and Overview
Sept. 6	Definitions, "Qualitativeness," World View, "Language" of Research, Search for "Meaning" Read: BB, Ch. 1; Patton, 1; *Bresler and Stake (1992); *Eisner (1996); **J-1**
Sept. 13	Research Questions, Problem Statements, Literature Review, Personal Frameworks Read: Patton, 2 and 3; **J-2**
Sept. 20	Philosophy, Epistemology, Ontology, Qualitative Designs Read: BB, Ch. 2; Patton, 4 and 5; **J-3**
Sept. 27	Continuation of Research Design Read: BB, Ch. 7; *Erikson (1994); *Bresler (1995); Conway and Borst (in press) (provided in class); *Conway (2000); **J-4**
Oct. 4	Selection, Ethics, and Access Issues Sample Studies Presentations Read: BB, Ch. 3 and 4; *Bresler (1995), (1996); *Roberts (1994)
Oct. 11	Observation Observation Assignment Due Read: Patton, 6
Oct. 18	Interview Interview Assignment Due Read: Patton, 7; *Kushner (1994)
Oct. 25	Generalizability, Triangulation, Reliability, Validity, Trustworthiness "Qualitativeness" Paper Presentations Read: Patton, 9; *Wolcott (1990)
Nov. 1	Catch Up Mini Study Part I Discussions/Due
Nov. 8	Analysis, Coding, and Categorization Read: BB, Ch. 5; Patton, 8; **J-5**

| Nov. 15 | Technology and Qualitative Analysis
Revisit of Theory
Read: *Weitzman (2000); Choose a Theoretical Framework Chapter from those provided in class; **J-6** |
| Nov. 29 | Writing the Qualitative Research Report, The Role of "Story" in Research, Journal Publication
Read: BB, Ch. 6 |
| Dec. 6 | Poster Presentation
Course Conclusions
Bibliography and Final Paper due on **Monday Dec. 11, 2000** |

READINGS IN COURSE PACK

Bresler, L., & Stake, R. E. (1992). Qualitative research methodology in music education. In R. Colwell (Ed.). *Handbook of research on music teaching and learning* (pp. 75–90). New York: Schirmer.

Bresler, L. (1995). Ethical issues in qualitative research methodology. *The Bulletin of the Council for Research in Music Education, 126,* 29–41.

Bresler, L. (1995). Ethnography, phenemenology and action research in music education. *The Quarterly Journal of Music Teaching and Learning, VI*(4), 4–16.

Bresler, L. (1996). Towards the creation of a new ethical code in qualitative research. *The Bulletin of the Council for Research in Music Education, 130,* 17–29.

Conway , C. M., & Borst, J. A. (2001). Action research and music education. *Update: Applications of Research in Music Education, 19*(2), 3–8.

Conway, C. M. (1999). The development of teaching cases for instrumental music methods courses. *Journal of Research in Music Education, 47*(4), 343–56.

Eisner, E. W. (1996). Qualitative research in music education: Past, present, perils, promise. *The Bulletin of the Council for Research in Music Education, 130,* 8–16.

Erikson, F. (1994). Where the action is: On collaborative action research in education. *The Bulletin of the Council for Research in Music Education, 123,* 10–26.

Kushner, S. (1994). Learning from experience: The construction of naturalistic methodology for evaluating music education. *The Bulletin of the Council for Research in Music Education, 123,* 97–111.

Richardson, L. (1990). *Writing strategies: Reaching diverse audiences.* Thousand Oaks, CA: Sage.

Roberts, B. A. (1994). The challenge of over-rapport. *The Bulletin of the Council for Research in Music Education, 123,* 90–96.

Seidman, I. E. (1991). *Interviewing as qualitative research.* New York: Teachers College Press.

Stake, R. E. (1995). *The art of case study research.* Newbury Park, CA: Sage.

Weitzman, E.A., & Miles, M.B. (1995). *Computer programs for qualitative data analysis.* Thousand Oaks, CA: Sage.

Weitzman, E. A. (2000). Software and qualitative research. In N. K. Denzin & Y. S. Lincoln (Eds.). *Handbook of qualitative research* (2nd ed., pp. 803–20).Thousand Oaks, CA: Sage.

Whyte, W. F. (Ed.). (1991). *Participatory action research.* Newbury Park, CA: Sage.

Wolcott, H.F. (1990). On seeking-and rejecting-validity in qualitative research. In E.W. Eisner & A. Peshkin (Eds.). *Qualitative inquiry in education: The continuing debate.* New York: Teachers College Press.

Wolcott, H. (1990). *Writing up qualitative research.* Newbury Park, CA: Sage.

Yin, R. K. (1993). *Applications of case study research.* Newbury Park, CA: Sage.

Yin, R. K. (1994). *Case study research: Design and methods.* (2nd ed.). Newbury Park, CA: Sage.

Other choices may be made by searching the Internet for books, mail lists, and/or Web sites which may be of interest to students in the class.

MUS 602: Introduction to Research in Music and Music Education
Dr. Marcelyn Smale and Dr. Marg Schmidt
St. Cloud State University
Fall 1999

Meetings:	Tuesdays, 6:40–8:30 p.m.	
Instructors:	Dr. Marcelyn Smale	Dr. Marg Schmidt
Office:	PAC 147	PAC 144
Phone:	(320) 255-2285	(320) 255-2295 (answering machine)
Fax:	(320) 255-2902	
E-mail:	smale@stcloudstate.edu	mschmidt@stcloudstate.edu

Course Objectives

- To become familiar with major resources and statistical tools for research in music teaching and learning
- To develop skills in identifying problems and formulating questions regarding music teaching and learning, and in determining appropriate strategies for investigating those questions
- To improve ability to analyze, evaluate, and use reports of research

Assignments

(1) Research tool projects (175 points, 25 points each)
> Observation notes and report
> Web site report
> Event graph
> Bibliography report
> Central tendency measures
> Standard deviation project
> Chi-square project

(2) Article analyses (400 points, 50 points each)
> Five assigned research analyses
> Three theme research analyses

(3) Final project (200 points)
> Research proposal, including:
>> Preliminary drafts of rationale, literature review, method, and bibliography
>> In-class presentation
>> Written research proposal

(4) Participation in class discussions, projects, and other class activities (200 points)

Grading

1000 points are possible:

900 = A	825 = B	750 = C

All assignments are due at the time specified. Late assignments will receive a proportion of the points otherwise earned:

One day: 90%	Two days: 70%	Three or more days: 0

At the discretion of the instructors, if you achieve less than 80% on an assignment, you may be given a second chance to demonstrate the objective.

RECOMMENDED RESOURCES
• A style manual such as *Publication Manual of the American Psychological Association* (4th Ed.), or *MLA Handbook for writers of research papers* (4th Ed.).
• http://leo@stcloudstate.edu: on-line reference manual (The Write Place)
• Colwell, R. (Ed.). (1992). *Handbook of Research on Music Teaching and Learning.* New York: Schirmer Books.

SCHEDULE—FALL 1999

Date	Topics	Assignments due
Sept. 14	Introduction, types of research Developing questions Observation techniques	
Sept. 21	Primary and secondary sources Historical research Reviews of literature Citations and style manuals	Observation report and notes Web site report Read Price and Madsen
Sept. 28	Library resources Bibliographies	Meet at 6:30 in CH 130 Analysis of Weber
Oct. 5	Systematic research methodology Defining the problem Basic statistics (levels of measurement)	Bibliography report Read Asmus & Radocy, 141–49
Oct. 12	Identifying resources Reviews of literature Basic statistics (central tendency)	Event graph Analysis of Bartel & Thompson
Oct. 19	Qualitative research Descriptive and inferential statistics	Central tendency project Analysis of Brendell
Oct. 26	Independent and dependent variables Experimental design	Analysis of Schmidt Theme analysis
Nov. 2	Standard deviation Validity and reliability	Two theme analyses Preliminary Statement of Purpose
Nov. 9	Basic statistics (Chi-square) Computer applications of statistics	Analysis of Kelly Read Busch & Sherbon, 124–29, 136–39
Nov. 16	Ethical issues in research Assessing research	Chi-square project Preliminary method
Nov. 23	Quantitative analysis Presenting research	Preliminary review of literature Revised purpose and method Read Abeles
Nov. 30	In-class presentations	Oral presentation of research proposal Preliminary bibliography
Dec. 7	Final in-class consultations	Draft of complete proposal
Dec. 21	Final written proposal due, 4:00 p.m.	PAC 238, St. Cloud State University 720 Fourth Ave. South St. Cloud, MN 56301-4498 FAX: (320) 255-2902

MUS 602—READINGS

Abeles H. (1992). A guide to interpreting research in music education. In R. Colwell (Ed.), *Handbook of research on music teaching and learning* (pp. 227–43). New York: Schirmer Books.

Asmus, E. P., & Radocy, R. E. (1992). Quantitative analysis. In R. Colwell (Ed.), *Handbook of research on music teaching and learning* (pp. 141–50). New York: Schirmer Books.

Atterbury, B. W., & Silcox, L. (1993). The effect of piano accompaniment on kindergartners' developmental singing ability. *Journal of Research in Music Education, 41*(1), 40–47.

Bartel, L. R., & Thompson, E. G. (1994). Coping with performance stress: A study of professional orchestral musicians in Canada. *The Quarterly Journal of Music Teaching and Learning, 5*(4), 70–78.

Brendell, J. K. (1996). Time use, rehearsal activity, and student off-task behavior during the initial minutes of high school choral rehearsals. *Journal of Research in Music Education, 44*(1), 6–14.

Busch, J. C., & Sherbon, J. W. (1992). Experimental research methodology. In R. Colwell (Ed.), *Handbook of research on music teaching and learning* (pp. 124–40). New York: Schirmer Books.

Kelly, S. N. (1997). Effects of conducting instruction on the musical performance of beginning band students. *Journal of Research in Music Education, 45*(2), 295–305.

Madsen, C. K. (2000). A personal perspective for research. *Music Educators Journal, 86*(6), 41–44, 54.

Price, H. E. (1998). Introduction. In H. E. Price (Ed.). *Music education research: An anthology from the Journal of Research in Music Education* (pp. xi–xviii). Reston, VA: MENC.

Schmidt, M. (1999). Defining "good" music teaching: Four student teachers' beliefs and practices. *Bulletin of the Council of Research in Music Education, 138,* 19–46.

Smale, M. (1991). Asking the right questions. *The Orff Echo, 23*(4), 13–14.

Weber, W. (1997). Did people listen in the 18th century? *Early Music, 25*(4), 678–91.

MUED 795: Research in Music Education/Pedagogy
Dr. Stephen Zdzinski
University of South Carolina
Fall 2000

Class Meetings:	6:00 p.m.–8:45 p.m., Mondays, Room 215
Instructor:	Dr. Stephen F. Zdzinski
Office:	320 Music
Office Hours:	By appointment
Phone:	777-0791
E-mail:	szdzinski@mozart.sc.edu

Course Description

An introduction to descriptive, experimental, philosophical, qualitative, and historical research in music education, with particular reference to principles of data collection, research design and effective research procedures. Students will prepare critiques of research material and will be guided in designing original research projects related to their own area of interest.

Texts
Required
Gall, M. D., Borg, W. R., & Gall, J. R., (1993). *Educational Research: An Introduction.* (GBG)

Price, H. (Ed.). (1998). *Music Education Research: An Anthology from the Journal of Research in Music Education* (P)

Huck, S. W., & Cormier, W. H. (1996). *Reading Statistics and Research,* 3rd ed. (HC)

Publication Manual of the American Psychological Association, 4th ed. (APA)

MUED 795 Stats Pak (#33, available at Addams Bookstore).

Recommended
SPSS. *SPSS 6.1 Student Edition for Windows/Macintosh.*

Reserve Materials
Boyle, J. David, and Radocy, Rudolf E. *Measurement and Evaluation of Musical Experiences.*

Colwell, R. (Ed.). *Handbook of Research on Music Teaching and Learning.*

Phelps, R. P., Ferrara, L., & Goolsby, T. W. *A Guide to Research in Music Education.*

Course Objectives
The objectives of this course are to enable the student to

(1) read, interpret, and evaluate the results of research studies in music education

(2) explain the differences among types of research activities (e.g., descriptive, experimental, historical) and choose the type appropriate for a given research problem

(3) demonstrate facility in consulting with a wide variety of standard library research tools in music, education, and music education

(4) intelligently read, abstract, and evaluate a wide range of research articles and reports as published in standard music, music education, education, philosophy, and psychology journals

(5) identify and explain basic terminology associated with educational measurement, research design, and statistical procedures

(6) identify factors possibly influencing the results obtained from data-gathering instruments, and describe the relative strengths and weaknesses of commonly used data-gathering techniques

(7) identify, describe, and compare standardized musical aptitude and achievement tests

(8) select and carry out appropriate statistical procedures by hand and/or computer

(9) identify appropriate statistical procedures for given research problems and interpret statistical results in a given research study

(10) conduct a review of literature on a given topic

(11) write critical reviews and summaries of research articles

(12a) write a proposal for a music education research study related to the student's own area of interest (doctoral music education majors/masters in thesis track)
or

(12b) write a paper that synthesizes systematic research literature in an area that is musically agreeable to the student and instructor (others)

TOPICS AND READINGS

Topic 1: Introduction to the Research Process in Music Education
GBG, Ch. 1

Schmidt, C. P,. & Zdzinski, S. F. (1993). Cited Articles in Music Education Research Journals 1975–1990: A Content Analysis of Selected Studies, *Journal of Research in Music Education.*

Sidnell, R. (1972) The Dimensions of Research in Music Education, *Council for Research in Music Education, 29,* 17–27.

Colwell, Ch. 4–5 (Mark and Cady)

Price, Ch. 1, 13

Topic 2: Planning a Research Project
GBG, Ch. 2–3

Castetter, W. B. & Heisler, R. S. (1988). Developing and Defending a Dissertation Proposal. [personal reserve]

Topic 3: Reviewing Research Literature
GBG, Ch. 2–4

HC, Ch. 1

Topic 4: Research Writing Style
APA Manual

Turabian Manual

Topic 5: Statistics I (Descriptive and Inferential)
GBG, Ch. 5

HC, Ch. 2–3, 5, 7–8

Topic 6: Data Collection Techniques
HC, Ch. 4

GBG, Ch. 6–9

Boyle & Radocy, *Measurement and Evaluation of Musical Experiences,* pp. 139–216.

Topic 7: Descriptive and Causal-Comparative Research
GBG, Ch. 10

HC, Ch. 11–12, 14–16

Descriptive Studies

        Wagner & Strul, 1979, *27*(2), 113–25 (Price, 301–13)

        Madsen & Duke, 1983, *3*(3), 205–14 (Price, 399–408)

        Yarbrough & Price, 1989, *37*(3), 179–87 (Price, 361–69)

        Taebel, 1990, *38*(1), 5–23 (Price, 373–91)

        Jellison & Flowers, 1991, *39*(4), 322–33 (Price, 603–14)

Causal Comparative Studies

    Hair, 1981, *29*(1), 11–21 (Price, 215–25)

    Geringer, 1983, *31*(2), 93–99 (Price, 244–50)

    Kuhn, 1974, *22*(4), 270–77 (Price, 273–80)

    Kuhn & Gates, 1975, *23*(3), 203–10 (Price, 291–98)

    Forsythe, 1977, *25*(2), 228–39 (Price, 314–25)

    Shehan, 1985, *33*(3), 149–58 (Price, 635–44)

    Standley & Madsen, 1991, *39*(1), 5–11 (Price, 392–98)

    Costa-Giomi, 1994, *42*(1), 68–85 (Price, 645–62)

    Fung, 1996, *44*(1), 60–83, (Price, 663–86)

Topic 8: Correlation Research

GBG, Ch. 11

HC, Ch. 10, 17

Correlational Studies

    LeBlanc, 1979, *27*(4), 255–70 (Price, 460–75)

    Zdzinski, S.F. (1992). Parental involvement, music aptitude, and musical achievement of instrumental music students, *Journal of Research in Music Education, 40,* 114–25.

    Zdzinski, S.F. (1996). Parental involvement, selected student attributes, and learning outcomes in instrumental music, *Journal of Research in Music Education, 44,* 34-48.

Topic 9: Statistics II (Advanced Statistics)

HC, Ch. 13, 18, 20

Colwell, Ch. 11 (Asmus & Radocy)

Topic 10: Evaluating Research

Bulletin of the Council for Research in Music Education, 97

Colwell, Ch. 14, 15 (Gonzo, Abeles)

Topic 11: Experimental Research

GBG, Ch. 12–13

HC, Ch. 21

Colwell, Ch. 10 (Sherbon)

Experimental Studies

    Madsen, 1966, *14*(4), 266–75 (Price, 263–72)

    Drake, 1968, *16*(4), 329–38 (Price, 281–90)

    Yarbrough, 1975, *23*(3), 134–46 (Price, 326–47)

    Dorow, 1977, *25*(1), 32–40 (Price, 529–37)

    Madsen, 1981, *29*(2), 103–10 (Price, 511–18)

    Price, 1983, *31*(4), 245–57 (Price, 348–60)

    Jellison, Brooks, & Huck 1984, 32(4), 243–64 (Price, 569–90)

    Sims, 1991, *39*(4), 298–310 (Price, 202–14)

    Price, 1992, *40*(1), 14–29 (Price, 424–39)

Topic 12: Qualitative Research

GBG, Ch. 14–15

Colwell, Ch. 6 (Bresler & Stake)

Council for Research in Music Education Bulletin, Issues #122, 123

    (entire issue on Qualitative Research)

Qualitative Studies

Campbell, M. R. (1999). Learing to teach music: A collaborative ethnography. *Council for Research in Music Education Bulletin, 139,* 12–36.

Norman, K. (1999). Music faculty perceptions of multicultural music education. *Council for Research in Music Education Bulletin, 139,* 37–49.

Freed-Garrod, J. (1999). Assessment in the arts: Elementary-aged students as qualitative assessors of their own and peers' musical compositions. *Council for Research in Music Education Bulletin, 139,* 50–63.

Topic 13: Historical and Philosophical Research

GBG, Ch. 16

Phelps, Ferrara, & Goolsby, Ch. 9

Colwell, Ch. 7, 8 (Jorgensen, Heller & Wilson)

Price, Ch. 2 & 3

Philosophical Studies

Reimer, 1962, *10*(2), 87–99 (Price, 15–27)

Mark, 1982, *30*(1), 15–21 (Price, 28–34)

Reichling, 1990, *38*(4), 282–93 (Price, 35–46)

Historical Studies

Livingstone, *15*(4), 243–77 (Price, 53–87)

Gates, *37*(1), 32–47 (Price, 88–103)

Heller, *27*(1), 20–8 (Price, 104–12)

McCarthy, *43*(4), 270–87 (Price, 113–30)

Topic 14: Action and Evaluation Research

GBG, Ch. 17

Action Research

Arnold, *Update 10*(1), 10–4

Topic 15: Student Presentation of Proposals

TENTATIVE WEEKLY SCHEDULE

Week	Topic	Assignment Due
1 (8/28)	Intro	
2 (9/4,6)	Planning	Research Ideas
3 (9/11)	Reviewing	Scavenger Hunt
4 (9/18)	Writing	Literature Search
5 (9/25)	Des/Inf Stats	Abstract
6 (10/2)	Data Collection	Stats I
7 (10/9)	Descriptive	Stats II
8 (10/16,18)	Causal/Comparative	Problem Statement Draft
9 (10/25)	Correlational	Literature Outline
10 (10/30)	Experimental	Stats III
11 (11/6)	Adv Stats	Stats IV
12 (11/13)	Evaluating	Stats V
13 (11/20)	Qual	Method Draft
14 (11/27)	Hist/phil	Stats VI
15 (12/4)	Act/eval	Critique
16 (12/14)	Presentations	Proposal/Synthesis Paper

EVALUATION

Class assignments

Library Assignments	10%
Library assignment I (scavenger hunt)	
Library assignment II (Literature search)	
Writing Assignments	25%
Research Types and Research Ideas	
Abstract	
Literature Outline	
Article Critique	
Problem Statement Draft	
Method Draft	
Statistics and Computer Assignments	20%
I. Descriptive and Inferential Stats Assignment	
II. Normal Curve, Variability, and Standard Scores Assignment	
III. Correlational, Reliability, and Regression Assignment	
IV. Validity and Experimental Design Issues Assignment	
V. ANOVA Assignment	
VI. Nonparametric Stats Assignment	
Weekly Quizzes on Readings (aural or written)/Participation	10%
Final Exam	15%
Proposal/synthesis paper	20%

LIBRARY ASSIGNMENTS

Complete the library familiarity assignment, which will be handed out in class and the Computer Search on your topic. It'll be a lot of fun.

SHORT WRITING ASSIGNMENTS

Complete several short writing assignments in which you will develop research writing and library skills and identify your topic area. Several writing assignments are also intended to provide an opportunity for you to submit rough drafts of sections of your research projects in progress.

RESEARCH STUDY ABSTRACT AND CRITIQUE

Construct a research abstract on a study related to your topic of interest. You will also review a music education research article (descriptive, quantitative, or historical). Each review is to be written as it might appear as a dissertation critique in the *Bulletin of the Council of Research in Music Education* (see issue #97 for guidelines). Each paper must be submitted typed, following APA style guidelines. The abstract should not exceed three pages; the critique should not exceed five pages in length.

STATISTICAL ANALYSIS AND COMPUTER ASSIGNMENTS

These short assignments will deal with the application of statistics in music education research. These assignments will be found in your Stats Pak. The focus in these assignments will be on the interpretation of statistics.

MAJOR PROJECT

Option A: Research Proposal

You will prepare a formal research proposal related to your particular music education research interest. Proposals should be typed and double-spaced, and should follow the writing style appropriate for the type of research proposed.

For quantitative and qualitative research proposals, the format should be that found in the *Publication Manual of the American Psychological Association,* 4th edition.

A quantitative proposal should include the following sections:

Ch. 1: Introduction
    (a) Statement of the Problem
    (b) Purpose of the Study
    (c) Research Problems/Questions
    (d) Delimitations and Definitions

Ch. 2: Review of Related Literature

Ch 3: Method
    (a) Subjects
    (b) Measurement Instruments
    (c) Data Collection
    (d) Data Analysis

A qualitative proposal should include the following sections:

Ch. 1: Introduction
    (a) Statement of the Problem
    (b) Purpose of the Study
    (c) Grand Tour Questions and Sub-questions
    (d) Delimitations and Definitions

Ch. 2: Review of Related Literature

Ch. 3: Procedures
    (a) Assumptions and Rationale for a Qualitative Design
    (b) The Type of Design Used
    (c) Data Collection Procedures
    (d) Data Analysis Procedures
    (e) Methods for Verification

For an historical research proposal, the format should be found in Turabian, *A Manual for Writers of Term Papers, Theses, and Dissertations.* The proposal should include the following sections:

Ch. 1
    (a) Rationale for the Study
    (b) Purpose of the Study
    (c) Research Questions
    (d) Delimitations
    (e) Definition of Terms

Ch. 2
    (a) Listing of Sources for Data to be Gathered and Location of Sources
    (b) Listing of the Nature of the Data
    (c) Description of Some of the Most Pertinent Materials
    (d) Plan for Interpretation of the Data and their Organization in the Final Report

Appendix (if applicable)

Working Bibliography

Option B: Research Synthesis Paper

Students who are not in the music education curriculum will write a paper, not to exceed 20 pages of text, which will synthesize research in a single area of personal interest. This paper should conform to APA style guidelines, and should be similar in format to research synthesis articles found in *Update, Council for Research in Music Bulletin,* or *The Quarterly.*

MISCELLANEOUS

MUSED 360: ADMINISTRATION OF SCHOOL MUSIC PROGRAMS
WILLIAM I. BAUER
BALL STATE UNIVERSITY
SPRING 2000

Professor: Dr. William I. Bauer
Office: MU 308
Office Hours: As posted or by appointment
Telephone: 285-5493
E-mail: wbauer@bsu.edu
WWW: http://bsuvc.bsu.edu/home/wbauer/
Meeting: M–W (10:00–10:50)

CATALOG DESCRIPTION

Explores practical ideas, print resources, and computer applications related to efficient administration of instrumental and choral music programs. Topics include recruitment, handbooks, scheduling, budgets, purchasing, libraries, inventories, fund-raising, parent groups, facilities, concerts, and trips.
Prerequisite: MUSED 200

REQUIRED TEXTS

Coursepack for MUSED 360. Available at T.I.S. College Bookstore, 1717 University Avenue.
Walker, Darwin E. (1998). *Teaching music: Managing the successful music program* (2nd ed.). NY: Schirmer Books.

OTHER RESOURCES

On-line resources have been established for use in this course. To access these, use a World Wide Web browser such as *Netscape* and open the following URL: http://www.bsu.edu/classes/bauer/mused360/

GOALS AND OBJECTIVES

By the conclusion of the course, the student will
- write a personal mission statement for music education
- explain the pros and cons of music contest/festival participation
- describe the process of planning the calendar of activities of music programs
- explain how to organize a music office, including the use of filing systems
- explain how to keep track of and organize inventory in a music program
- describe procedures for organizing and maintaining school music libraries
- explain the general procedures involved in budgeting, requisitioning, and purchasing as it applies to school music programs
- describe procedures for promoting the music program through public relations/advocacy techniques
- discuss basic procedures to be followed when fund-raising for school groups
- describe the role(s) and management of music booster organizations
- discuss basic procedures to be followed when traveling with school groups
- organize and assemble a notebook of materials from this course for use as a resource in his or her teaching career

Note: If you need course adaptations or accommodations because of a disability, if you have emergency medical information to share with me, or if you need special arrangements in case the building must be evacuated, please make an appointment with me as soon as possible. My office location and hours are listed on the first page of this syllabus.

EXPECTATIONS

Attendance. Prompt attendance is expected as a demonstration of professional commitment. The heart of education at Ball State is the teaching/learning interaction between you, the student, and your instructors. Because of this belief, class attendance is regarded as an essential part of the "contract" between you and the University. You are expected to attend all classes for which you are registered.

If you know you must be absent from this class, you should speak, before your absence, with Dr. Bauer, stating the reasons for your absence and agreeing upon a way to make up the work. Absences for illness and other valid reasons will be excused when *advance notice* is provided. If you have a valid reason for an absence on an examination day, and you *let me know in advance,* you will be permitted to make up the test at a mutually convenient time. Exams must be made up as soon as possible after your return to class, and no later than one week following your return.

Because attendance and punctuality are such an important part of being a professional music educator, you will receive full attendance credit for being on time to class and partial attendance credit for being in class but arriving after class has begun. No attendance credit will be given for arrival to class later than ten minutes into the class period. Faculty members are responsible for keeping a record of attendance of all students registered in the class. Significant absences may be reported to the Registrar's Office.

Class Participation. Because active and articulate oral interchange increases verbal skills and promotes a stimulating classroom atmosphere, the instructor will evaluate the quality, quantity, and appropriateness of each student's oral contributions to the class. Although no attempt will be made to translate this evaluation into an objective number of points, the instructor will use his subjective judgment of this behavior in the determination of borderline final grades. The dynamics of this class, and its ultimate value to you, require you to come to class prepared (read assignments), bringing questions and comments to stimulate discussions.

Honor Policy. Students of the university must conduct themselves in accordance with the highest standards of academic honesty and integrity. Academic dishonesty by a student will not be tolerated and will be treated in accordance with the "Student Academic Ethics Policy." Please see the Student Code in the Ball State University Calendar Book.

Copyright Policy. Plagiarism or violations of copyright policies are a form of academic dishonesty and are treated as an ethics violation. See the "Student Academic Ethics Policy" for more details.

MENC. It is *strongly* suggested that all students enrolled in this course become members of the MENC Chapter. Belonging to and participating in professional organizations are an important part of being a professional music teacher. Student MENC members also receive the *Music Educators Journal, Teaching Music,* and the *Indiana Musicator.* See Dr. Burns and/or Dr. Woody for more information on the MENC chapter.

ASSIGNMENTS

All assignments are due on the date specified. Grades on late assignments will be lowered by 10% for each day they are late. No credit will be given for assignments received later than two weeks past the due date. An exception to this policy is if the student is personally ill (doctor's excuse appreciated) or has a death in his or her immediate family. The student should see the instructor immediately upon returning to class to make arrangements to complete missed assignments at the earliest possible date.

Reading Quizzes. Students will take an on-line (accessed through course Web page) reading quiz for each daily class reading assignment. Reading quizzes must be completed *prior* to the start of the class for which the reading is assigned.

On-line Activities. Students will participate in a variety of on-line activities. More discussion of these will take place in class and on the course Web site.

Music Education Mission Statement. Each student will prepare a personal mission statement which outlines his or her personal philosophy/rationale on music teaching and learning. More discussion of this assignment will occur in class.

Budget Project. Using the sample on pages 96–107 of Walker as a guide, compile a budget for a high school band, choir, or orchestra program. The Budget Project may be completed with the use of a spreadsheet program or done manually within a word-processing program. Your budget request should include: (1) cover letter, (2) budget summary, (3) budget description by line-item categories, and (4) support information. Remember to include income and expenses. This project must be word processed. More discussion of this assignment will take place in class.

Cover Letter and Resume. Each student will write a cover letter and develop a resume like ones which would be used in the search for professional employment. Further information about this project will be provided in class and will be found on-line.

Group Projects. Small groups of students will form committees to work together on a project relating to one of the following topics: (1) Public Relations/Advocacy, (2) Fund-Raising, (3) Booster Groups, (4) Trips/Travel, or (5) Music Education Technology. Each group will compile a packet of resource materials on these subjects. Group members will also present an overview of their findings to the class. More details on the projects and the project presentations will be provided in class. The Walker text should serve as a starting point for researching your project expanded on by other material from outside sources. These outside sources might include traditional library resources, interviews, information found on the Internet, information from HS music teachers, etc.

Notebook. Each student will complete a notebook of materials from this class for use as a resource during student teaching and the early years of his or her teaching career. The notebook must be one with *large* rings so that pages can be easily turned. If the notebook has pockets, nothing should be placed in these pockets. In the front of the notebook should be the syllabus for this class followed by a *typed* table of contents (put your name on the table of contents someplace). Use the table of contents found in your coursepack as an example of the type of table of contents you should develop for your notebook.

The notebook should be separated into appropriate content areas with divider pages that have *typed* index tabs. The coursepack should be divided up and placed into these content areas. For ease of retrieval, sections in the notebook should be alphabetized. Sections should also not contain too many topics. Possible sections for the notebook might include: Philosophy, Planning, Assessment, Classroom Management, Competition, Finances, Public Relations, Booster Groups, Fund-Raising, Trips/Travel. (This is just an example; you do not have to use these exact sections.) Be sure to include a spot for each of the group presentations, even though those will have not taken place by the time you turn in your notebooks.

Professional Development. Continual growth and development as a musician and teacher throughout a career is essential. For this class, students will exhibit a commitment to professional growth and development by completing four professional development hours through at least two different activities. MENC meetings, ASTA meetings, and Career Services workshops are among those events that can be used to fulfill this requirement. Other events will be discussed in class. Students should obtain the permission of the instructor prior to attending any event that has not been discussed in class in order to receive professional development credit. Turn in the professional development log form to Dr. Bauer no later than the due date indicated on the course calendar.

Please Note

- A music-teaching experience (for example, teaching a private lesson or directing a church choir) can be used for one of the four required professional development hours. A reflective essay on lesson content and how your teaching is evolving needs to be stapled to the professional development log.
- Fraternity or sorority events and meetings do not count toward this requirement
- A BSU faculty member or speaker must sign the professional development log for you to receive credit for the event. Student officers/leaders' signatures will not be accepted.

ASSESSMENT

Assignment	Grading Criteria	Weight
Attendance	Prompt attendance at each class session	.05
On-line Reading Quizzes	Percentage of correct responses	.10
Personal Mission Statement for Music Education	Clarity, depth of thought, grammar, spelling, punctuation, neatness	.05
Budget Project	Content, comprehensiveness, organization, accuracy, spelling, grammar, neatness	.05
Cover Letter/Resume	Proper format, spelling, grammar, punctuation, sentence structure, depth of thought	.05
Group Project	Content, comprehensiveness, organization, neatness, handout materials, presentation	.20
On-line Activities	Satisfactory completion of all on-line activities, on time	.05
Notebook	Content, organization, neatness	.07
Professional Development	Professional development log completed in the manner indicated in the syllabus	.03
Midterm	Percent of correct answers, depth of thought, clarity of expression	.20
Final Exam	Percent of correct answers, depth of thought, clarity of expression	.15

Grading Scale

99 –100	A+	
93 – 98	A	
90 – 92	A-	
87 – 89	B+	
83 – 86	B	
80 – 82	B-	
77 – 79	C+	
73 – 76	C	
70 – 72	C-	
67 – 69	D+	
63 – 66	D	
60 – 62	D-	
59 & below	F	

Letter to Numerical Grade Conversion

Letter Grade	Numerical Equivalent
A+	100
A	95
A-	91
B+	88
B	85
B-	81
C+	78
C	75
C-	71
D+	68
D	65
D-	61

COURSE CALENDAR

Key: CP = Coursepacket   O = On-line—see course Web page
         W = Walker Text   ER = Electronic Reserve

Date	Topic	Assignment	
Jan. 10	Course Overview/Syllabus/ Web site		
Jan. 12	A Philosophy and Rationale for Teaching and Learning	Read:	ER, "Music in Today's Schools: Rationale and Commentary"
Jan. 17	Philosophy of Music Education	Read:	W, Ch. 14 CP, "Aesthetic Education in the Performance Classroom"
Jan. 19	Philosophy/Personal Mission Statement	Due: Read:	*Personal Home page* CP, "Teaching Music in the Ensemble Rehearsal through Multiple Intelligences," "Where We Stand," "Leading the Way"
Jan. 24	Making Music Education Curricular	Read: Due:	ER, "Making Arts Education Curricular" CP, "Music Education in the Twenty-First Century" O, Opportunity to Learn Standards [OPTLS] (section on Curriculum and Staffing) *Personal Reaction to "Making Arts Education Curricular"*
Jan. 26	Curriculum/Planning Sign Up for Group Projects	Read:	CP, "Summer Tasks for the First-Year Band Director," "Surviving the Opening of School" W, Ch. 4
Jan. 31	Planning	Read:	CP, "A Filing System: The Process of Keeping Organized," "Things You Might Include in a Band/Orchestra Handbook," *Firestone HS Band Handbook,* "There's More to a Concert Than Just the Music," Concert Checklist
Feb. 2	Preparing and Presenting Group Presentations	Due:	*The First Day of School Newsgroup Posting*
Feb. 7	Assessment	Read:	W, Ch. 9
Feb. 9	No class meeting—work on group projects	Read:	CP, "Evaluating Student Achievement"
Feb. 14	Assessment	Due: Read:	*Personal Mission Statement for Music Education* CP, "Assessment—Applying the Yardstick to Musical Growth," "Criteria for Evaluating Performance Assessment," "Tools for Assessing Musical Skills," "Can Portfolios Be Practical for Performance Assessment?"
Feb. 16	Assessment	Read:	CP, "Reporting Progress with Developmental Profiles"; browse the remainder of this section of the coursepack.

Feb. 21	Classroom Management	Read:	W, Ch. 3 CP, "Classroom Management for Beginning Music Educators"
Feb. 23	Classroom Management	Read:	CP, "Classroom Management for Ensembles"
Feb. 28	Motivation	Read:	CP, "Pieces to the Motivation Puzzle," "Choosing Music that Motivates," "Student Motivation"
Mar. 1	Midterm		
Mar. 6, 8	Spring Break		
Mar. 13	Group Project Meetings	*Due:*	*Preliminary outline of Group Projects*
Mar. 15	Discuss Midterm/Competition	Read:	W, Ch. 10
Mar. 20	Competition/Cooperative Learning	*Due:* Read:	*Web site review* CP, "Competition: Is Music Education the Loser?" "Cooperative Learning for Better Performance," "Do We Need Chairs?"
Mar. 22	ISSMA	Read:	CP, ISSMA selected forms.
Mar. 27	Finances and Budgets	*Due:* Read:	*Web Site Follow-up Newsgroup Posting.* W, Ch. 5 CP, Sample Budget Request
Mar. 29	Facilities and Equipment/ The School Music Library	Read:	W, Ch. 6, 8 CP, "Data Control for Program Longevity," Inventory Form O-OTLS (section on Materials and Equipment, Facilities)
April 3	Scheduling	Read:	CP, "Why High School Students Should Study the Arts" ER, "Scheduling Time For Music" O-OTLS (section on Scheduling)
April 5	Travel Group Presentation	Due:	Budget Project
April 10	The Job Search	Read:	O, See course Web page
April 12	Fund-raising Group Presentation	*Due:*	*Block Scheduling Newsgroup Posting*
April 17	Booster Group Presentation	*Due:*	*Cover Letter/Resume*
April 19	Public Relations/Advocacy Group Presentation	*Due:*	*Notebooks*
April 24	Music Education Technology Group Presentation		
April 26	Personal/Professional Growth and Development/ Final Exam Review	*Due:* Read:	*Professional Development Log* CP, "Burnout: How to Spot It, How to Avoid It," "Time for Professional Development," "Using the Internet for Professional Development"
May 2	Final Examination @ 9:45–11:45		

This syllabus is a guide. It may be varied as needed.

ELECTRONIC RESERVE ITEMS

Lehman, P. R. (1987). *Music in today's schools: Rationale and commentary.* Reston, VA: Music Eductors National Conference.

Shuler, S. C. (1990). *Making arts education curricular.* Reston, VA: Music Educators National Conference.

COURSEPACK ARTICLES LIST

Asmus, E. P. (1999). Music assessment concepts. *Music Educators Journal, 86*(2), 19–24.

Austin, J. (1990). Competition: Is music education the loser? *Music Educators Journal, 76*(6), 21–25.

Bauer, W. I. (1998, September). Teaching music in the ensemble rehearsal through multiple intelligences. *Indiana Musicator,* 37–39.

Bauer, W. I. (1997). Using the Internet for professional development. *Music Educators Journal, 83*(6), 22–27.

Brophy, T. S. (1997, July). Reporting progress with developmental profiles. *Music Educators Journal,* 24–27.

Consortium of National Arts Education Associations. (1999, January). The value and quality of arts education. *Music Educators Journal,* 39–42.

Detgen, D. (1996, January–February). There's more to a concert than just the music. *Bandworld, 26.*

Di Natale, J. J., & Russell, G. (1995). Cooperative learning for better performance. *Music Educators Journal, 82*(2), 26–28.

Hamann, D. L. (1990). Burnout: How to spot it, how to avoid it. *Music Educators Journal, 77*(2), 30–33.

Keenan-Takagi, K. (1999). Embedding Assessment in Choral Teaching. *Music Educators Journal, 86*(4), 42–46, 63.

Kirk, J. D. (1985, December). The use of the tape recorder in instrumental music rehearsal. *TRIAD,* 24–25.

Lehman, P. R. (1999, March). Making standards work for you. *Indiana Musicator,* 20–23.

MENC. (1997, September). Where we stand. *Music Educators Journal,* 41–44.

MENC. (1994). Time for professional development. *Teaching Music, 1*(6), 36–37.

Merrion, M. (1991). Classroom management for beginning music educators. *Music Educators Journal, 79*(2), 53–56.

Niebur, L. (1994). Assessment as a class activity. *Music Educators Journal, 80*(5), 23–25, 47.

Powell, L. (1984). Pieces to the motivation puzzle. *Music Educators Journal, 70*(6), 31–32.

Nierman, G. E. (1997). Assessment—Applying the yardstick to musical growth. *Indiana Musicator, 53*(1), 34–35.

Nierman, G. E. (1997). Criteria for evaluating performance assessment. *Indiana Musicator, 53*(2), 60–61.

Nierman, G. E. (1998). Tools for assessing musical skills. *Indiana Musicator, 53*(3), 18–21.

Nierman, G. E. (1999). Can portfolios be practical for performance assessment? *Indiana Musicator, 53*(4), 10–12.

Prentice, B. (1986). Surviving the opening of school. *The Instrumentalist, 41*(1), 30, 32, 36, 38, 40, 42.

Rideout, R. (1987). Summer tasks for the first-year band director. *The Instrumentalist, 41*(8), 50, 52, 54.

Rudgers, G. B. (1996). Aesthetic education in the performance classroom. *Teaching Music, 4*(3), 35–37.

Shuler, S. C. (1996, July). Why high school students should study the arts. *Music Educators Journal,* 22–26.

Werpy, S. (1987). Choosing music that motivates. *Music Educators Journal, 74*(1), 50–52.

MUS 460: Computers in Music Education
Colleen Conway
Michigan State University
Spring 1999

Instructors: Dr. Colleen Conway   Mr. Erick Senkmajer
E-mail: conwayc@pilot.msu.edu,   Senkmajer@voyager.net
Phone: 355-7658
Office: 206 MBP
Office Hours: M, 1:00–3:00; T/R, 10:00–12:00

Required Texts
Rudolph, T. E. (1996). *Teaching music with technology.* Chicago: G.I.A. Publications.

Course Description
Computers in Music Education will explore the general uses of technology in music education including: administrative applications; funding and proposal writing; uses of the Internet; uses of technology to meet the National Standards; notational software; and a basic overview of available hardware, software, and MIDI.

Course Requirements
Class Participation. Attendance is required, and class participation is expected. More than two unexcused absences from class will result in one grade lower. Each continuing absence will result in the lowering of another grade. (20% of course grade/ pass or not pass)

Technology Portfolio. Portions of the Technology Portfolio will be graded at the completion of each unit. Any missing unit, regardless of that unit's value, will result in one grade lower. See the course assignment schedule for specific details regarding these assignments (80% of course grade, grading rubrics developed in class).

Course Calendar/Assignment Schedule
Jan. 11/13. Course Introduction and Overview, Scheduling of Lab Class, Development of Grading Rubrics (Read Ch. 1 and 2)

Jan. 18. No Class

Jan. 20, 25; Feb. 1, 8. Administrative Applications (Read Ch. 14)
Administrative Applications Assignment. Due by Monday, Feb. 15 (20% of course grade). Choose (or create) a K–12 music setting as your context for this entire unit. At the beginning of the portfolio unit, describe the district, the school, and your teaching responsibilities.
(1) Word Processing (5% of grade). Choose one of the following: Generate your own data.
    (a) You have a concert in two weeks. Assemble a "copy-ready" program that includes the following:
        (i) Cover page: School district, groups performing (2+), date, time, location, directors, graphics
        (ii) Program order: groups performing, directors, titles, composers, arrangers
        (iii) Personnel: Full name, instrument/voice, indication of principal/lead
        (iv) Other: program notes, etiquette, calendar of upcoming events, district personnel, advertisements, etc. Be creative!
    OR
    (b) Assemble a two to three page newsletter for students/parents which includes:
        (i) "Banner" with title, date and groups represented, newsletter editor and student assistants
        (ii) Three or four short "articles" discussing issues relevant to your program (i.e., booster news, uniforms, fund-raisers, solo and ensemble, trips, auditions, private lessons)
        (iii) Upcoming Events Calendar

(2) Database (5% of course grade). Create either an instrument or uniform inventory using a database. Generate your own data.
  (a) Instrument Inventory
      (i) Include at least the following fields: instrument, serial number, make, condition, approximate replacement value (for insurance purposes—update yearly!), building storage location
      (ii) Sort and print by instrument only and by building location and instrument
  OR
  (b) Uniform Inventory
      (i) Include at least the following fields: garment, manufacturer, serial number, condition, approximate replacement value, storage location
      (ii) Sort and print by garment only and by building location and garment
(3) Spreadsheet (5% of course grade). Using a spreadsheet, generate a budget that will calculate your financial needs for the year including:
  (a) At least two buildings with two groups in each building on the vertical axis
  (b) At least four categories of expenditure (i.e., music, uniforms, repair, fees)
  (c) At least three total lines: one for each school and one "grand total" line
  (d) Print out two copies, one with your requested budget and one which reflects feedback given by an administrator
(4) Grading Software or Spreadsheet (5% of course grade). Using grading criteria which you establish (describe your grading policy as part of the unit), generate sample grades for a class of ten students. Include at least four categories of grades (i.e., performance, attendance, playing/quartet tests, homework, practice sheets) and at least twelve assignments.

Feb. 15. Grant and Proposal Writing (Read Ch. 17)
Grant and Proposal Writing Assignment. Due Monday, Feb. 22 (10% of course grade). Choose (or create) a different K–12 music setting as your context for this unit. Describe the district, the school, and your teaching responsibilities.
(1) You have been asked by your principal to present for 10 minutes at a school board meeting regarding the need for funding for technology for the music program. Write out what you will say (3–4 pages). Include information regarding what is needed for the program and why. Be sure to discuss how the program will benefit students. You will strengthen your case by referring to published literature on this topic (try the *Music Educators Journal, Teaching Music,* and the materials we provided!).
(2) Restructure your school board speech to meet the criteria on the grant application which is provided.

Feb. 22. Use of the Internet and Incorporation of the National Standards (Read Ch. 13).
Use of the Internet Assignment. Due Monday, March 1 (10% of course grade). Using the Web site list provided, find three sites that interest you and write two or three paragraphs describing each site. Print the home page from the site to include with your paper. Make copies of your paper for the rest of the class.

March 1. Technology at Sexton and East Lansing (No assignment).

March 15, 22, 29; April 5. Notational Software (Read Ch. 6).
Notational Software Assignment. Due April 19 (20% of course grade). Using the *Finale* program, provide a transcription of 32 measures of one of the piano pieces provided for a small ensemble of your choice (i.e., brass quintet, woodwind quintet, string quartet, sax quartet, or others). Provide a score and transposed parts and present the transcription in two different keys.

April 12, 19, 26. Overview of Available Hardware, Software, and MIDI Applications.
Final Paper. Due Monday, May 3 (20% of course grade, grading rubric developed in class). Based on four field visits to Sexton and East Lansing High Schools, write a 8–10-page paper which describes your observations and reflections regarding the use of technology in music classrooms. Include at least five references to support your views.

MUED 200: Music Education Practicum
Stephen F. Zdzinski
University of South Carolina
Fall 2000

Professor: Dr. Stephen F. Zdzinski
Office: Rm. 320
Office Hours: by appointment
Phone: 777-0791 (office)
E-mail: szdzinski@mozart.sc.edu

Course Description
Students in this course will participate in field experiences, lectures, readings, discussions, and writing assignments designed to provide an introduction to the profession of music education. Emphasis will be placed on personal, professional, and musical skills necessary for successful music teaching and learning.

Text
Music Educators Journal (The *MEJ* articles are announced each week as the journal articles come out.)

Class Meeting Time
1:25–2:15 p.m., Fridays, Room 016

Course Objectives
As a result of this course, the student will be able to
- Describe the process of music learning
- Describe why music should be included in the schools
- Describe the student-teaching and teacher-induction process
- Create a personal philosophy of music education statement
- Discuss how special learners and students with diverse abilities and background impact upon music teaching and learning
- Discuss the role of classroom management in music teaching and learning
- Discuss how student response is related to teacher behaviors
- Discuss teaching and rehearsal techniques used by successful music teachers
- Compare students in different areas (general, band, choral, string), and at different ages
- Discuss the importance of non-teaching duties that music teachers perform
- Discuss the role of competition in music education
- Discuss how multiculturalism impacts upon music education
- Discuss the impact and implementation of the MENC National Standards for Music Education
- Discuss the impact and implementation of block scheduling for music education
- Discuss the impact of technology on music education

Course Requirements
(1) Attend a minimum of 13 class meetings (as per university policy), unless formally excused from class with written note approved prior to the absence. More than a single absence means that you will fail the course.

(2) Complete six written observations of public school music classes, three in your main area of interest, three outside your main area of interest. *You are responsible for contacting the music teacher(s) you wish to observe and scheduling observations prior to making observations.* It is suggested that you observe a variety of teachers and classes. You must complete and submit the appropriate written

observation form for each class you observe. All completed written observation forms are due by December 1. It is suggested that you begin scheduling and completing your observations as soon as possible. Please submit the completed set of six written observation forms on or before December 1. You may hand them to Dr. Zdzinski before or after class. When scheduling and completing observations, use the following procedure.

(a) Contact the music teachers you wish to observe and ask for permission to do so.

(b) Explain that you are observing music teachers in order to fulfill class requirements for MUED 200 at the University of South Carolina School of Music.

(c) Secure observation dates that pose no conflicts for you or the teacher, and thank the teacher for his or her cooperation.

(d) Arrive at the school 10 minutes prior to the start of your observation, dressed professionally.

(e) Go immediately to the main office and register your name in the Visitor's Log.

(f) Go to the classroom and enter between classes.

(g) Introduce yourself to the teacher and thank him or her again.

(h) Ask the teacher where he or she would like you to be and what you should do during class.

(i) Sign out in the Visitor's Log before leaving the building.

(j) Complete the observation(s) and once again thank the cooperating teacher.

(k) Complete the written observation forms as soon as possible.

(l) Submit a completed set of six written observations to Dr. Zdzinski.

(3) Apply to the Professional Program in the College of Education Student Affairs office by the last day of class.

(4) Complete reading and writing assignments. Submit writing assignments with correct usage of grammar, spelling, and punctuation by the due date.

(a) Musical Autobiography

(b) Philosophy of Music Education

(c) Listserv Reflective Journal

(5) Pick up your application for the Praxis 1 Exam in the College of Education Student Affairs office Rm. 113, Wardlaw (7-6732), by the last day of class. Simply go to Rm. 113 in Wardlaw and have your student identification card with you. Pick up a Praxis 1 packet and sign your name on the appropriate list to indicate that you have received the packet. Sign the Praxis completion sheet and hand it in to Dr. Zdzinski.

(6) Join Collegiate MENC Chapter 33 by the second class meeting. This will allow you to receive the text for the course as well as other professional materials that will aid you in your achievement of becoming a professional educator.

GRADING POLICY

This is a Pass/Fail course. No late work will be accepted. If your work is late, you will fail the course. Your work includes (1) written assignments (musical autobiography, philosophy, listserv assignments, and observation reports), (2) application to the Profession Program on file in the College of Education by the last day of class, (3) application to take the Praxis I exam.

TENTATIVE TOPIC OUTLINE (SUBJECT TO CHANGE)

	Topic	Speaker	Due
(1) Aug. 25	Introduction to Class/ History of Music Education	SFZ	
(2) Sept. 1	CMENC		Join MENC
(3) Sept. 8	String Music Education	Dr. Barnes	Musical Autobiography

(4) Sept. 15	Student Teaching	Mr. Pruzin	
(5) Sept. 22	Choral Music Education	Dr. Wyatt	
(6) Sept. 29	Early Childhood Music Ed.	Dr. Valerio	
(7) Oct. 6	Band Music Education	Dr. O'Shields	
(8) Oct. 13	Multicultural and International Music Education	SFZ	Listserv #1 Check
(9) Oct. 20			
(10) Oct. 27	Administration	Dr.Gowan	Philosophy Paper
(11) Nov. 3	Music for Special Learners	SFZ	
(12) Nov. 10	Testing, Testing, Testing	SFZ	
(13) Nov. 17	National Standards, SC Framework		
(14) Nov. 23	Thanksgiving	Football	Stay Home
(15) Dec. 1	Technology in Music Education	Dr. Bain	Listserv #2 Check
(16) Dec. 8	First-Year Teachers/Student Teachers		Observation Reports Test Registration

MUSICAL AUTOBIOGRAPHY

You are to write a two- to three-page story of your musical life. We are interested in finding out about your musical backgrounds, seeing what musical experiences you have had in school or at home, and having you think about other musical influences that may have happened in your life, either through listening to music, watching TV, or going to concerts and performances. Give us as much detail as you can. The assignment is also designed to provide information about you in order to serve you better.

MUED 200 DISCUSSION WEB SITE

You are required to contribute your ideas on music education as part of MUED 200 to the course discussion Web site. To complete this part of the course, you must react to each of the questions posed in the discussion area.

This should serve as a professional growth activity: what is the meaning of what you are seeing and doing in the classroom; how do the ideas you have relate to larger issues of educational theory, practice, and philosophy; and how does this impact and change your own teaching practice? These discussion activities are not meant to be a critique of the classroom or the cooperating teacher that you are observing, but rather is a reflection of your professional growth and development.

You will be asked to respond periodically to discussion topics from both faculty and students. The entries will consist mostly of your thoughts and ideas about music teaching and learning. Personal experiences and, indeed, recollections and thoughts about your own music education which led to your admission to a university degree program majoring in music and music education at USC should be considered for inclusion into your journal. Observations of teachers at USC (no names please!) or in public schools would also be particularly pertinent for this activity. The journal should also help you to begin articulating your own philosophy about music education. There will be a weekly topic which you will be asked to respond to, and your responses will be circulated to all other members of the class. Students from other universities across the country may also be participating in these discussions, in order to provide us with a broader perspective.

MUSIC EDUCATION PHILOSOPHY

Write a personal philosophy of music education, suitable for inclusion in a job application. Be prepared to discuss in class your written statement.

MUED MUSIC EDUCATION PRACTICUM OBSERVATION FORM

Student _____

Cooperating Teacher _____Date _____

School _____

Class Observed _____Time _____

Please complete the following, using complete sentences (typed) on a separate piece of paper. Staple this page to your answer sheet(s) before submitting them to Dr. Zdzinski.

(1) Describe the physical arrangement of the room. Explain how this arrangement facilitated learning.

(2) Describe three or more qualities or teaching techniques you observed during this class that enhanced classroom management. Teaching techniques are how the teacher facilitated classroom management.

(3) Describe three or more teaching techniques you observed during this class that facilitated student responses. Teaching techniques are how the teacher delivered material and facilitated student responses.

(4) What method or methods did the instructor use to teach the content of the course? Method refers to the orderly sequencing of music content and skills.

(5) What actions did the teacher take to determine how well the students learned what was being taught? If such actions were taken, how well did it appear that the students had learned?

(6) Comment on how you will incorporate teaching techniques, teaching content, or classroom management techniques you observed during this class into your own teaching method.

Music 570:050: Introduction to Music Education
Dr. Debra Gordon
University of Northern Iowa

Time: 9:00 Mon., Wed.
Location: #30 GBPAC
Office: #42 GBPAC
Phone: 273-6865

Textbooks and Resources
Required reading (available at UB & S)
Hoffer, C. R. (1993). *Introduction to Music Education.* Belmont, CA: Wadsworth Publishing Company.

Articles are on reserve in a handbook in both Rod Library (basement reserve desk) and the IRTS lab in SEC.

There are various methods and supplemental texts housed both in the GBPAC classroom (#30) library and Rod Library in the music section. For General Music, the *Holt Music* texts, both teacher and student copies, are available in the music classroom in GBPAC. You will need to make arrangements with Carolina in the office or me to gain access to these. There are accompanying recordings and notebooks for additional activities. Additionally, the McGraw-Hill and Silver Burdett Ginn texts and some recordings are also available. Older Holt texts are also available at the IRTS curriculum lab in the SEC.

Goals for the Class
- To introduce you to a variety of facets of music teaching and pedagogy through observation, reading, and discovery experiences
- To acquaint you with the elements of learning and teaching
- To provide meaningful micro-teaching experiences with a variety of methods
- To initiate the assembly of a professional portfolio
- To prepare a short research paper regarding a topic of personal and professional interest to extend musical knowledge in a specific area

Important Information about the Class
The Americans with Disabilities Act provides for students requesting instructional accommodations, arranged through the Office of Disability Services, 213 Student Services Center, 273-2676.

Overview. This is a tentative schedule for the class. As the instructor, I reserve the right to modify the schedule to accommodate the needs of the class. Please realize that many factors contribute to the schedule remaining intact. Note that oral, written, reading, and teaching assignments are due on the scheduled dates unless prior notice is given by the instructor. Any incomplete assignment will warrant a grade reduction. Any unprepared assignment will earn a "zero" grade.

Since this is a participation-based class, *you are expected to attend every class, to be on time, and to have quality work prepared, whether written or in assigned reading or presentation formats. Please notify me if you are ill.* There are two acceptable reasons for missing class: your illness or a death in your *immediate* family.

Student Responsibilities. To read and gain a working knowledge of the information in the text and articles so that classroom discussion, application, and evaluation can successfully occur. We cannot cover all readings in class; therefore, it is your responsibility to know this information *in addition to* the topics covered in class.

All written work is expected to be submitted in class on the due dates, to be professionally presented in word-processed form, and to be quality, collegiate writing. In addition, you are expected to collaborate on classroom assignments, but to present individual work on written assignments and projects.

Exams
There are both unscheduled and scheduled quizzes and scheduled exams that will be conducted during the class meetings. Be well prepared for these.

Grades are earned in the following manner:

        Midterm, quizzes, other exams, and final = 20%
        Micro-teaching presentations = 20% (see grading criteria)
        Portfolio = 15% (see grading criteria)
        Research paper = 20% (see grading criteria)
        Philosophy of music education document and observations = 20%
        Attendance and punctuality = 5%

SCHEDULE

Please prepare all readings and assignments for the date indicated. Note that the course is divided into three topical areas of study.

The School Environment: The Music Program in Public Schools

Date	Topic for Class	Assignment due for today
8-21	Course Overview: Qualities of Effective Music Programs	Assign research for 8-23.
8-23	A History of Music Education in America. Each student will be assigned a particular area to research and present orally to the class. Present a comprehensive but short synopsis of your research (limited to three minutes each).	Read Ch. 1 of Abeles, Hoffer, Klotman, pp. 3–36 (on reserve)
8-28	Finish the History of Music Education in America.	
8-30	The General Music Program.	Read Hoffer, pp. 79–103; and Brophy, "Making the Elementary Music Program Essential."
9-6	The Band Program.	Read Hoffer, pp. 54–64; and Robinson, "To Sing or Not to Sing in Instrumental Class."
9-11	The String Program.	Read Hoffer, pp. 104–114; and Reviere, "Singing Strings."
9-13	The Choral Program.	Read Hoffer, pp. 21–31; and Armstrong & Armstrong, "The Conductor as Transformational Leader."
9-18	Class discussion: School Music Programs—Positive and Negative Components.	Read Morrison, "Music Students and Academic Growth"; and Schuler, "Why High School Students Should Study the Arts."
9-20	Library Resources: Meet at the front desk in Rod Library.	
9-25	Classroom Management and Discipline.	Read McDaniel, "Practicing Positive Reinforcement."

Teaching and Teachers

Date	Topic for Class	Assignment due for today
9-27	Classroom discussion: What is teaching? Effective teaching? What qualities are characteristics of effective teachers?	Read Hoffer, pp. 2–20, 32–41, and Ornstein, "How to Recognize Good Teaching" *Due in Class: Identify the topic of your research paper.*
10-2	Classroom discussion: What is learning? Effective learning? Music learning? Learning styles?	Read Hoffer, pp. 42–52; Silverman, "The Visual-Spatial Learner"; and Begley, "Your Child's Brain."
10-4	Personality Profiles and Self-Assessments: What do you know about yourself? How do these factors relate to your classroom?	Read Stufft, "Assessing Your Emotional IQ." *Due in Class: Observation #1*

10-9	Reserved for continuation of previous topics. Overview of the portfolio. Preparation for scheduled quiz.	Read Wolf, "Developing an Effective Teaching Portfolio."
10-11	Quiz: Assigned Reading and Classroom Discussions. Creating Powerful Lessons for the Music Classroom. Active vs. Passive Learning: Engaging the Students.	Read Hoffer, pp. 67–77.

Curriculum for the Music Classroom

10-16	Technology in the Music Classroom (meet in the music lab, #120 Russell Hall).	
10-18	The Components of the Spiral Curriculum. Composing Goals, Objectives, and Philosophy.	Read Hoffer, pp. 134–50. *Due in Class: Typed outline of the research paper including title, literature review, points of discussion, proposed conclusions.*

10-23 *Midterm Exam*

For the following, use the critiquing sheets in your classroom packet. You will critique each lesson and include these in your portfolio. There are 10 micro-teaching assignments. Each of you will collaboratively plan and deliver (among a team of five teachers) two 25-minute lessons within the 10 teaching assignments.

10-25	The Kodály Method: Micro-Teaching.	Read Hoffer, pp. 123–28; and Howard, "Kodály Strategies for Instrumental Teachers."
10-30	The Orff Approach: Micro-Teaching	Read Hoffer, pp. 118–22. *Due in Class: Philosophy of Music Education Statement.*
11-1	The Dalcroze Approach: Micro-Teaching.	Read Hoffer, pp. 115–17.
11-6	The Suzuki Talent Education; Roland, Applebaum, Menuhin, and Szilvay String Methodologies: Micro-Teaching.	Read Hoffer, pp. 129–33; and Kendall, "Suzuki's Mother Tongue Method."
11-8	Quiz on assigned readings and classroom activities.	
11-13	Structuring the research paper: format and citations.	
11-15	Gordon (Edwin) and Carabo-Cone Approaches: Micro-Teaching.	*Due in Class: Observation #2.*
11-20	Band Methodologies: Colwell; Westphal & Hunt; Barnhouse; Wiley: Micro-Teaching.	
11-27	Choral Approaches: Brinson; Kirk; Ashworth-Bartle: Micro-Teaching	
11-29:	Manhattanville Music Curriculum Program (MMCP), Contemporary Music Project, and Comprehensive Musicianship: Micro-Teaching.	*Due in Class: Research paper in final form.*
12-4	The Eclectic Approach: Micro-Teaching.	
12-6	The National Standards for Music Education.	Read: The National Standards for Arts Education (read the sections on music, K–4, 5–8, and 9–12) *Due in Class: Your Finished Portfolio*
12-13	Final Exam, 10 a.m.	

Reference List for Class Readings

Abeles, H. F., Hoffer, C. F., & Klotman, R. H. (1994). *Foundations of music education.* New York: Schirmer Books.

Armstrong, S., & Armstrong, S. (1996). The conductor as transformational leader. *Music Educators Journal, 82*(6), 22–25.

Begley, S. (1996). Your child's brain. *Newsweek, 127*(8), 55–61.

Brophy, T. (1994). Making the elementary music program essential. *Music Educators Journal, 81*(2), 29–32.

Consortium of National Arts Education Associations (1994). *The national standards for arts education.* Reston, VA: MENC.

Hoffer, C. R. (1993). Introduction to music education. Belmont, CA: Wadsworth Publishing Company.

Howard, P. M. (1996). Kodály strategies for instrumental teachers. *Music Educators Journal, 82*(5), 27–33.

Kendall, J. (1996). Suzuki's mother tongue method. *Music Educators Journal, 72*(6), 47–50.

McDaniel, T. R. (1987). Practicing positive reinforcement: Ten behavior management techniques. *The Clearing House, 60*(9), 389–92.

Morrison, S. J. (1994). Music students and academic growth. *Music Educators Journal, 81*(2), 33–36.

Ornstein, A. C. (1993). How to recognize good teaching. *The American School Board Journal, 180*(1), 24–27.

Reveire, J. (1996). Singing strings. *Teaching Music, 3*(6), 36–37.

Robinson, M. (1996). To sing or not to sing in instrumental class. *Music Educators Journal, 83*(1), 17–21, 47.

Schuler, S. (1996). Why high school students should study the arts. *Music Educators Journal, 83*(1), 22–26, 49.

Silverman, L. K. (1989). The visual-spatial learner. *Preventing School Failure, 34*(1), 15–20.

Stufft, W. D. (1996). Assessing your emotional IQ. *Teaching Music, 4*(1), 42–43.

Wolf, K. (1996). Developing an effective teaching portfolio. *Educational Leadership, 53*(6), 34–37.

Specific Assignments for the Class

(1) You will be assigned informal research projects in which you will present information to the class in capsulized form. Be prepared to share the information in a professional manner so that the class can quickly take notes and glean a basic understanding of your assigned research topic.
Due: 8-23

(2) Micro-teaching assignments will consist of teams of students who will formally research a particular methodology and present a 25-minute lesson to the class. Each class member is expected to present a minimum of five minutes of each assigned lesson, not to be read from a text, but rather taught to the class in an interesting, engaging, and enlightening way. Each teacher will be modeling methodology and/or pedagogy. The class members will complete critiques of your teaching and lesson that will be shared in class.
Due: See Syllabus and Class Sign-in Sheets

(3) You will create a professional statement of philosophy regarding music education. These are typically one to two paragraphs in length and specify the general and specific contents of your music program. This is one of the most critical documents you will formulate throughout your coursework. Expect to continue to modify and refine this throughout your coursework and teaching. Prospective employers will scrutinize this as you seek employment opportunities.
Due: 10-30

(4) You will construct a professional portfolio of your assignments, critiques, papers, assessments, and all other assignments, all of which must be complete and well organized. These will be graded only once during the semester. The inclusions are
  • all research assignments presented both formally and informally
  • your philosophy of music education
  • critiques of each micro-teaching presentation
  • title page with your name and the class name
  • organized divisions of the contents of the portfolio
  • notes from each class meeting noted with the specific topic attached

Please organize the portfolio in the following way. You should present a notebook which has met the following criteria:
- new notebook free of scratches, writing, or stickers
- typed name in large, bold print on the cover
- title page with your name in large, bold print (as your p. 1)
- table of contents
- typed tabs designating the specific components of the portfolio (see the accompanying class handout for details)
- current resume conforming to the College of Education requirements
- separation of pages in multi-paged documents to facilitate easier reading
- statement of philosophy which presents both a general view of your music program and delineates the specific skills and knowledge your students will gain as a result of participating in that program (lifelong skills are important!)
- highlight your name in programs and documents which aren't related solely to you and your experiences

Numbered dividers are not recommended, so please type the tabs and coordinate these with the table of contents. It is expected that your portfolio will be professionally assembled and represent a comprehensive, printed form of "you."
Due: 12-6

(5) You will make two formal observations of music educators and their programs for submission of a formal observation paper. The teachers should not be your recent high school music teachers, but rather those who have unfamiliar programs. The essence of this assignment is to acquaint you with new people, to network, and to provide other "ways of doing business." It is your responsibility to contact the school and the teacher to make an appointment for the observation. Please attend the class as an observer, approaching this in a most professional manner. Please do not talk with other observers or distract the teacher or students during this observation. Following the observation, provide a two- to three-page paper including the following: the school's name; the teacher's name; the class observed; the date of the observation; and an overview of the kinds of activities and inclusions observed in the lesson/rehearsal/class. I will provide a list of teachers who can be observed.
Due: 10-4 (from one school at one level in one music discipline, i.e., CF High School Orchestra) and **11-15** (from a different school at a different level in a different music discipline, i.e., Waverly third grade general music).

(6) You will research and compose a paper regarding one facet of music education that is of primary interest to you. The requirements include the following: five to seven pages in length, double-spaced; title page with pertinent information; reference list with a minimum of six entries; the body of the paper should be well organized and include citations from your reference list in APA format; there should be introductory and concluding paragraphs. Proofread your work carefully. The following criteria apply for the paper to receive a grade of "A":
- the title page presents a title which accurately reflects the contents of the paper
- the paper is logically presented with an introductory paragraph, the body containing the main discussion, and a concluding paragraph, all of which are related to one topic
- the arguments and discussion in the paper are relevant, accurate, and cogently presented
- the paper includes citations from the six sources which are appropriately and correctly presented in APA format
- grammar and spelling are correct and reflective of collegiate work
- the reference list is properly presented in APA format
- the paper consistently presents the topic of discussion without extraneous and superfluous information, exemplifying the research paper.

Music 52-691-31: Music Education for the Special Learner
Verna Brummett
Ithaca College
Summer 98

Instructor:	Dr. Verna Brummett
Office:	207 Ford Hall
Office Hours:	Daily 9:00–10:30, and by app't.
Phone:	274-3386 (office)
E-mail:	brummett@ithaca.edu
Credits:	3 credit hours

Textbooks

- Schaberg, *Tips: Teaching Music to Special Learners*
- Atterbury, *Mainstreaming Special Learners in Music* (This book has been photocopied by permission of author.)

Both books are available at the IC Bookstore. Also, purchase a three-ring binder.

- *A New Vision* (MENC) should also be purchased as a required text. As the course develops, the National Standards for Music Education will serve as the curricular framework. Accommodations for the various exceptionalities with regard to the content standards will be discussed throughout the course.

Attendance

Class will meet daily 10:45 a.m.–12:15 p.m. As a graduate course, your final grade will be dropped a letter grade for each absence after the one excused absence. Please see me in case of an emergency.

Course Objectives

Students will develop

- an understanding of the various exceptionalities
- appropriate vocabulary pertinent to students with a disability
- familiarity with adaptive instruments and music reading useful in the mainstreamed music classroom
- familiarity with current literature and resources related to the music education of exceptional students
- an awareness of attitudes which facilitate and/or hinder mainstreaming of exceptional students
- instructional strategies regarding the mainstreamed music classroom

Requirements and Evaluation

60%	Performance (five reflection papers, daily assignments, notebook, and class contribution)
40%	Final Project (topic and approach approved by instructor) and exit interview

Daily Assignments. Reading from texts, reserve books and articles, and viewing of videotapes will comprise the daily assignments. Be prepared to discuss assignments on days they are due.
There will also be five "Reflection" papers; one due at the end of each week. These should be one to two pages typewritten. In addition, I will pose several scenarios or philosophical/pedagogical questions on-line. You should respond at your leisure, but before the final day of class.

Notebook. Organizing class notes, handouts, and other materials will provide a "sourcebook" for your later use. Begin organizing this resource from the initial class meeting. A large loose-leaf three-ring binder should be purchased immediately.

Final Project.

Part A: Development of the Project. Within the first week, you should select two or three possible topics which are of particular interest to you. Meet with the instructor to finalize the topic and approach. This project should develop over the five weeks. The final class sessions will be devoted to class presentations of final projects.

Some ideas for the final project:
- investigate legislation, especially 1975 and 1990+, and indicate implications for your teaching
- select one exceptionality and thoroughly research it. Prepare program accommodations for your use.
- annotated bibliography of helpful resources
- prepare materials for use in your program
- investigate accommodations for VI and HI students in music (braille music, appliances, etc.)
- prepare actual visuals, instrumental accompaniments, etc. for use with your students
- do an in-service presentation for your colleagues at your school
- sign one or two songs

During the course, do an on-line search for information relating to your final project. Please include the search results with the project.

Part B: Class Presentation of Project. The culmination of the project will be a presentation for class. You will sign up for a specific day. Please follow these guidelines:
- Ten to fifteen minutes in length (not to exceed 15 minutes! You will be stopped at that point so "rehearse" the presentation beforehand.)
- Formal, professional presentation which is engaging and informative
- One-page handout for class members with helpful information regarding your topic. Be sure to include your name, address, phone, and e-mail.

Exit Interview. An interview will be scheduled during the final week of classes with each student. You should be prepared to discuss the implications of mainstreaming within the context of your teaching, as well as insights you have gained based upon information and experiences during the course.

Remember the Core Question. *What does this course and the information gained have to do with my teaching?* (How has my practice been enhanced with the information in this course? How has this experience provided further foundation to my teaching?)

CALENDAR

7/6	Introduction/Overview
7/7	Cognitive Exceptionalities Preface, Ch. 1, 2, & 4 (Mental Development)
7/8	Ch. 3, Learning Disabled
7/9	Multiple Intelligences (*Ithaca Conference '96 Music as Intelligence Sourcebook*)
7/10	Ch. 5, Putting It All Together
7/13	Perceptual/Physical Exceptionality Reflection Paper #1 Due Ch. 6, Hearing Impaired
7/14	Ch. 7, Visually Impaired
7/15	Ch. 8, Physically Handicapped
7/16	Ch. 9, Emotionally Disturbed/Behavior Disorder

7/17	Ch. 10, Putting It All Together
7/20	Ch. 11, Self-Contained Classes for Multiply Handicapped Students Reflection Paper #2 due today
7/21	Being Involved in Mainstreaming Decisions The IEP
7/22	Basic Concepts in Music Education II, ed. Colwell, Ch. 44; Graham, pp. 222–36
7/23	Full Inclusion (handouts)
7/24	Self-Contained, Mainstreamed, Inclusive Classrooms
7/27	*My Left Foot* (videotape) Reflection Paper #3 due today
7/28	*Children of a Lesser God* (videotape)
7/29	Multilevel/Multisensory Planning
7/30	Multilevel/Multisensory Planning
7/31	Colwell Handbook, Gfeller, pp. 615+
*8/3	Ch. 12 Reflection Paper #4 due today
8/4	*TIPS: Teaching Music to Special Learners* Notebook due
8/5	Class Presentations on Final Projects
8/6	Class Presentations on Final Projects
8/7	Class Presentations on Final Projects Reflection Paper #5 due today

*Exit interviews scheduled with professor during this final week. Please allow 15–20 minutes.
Graham & Gfeller readings are available on fifth-floor library reserve and on-line (*brum* and *special*)
Music library (fifth floor) is open M–F 2:30–8:00 p.m.; Sat 1:00–5:00 p.m.; Sun 4:00–8:00 p.m.

RESOURCES

Graham, R. (1991). Music education of exceptional children. In R. Colwell (Ed.), *Basic Concepts II*.
    Niwot, CO: University Press.
McKlesky, J. & Waldron, N. (2000). *Inclusive schools in action: Making differences ordinary*.
    Alexandria, VA: Association for Supervision and Curriculum Development.

MUS 961: Seminar in Music Teacher Education
Colleen Conway
Michigan State University
Fall 1999

Instructor: Dr. Colleen Conway
Office: 206PB
Telephone: 355-7658
E-mail: conwayc@pilot.msu.edu
Office Hours: Monday, 10:00–12:30, Wednesday, 2:00–6:00 (except on Seminar Days!), Friday, 11:30–12:30, or by appointment

Required Texts

Holmes Group (1996). *The Holmes trilogy.* East Lansing, MI: Holmes Group.
McKeachie, W. J. (1999). *McKeachie's teaching tips: Strategies, research, and theory for college and university teachers* (10th ed.). New York: Houghton Mifflin Co.
Course Pack (Available at Neds)

Recommended Texts

Hall, L. O., Boone, N. R., Grashel, J., & Watkins, R. (1997). *Strategies for teaching: Guide for music methods classes.* Reston, VA: MENC.
Society for Music Teacher Education. (1995). *Syllabi for music methods courses.* Reston, VA: MENC.
MENC. (1996). *Teacher education for the arts disciplines.* Reston, VA: MENC.
American Psychological Association. (1994). *Publication Manual of the American Psychological Association* (4th Ed.). Washington, DC: American Psychological Association.

Course Description

Seminar in Music Teacher Education will include study and discussion of research and scholarship pertaining to undergraduate music teacher education. The course will begin with an overview of current teacher education trends in general education. It will continue with issues in music teacher education (including the incorporation of the MENC National Standards for Music Education, new requirements in technology for teacher education, and multicultural and multiethnic music teacher education). The course will conclude with strategies for success in undergraduate teaching (including course design, various instructional techniques, the use of case studies, and various assessment techniques for teacher education).

Course Objectives

- To become familiar with current trends in teacher education research including Holmes Group and Carnegie Foundation recommendations.
- To gain a working knowledge of curricular and instructional issues in music teacher education including the incorporation of the MENC National Standards for Music Education, technology for music educators, multicultural and multiethnic music education, extended fieldwork, and high-stakes state certification testing.
- To become familiar with research designs and scholarship in music teacher education research.
- To study and review strategies for success in undergraduate teaching including course design, syllabi development, various instructional techniques, the use of case studies as instructional tools, Internet-based class assignments, and various assessment techniques for teacher education.

Course Requirements

Class Participation. Attendance is required, and class participation is requested. There will be occasional class activities based on course readings. (10% of course grade)

Weekly Journal. Students are asked to e-mail the class on the Monday evening before the Wednesday class regarding personal reflections on the week's reading. There will be eight journal entries marked with a "J" on the syllabus. (20% of course grade/pass or not pass)

Teacher Education Research Reviews and Presentation. Students are required to write two reviews (3–4 pages max.) of research articles from the teacher (nonmusic) education literature. Reviews will be presented to the class in a mini-lecture/presentation. (15% written; 5% oral, rubric developed in class)

Review of Literature Paper/Presentation. Each student will prepare a 10–15 page review of the relevant research literature in one specific area of music teacher education (i.e., general music education, instrumental music education, student teaching). Papers should be formatted for submission to *Update: Applications of Research in Music Education* and should include implications for teachers and suggestions for further research. A grading rubric will be developed in class. (20%)

Issues in College Teaching Book "Report"/Presentation. Students are asked to write a three-to-five-page book review on a book that explores issues in college teaching. Books may be chosen from the references in McKeachie and must be approved by the instructor. A grading rubric will be developed in class. (10%)

Sample Undergraduate Course Syllabus. At the last class meeting on December 8, 1999, students will be asked to share a course syllabus (make enough copies for everyone) for an undergraduate music teacher education course. The syllabus should include: required texts, a course description, course requirements, grading procedures, and a course calendar detailing content for each class meeting. At least one of the projects for the course must include instructional technology. In addition, a course bibliography must be provided. We will develop a grading rubric for this assignment as well. (20%)

EVALUATION

- Pass/not pass assignments are "grade neutral" in the sense that as long as you complete the assignment, your course grade will not be affected. If you do an exceptionally fine job, your grade could be made higher.
- Rubrics will be developed by the class to include criteria for grading the research reviews, the book review, the review of literature paper, and the course syllabus.
- The following qualities will be valued in your written work
    (1) Attention to APA editorial style
    (2) Relevance. Connections between your work and the content and orientation of this course should be clear. Your work should show evidence of your understanding of course readings and discussions.
    (3) Responsiveness to the task or question. Are you fulfilling the requirements of the assignment? Or are you answering your stated research questions?
    (4) Conciseness. Clear and organized writing style will be valued. Writing should be concise yet complete. Write as though your audience is not an expert on your topic.

COURSE CALENDAR/ASSIGNMENT SCHEDULE

All readings marked with a * are in the course pack.
Sept. 1, 1999   Course Introduction and Overview

Research in Teacher Education

Sept. 8, 1999	J-1
	*(1 and 2) Sikula Handbook—Forward, Preface, Introduction, and Ch. 1 and 2
	Holmes Group—*Tomorrow's Teachers*
Sept. 15, 1999	J-2
	Holmes Group—*Tomorrow's Schools, Tomorrow's Schools of Education*
Sept. 22, 1999	*(3) Sikula Handbook—Ch. 48
	Teacher Education Research Review Presentations and Paper Due

	Research and Scholarship in Music Teacher Education
Sept. 29, 1999	J-3
	*(4–8) Verrastro and Leglar, Leonhard, Boardman Meske, Price, Leglar
Oct. 6, 1999	J-4
	*(9–12) L'Hommeadieu, Asmus, Elliott, Reimer, Parr
Oct. 13, 1999	J-5
	*(13–16) Hope, Shuler, Woody, Conkling and Henry
Oct. 20, 1999	J-6
	*(17–20) Leonhard, May, Wing, Wing
Oct. 27, 1999	J-7
	*(21–25) Conway, Atterbury, Gromko, Harwood, Robbins
Nov. 3, 1999	*(26–29) Legette, Bowles and Runnels, Collins, Conway
	Literature Review Paper Due—Presentations
	Teaching in Higher Education
Nov. 10, 1999	J-8
	McKeachie, Ch. 1–8
Nov. 17, 1999	McKeachie, Ch. 9–24
	*(30) Conway
Dec. 1, 1999	Book Report Presentations
Dec. 8, 1999	McKeachie, Ch. 25–34
	Course Conclusions/Syllabi Presentations

COURSE PACK REFERENCES

1. Sikula, J. (Ed.). (1996). *Handbook of research on teacher education* (2nd ed.). New York: Macmillan. Foreword, Preface, and Introduction. (pp. ix–xxiii).

2. Sikula, J. (Ed.). (1996). *Handbook of research on teacher education* (2nd ed.). New York: Macmillan. Chapters 1 and 2 (pp. 3–37).

3. Sikula, J. (Ed.). (1996). *Handbook of research on teacher education* (2nd ed.). New York: Macmillan. Chapter 48 (pp. 1108–49).

4. Verrastro, R., & Leglar, M. (1992). Music teacher education. In. R. Colwell (Ed.). *The handbook of research on music teaching and learning* (pp. 676-96). New York: Schirmer.

5. Leonhard, C. (1985). Forward and Toward reform in music teacher education. *Bulletin of the Council for Research in Music Education, 81,* 1–3, 10–17.

6. Boardman M. E. (1985). Teacher education: A wedding of theory and practice. *Bulletin of the Council for Research in Music Education, 81,* 65–76.

7. Price, H. E. (1993). Applications of research to music teacher education. *The Quarterly Journal of Music Teaching and Learning, IV*(1), 36–44.

8. Leglar, M. A. (1993). A profile of research in music teacher education. *The Quarterly Journal of Music Teaching and Learning, IV*(1), 59–67.

9. L'Hommedieu, R. (1998). Opportunities and challenges. *Journal of Music Teacher Education, 8*(1), 3–4.

9a. Asmus, E. (1998). A look at the past and the future. *Journal of Music Teacher Education, 8*(1), 5–6.

10. Elliott, D. J. (1992). Rethinking music teacher education. *Journal of Music Teacher Education, 2*(1), 6–12.

11. Reimer, B. (1993). Avoiding extremes of theory and practice in music teacher education. *Journal of Music Teacher Education, 3*(1), 12–22.

12. Parr, N. C. (1999). Towards a philosophy of music teacher preparation. *Philosophy of Music Education Review, 7*(1), 55–64.

13. Hope, S. (1993). Teacher preparation and the voluntary K–12 music standards. *The Quarterly Journal of Music Teaching and Learning, IV*(2),14–21.

14. Shuler, S. C. (1995). The impact of the National Standards on the preparation, in-service professional development, and assessment of music teachers. *Arts Education Policy Review, 96*(3), 2–15.

15. Woody, R. H. (1999). Music teacher education and the Holmes Group. *Contributions to Music Education, 25*(2), 27–37.

16. Conkling, S. W., & Henry, W. (1999). Professional development partnerships: A new model for music teacher preparation. *Arts Education Policy Review, 100*(4), 19–23.

17. Leonhard, C. (1993). The challenge. *Bulletin of the Council for Research in Music Education, 117,* 1–8.

18. May, W. T. (1993). Why teachers cannot respond to Leonhard's proposal. *Bulletin of the Council for Research in Music Education, 117,* 167–91.

19. Wing, L. (1993). Music teacher education: Coming to our senses. *Bulletin of the Council for Research in Music Education, 117,* 51–65.

20. Wing, L. (1993). Teachers in the study of music teacher education: Finding voices. *The Quarterly Journal of Music Teaching and Learning, IV*(2), 5–12.

21. Conway, C. M. (1998). Reflection and the music methods course. *Southeastern Journal of Music Education, 10,* (in press).

22. Atterbury, B. W. (1994). Developing reflective music educators. *Journal of Music Teacher Education 4*(1), 6–12.

23. Gromko, J. E. (1995). Educating the reflective teacher. *Journal of Music Teacher Education, 4*(2), 8–13.

24. Harwood, E. (1993). Learning characteristics of college students: Implications for the elementary music education methods class. *The Quarterly Journal of Music Teaching and Learning, IV*(1), 13–19.

25. Robbins, J. (1993). Preparing students to think like teachers: Relocating our teacher education perspective. *The Quarterly Journal of Music Teaching and Learning, IV*(1), 45–51.

26. Legette, R. M. (1997). Enhancing the music student-teaching experience: A research review. *Update: Applications of Research in Music Education, 16*(1), 25–28.

27. Bowles, C., & Runnels, B. D. (1999). The need for collaboration in the student teaching experience. *Journal of Music Teacher Education, 8*(1), 15–24.

28. Collins, I. H. (1996). Assessment and evaluation in music teacher education. *Arts Education Policy Review, 98*(1), 16–21.

29. Conway, C. M. (1997). Authentic assessment in undergraduate brass methods class. *Journal of Music Teacher Education, 7*(1), 6–15.

30. Conway, C. M. (1999). The case method and music teacher education. *Update: Applications of Research in Music Education, 17*(2), 20–26.

CONTRIBUTORS

William Bauer
Case Western Reserve University

Virginia Bennett
Drake University

Verna Brummett
Ithaca College

J. Bryan Burton
West Chester University of Pennsylvania

Colleen Conway
Michigan State University

Lynn Cooper
Asbury College

Ed Duling
Bowling Green State University

Victor Fung
Bowling Green State University

Robert Gillespie
Ohio State University

Debra Gordon
University of Northern Iowa

Sharon Davis Gratto
Gettysburg College

Kathleen Jacobi-Karna
University of Oregon

Pat Krueger
University of Puget Sound

Nolan W. Long
University of North Dakota

Caroline Perkins
DePauw University

Diane Persellin
Trinity University

Susan Quindag
Bob Jones University

Margaret Schmidt
Arizona State University

Marcelyn Smale
St. Cloud State University

Sandra Frey Stegman
Northern Illinois University

Lewis Strouse
Carnegie Mellon University

Victor Vallo, Jr.
Anderson College

Stephen Zdzinski
University of South Carolina

Syllabi
for Music Methods Courses
Second Edition

Since MENC published its first collection of music methods syllabi in 1992, many changes have taken place in music education. The development of the National Standards for Music Education and the growth of technology have affected how prospective music teachers are taught. This new collection of syllabi, reviewed and selected by a committee from the Society for Music Teacher Education, offers a look at what is currently being taught in music education courses across the country. This volume consists of syllabi for the following types of courses:

- General Music
- Music for the Classroom Teacher
- Choral Methods
- Instrumental Methods
- Graduate Level Classes

The undergraduate and graduate courses represented in this volume include music methods for the elementary and secondary level; methods for brass, strings, and other instruments; research methods; the use of computers; practicum experiences; and curriculum development. By examining these syllabi and learning what their colleagues are teaching, music education professors can find ideas for their own classrooms.

Editor **Barbara Lewis**, who oversaw the solicitation and review of syllabi submissions, is associate professor of music education at the University of North Dakota in Grand Forks.

MENC MENC *The National Association for*
MENC MENC **MUSIC**
MENC MENC **EDUCATION**
1806 Robert Fulton Drive ■ Reston, VA 20191
703-860-4000 ■ Fax 703-860-1531 ■ www.menc.org

1052
ISBN 1-56545-151-1